'While the twenty-four stories [in this collection]
range from colonial to contemporary, there is a
common theme—a pervading sense of place...
Ralph Crane and Danielle Wood's stories can be
approached as pieces in a mosaic that presents a broader,
historically deeper picture of Tasmania, but the writing
can just be enjoyed: in "The Castle Morton Jerry",
Nicholas Shakespeare demonstrates that history
can be a source of good old ribald humour.'
Saturday Age

'A strong, spirited collection: twenty-four stories
written across one hundred and fifty years...
Quality is high and range wide.'
Weekend Herald NZ

'Beautifully presented...Co-editor Danielle Wood
[has] a wonderful contemporary story in the book,
portraying a sleep-deprived new mother coming
to terms with the changes in her world.'
Readings Monthly

'The editors pull no punches...the collection is strong.'
Sun-Herald

'Repeating motifs and discrete conventions have made
the Tasmanian story its own subgenre...Stylish, assured
writing...Offers readers a glimpse into the imagery and
symbolism that has come to shape how outsiders perceive
the island...There's a topographical intimacy that inflects
the collection's overarching tone, solidifying its coherency.'
Weekend Australian

Ralph Crane is the author or editor of sixteen academic books. He lives in Hobart and is Professor of English at the University of Tasmania.

Danielle Wood is the author of a novel, *The Alphabet of Light and Dark* (2003; winner of the *Australian* / Vogel and Dobbie awards); a collection of short stories, *Rosie Little's Cautionary Tales for Girls* (2006); and a non-fiction work, *Housewife Superstar: The Very Best of Marjorie Bligh* (2011). She lives in Hobart and teaches at the University of Tasmania.

Deep South

Stories from Tasmania

Edited by Ralph Crane
& Danielle Wood

TEXT PUBLISHING MELBOURNE AUSTRALIA

textpublishing.com.au
The Text Publishing Company
Swann House
22 William Street
Melbourne Victoria 3000
Australia

Copyright © Ralph Crane & Danielle Wood 2012
Where applicable, copyright in individual stories remains with the authors or their estates

All rights reserved. Without limiting the rights under copyright above, no part of this publication shall be reproduced, stored in or introduced into a retrieval system, or transmitted in any form or by any means (electronic, mechanical, photocopying, recording or otherwise), without the prior permission of both the copyright owner and the publisher of this book.

First published in 2012 by The Text Publishing Company
This edition published 2013

Page design by Text
Typeset by Imogen Stubbs
Jacket design by WH Chong
Jacket image by Olegas Truchanas: Three Truchanas children at Lake Pedder in 1971, before its flooding by the Tasmanian Hydro-Electric Commission. Used with the kind permission of the Truchanas Family Collection. (National Library of Australia file 3969586, digital reproduction of slide.)

Printed in Australia by Griffin Press, an Accredited ISO AS/NZS 14001:2004 Environmental Management System printer

National Library of Australia Cataloguing-in-Publication entry:
Title: Deep south: stories from Tasmania, editors, Ralph Crane, Danielle Wood.
Edition: 2nd ed.
ISBN: 9781922147592 (pbk.)
ISBN: 9781921961274 (ebook)
Subjects: Short stories, Australian—Tasmania. Tasmania—Fiction.
Other Authors/Contributors: Crane, Ralph J. (Ralph Jonathan), 1957-
       Wood, Danielle, 1972-
Dewey Number: A823.01

This book is printed on paper certified against the Forest Stewardship Council® Standards. Griffin Press holds FSC chain-of-custody certification SGS-COC-005088. FSC promotes environmentally responsible, socially beneficial and economically viable management of the world's forests.

Contents

INTRODUCTION	1
Black Crows: An Episode of 'Old Van Diemen' *A. Werner*	11
Nectar of the Gods *H. W. Stewart*	21
Death of a Ladies' Man *James McQueen*	31
Great-Aunt Fanny's Picnic *Hal Porter*	51
Faith, Hope and Charity *Philomena van Rijswijk*	71
The Woodpecker Toy Fact *Carmel Bird*	87
A Jar of Raspberry Jam *Barney Roberts*	97
How Muster-Master Stoneman Earned His Breakfast *Price Warung*	105
A 'Model' Dream *Theresa Tasmania*	117
An Old-Time Episode in Tasmania *Tasma*	133
The Seizure of the *Cyprus* *Marcus Clarke*	153
The Hermit of the Huon *Henry J. Goldsmith*	165

The Castle Morton Jerry *Nicholas Shakespeare*	185
Orange Bathers *Adrienne Eberhard*	197
The Needle in the Shoe *Rohan Wilson*	205
None of the Above *Danielle Wood*	215
In the River *Tahune Linah*	227
The Salted Claim *A. J. O.*	231
The Tasmanian Devil *James Leakey*	243
The Magistrate *Roy Bridges*	269
The Meat Merchant *Geoffrey Dean*	283
Preserves *Margaret Scott*	289
The Mysterious Handbag *Rachael Treasure*	309
The Conquest of Emmie *Joan Wise*	315
BIOGRAPHICAL DETAILS	321
ACKNOWLEDGEMENTS	329

Introduction

> 'A sort of bringing of heaven and hell together'
> —*Mark Twain*

The literature of Tasmania has made, and continues to make, a remarkable contribution to the literature of Australia. David Burn's *The Bushrangers*, reputedly the first Australian play to be staged, was performed in Edinburgh in 1829. In 1830 Henry Savery published the first collection of Australian essays, *The Hermit in Van Diemen's Land*, and the following year he published the first Australian novel, *Quintus Servinton*. Thomas Richards, who wrote extensively for various periodicals, including the *Hobart Town Magazine* (Australia's first literary journal), is widely regarded as Australia's first dramatic critic, and among the earliest Australian short-story writers and literary essayists. Charles Rowcroft's *Tales of the Colonies, or, the Adventures of an Emigrant* (1843) was the first novel to explore the migrant experience in Australia. Caroline Leakey's *Broad Arrow* (1859) was the first convict novel, a genre made famous by Marcus Clarke's *For the Term of His Natural Life* (1874).

The short story, like poetry, has been prominent in Tasmanian literature since colonial days. Stories were published in serial form in early literary periodicals from the 1830s, such as Thomas Richards' unfinished 'The Bushrangers Confederate', published across five editions of the *Hobart Town Magazine* in 1834 (and far too long to include in this collection). Not all the stories published in or about Tasmania in the first half-century of white settlement, when the colony was still Van Diemen's Land, have much artistic merit today. From the 1860s on, though, there is no shortage of high-quality short fiction from the island state.

The earliest stories in this book—Theresa Tasmania's 'A "Model" Dream', Marcus Clarke's 'The Seizure of the *Cyprus*', Henry J. Goldsmith's 'The Hermit of the Huon' and James Leakey's 'The Tasmanian Devil'—attest to this quality and give us a clear idea of the types of fiction that were being read in Tasmania and Australia in the 1860s and 1870s. Clarke's story was published in the *Australasian*, while the stories by Tasmania and Goldsmith both appeared in the *Australian Journal*.

These periodicals, along with the *Bulletin*, the nation's most famous literary and current affairs magazine, were the most important forums for short fiction in Australia in the later decades of the nineteenth century and through the first half of the twentieth. They provided a platform for short-fiction writers, freed of imperial shackles, to develop an Australian voice—in the case of the stories in this volume, a distinctly Tasmanian one—to write about Australia, for Australians. Under the editorship of Marcus Clarke (1870–71) the *Australian Journal* announced a policy of publishing only fiction set in the colonies or of colonial interest, while the *Bulletin* cultivated an anti-British literary nationalism. To write for local periodicals was, and is, to engage with a local readership. The short story is thus the form in which many of the preoccupations of Tasmanian colonial and postcolonial literature have manifested over almost two centuries.

If the *Australasian*, the *Australian Journal* and the *Bulletin* provided an Australian context for writers in the nineteenth century, the launch in 1979 of the *Tasmanian Review*—'a literary and arts quarterly produced in Tasmania' that would later become *Island Magazine*, then the current *Island*—provided a specifically local context for the state's writers. It quickly established itself as an important outlet for the work of Tasmanian and other short-story writers, and indeed four of the stories in this collection—James McQueen's 'Death of a Ladies' Man', Nicholas Shakespeare's 'The Castle Morton Jerry', Adrienne Eberhard's 'Orange Bathers' and Danielle Wood's 'None of the Above'—were first published in this Tasmanian literary icon.

But back copies of journals are rarely read, and unless they are anthologised it is the fate of short stories to be quickly forgotten. This book sets out to rectify that loss, to rediscover Tasmania's literary and cultural history through its short fiction. These twenty-four stories talk to each other; they form a narrative, and not simply a historical one (which is why we eschewed chronological order), of the way Tasmania perceives itself.

The short stories in this book can be approached as pieces in a mosaic: each is engaging on its own, but when pieced together they present a broader, historically deeper picture of Tasmania.

The devastating impact of white settlement on the Indigenous population is the starting point of our anthology. The opening story, A. Werner's 'Black Crows: An Episode of "Old Van Diemen"', could almost have been in Mark Twain's mind when in *Following the Equator* (1895) he wrote: 'it was in this paradise that the yellow liveried convicts were landed, and the Corps-bandits quartered, and the wanton slaughter of the kangaroo-chasing black innocents consummated.' Set several millennia earlier, H. W. Stewart's 'Nectar of the Gods' depicts Tasmania's first inhabitants in a lost Arcadian landscape, untouched by the brutality of colonisation that marks Werner's narrative. Stewart's story celebrates the innocence of the Aborigines, and its humour assiduously avoids condescension. Though the racist language used by the narrator of James McQueen's gritty 'Death of a Ladies' Man' is confronting, this story is unusual in its refusal to locate Tasmanian Aboriginality in the distant past or within a narrative of extinction. Set on Flinders Island, McQueen's moving tale tells of family bonds strong enough to prevail over ingrained prejudice.

Place, family and identity, all important aspects of McQueen's story, are tightly interwoven in Tasmania's relatively small and stable population. Notions of memory and inheritance, too, pervade the fiction produced here. Hal Porter covers all this territory in 'Great-Aunt Fanny's Picnic', in which the machinations of the dynastic and parochial

Otterwell clan are depicted with the author's characteristic wit. Philomena van Rijswijk's 'Faith, Hope and Charity', named for the three major islands in Port Esperance in the south, delves into the darker memories of a family's seaside holidays, while in 'The Woodpecker Toy Fact' Carmel Bird is appropriately bowerbird-like in her bringing together of bright bits and pieces from her narrator's childhood, heritage and flights of fancy. Bird's story is set in the northwest of the island, not far from Flowerdale, where Barney Roberts was born, lived and set most of his tales, including 'A Jar of Raspberry Jam', in which a young boy observes the impermanence of the world around him.

In many of the stories Tasmania tells to itself and to its visitors the past remains omnipresent. Perhaps the least escapable aspect of its narrative inheritance comes from the convict era, which continues to provide writers and filmmakers with opportunities for high drama and sentimentality, skulduggery and bloody violence. Price Warung's wonderfully titled 'How Muster-Master Stoneman Earned His Breakfast', set in the early 1830s, may draw on the careers of the muster-master Thomas Mason (hence Stoneman) and the convict Joseph Greenwood, but here, as in the author's other convict tales, historical accuracy does not get in the way of convict legend, in which the felon is usually the hero. Again, the author's sympathies are on the side of the convict mutineers in Marcus Clarke's 'The Seizure of the *Cyprus*' who are desperate to gain their freedom rather than complete the journey to incarceration at Macquarie Harbour. Theresa Tasmania's chilling story 'A "Model"

Dream' graphically portrays the horror of Port Arthur, in particular its panopticon, while Tasma's deft handling of character in 'An Old-Time Episode in Tasmania' brings to the fore the distorted social hierarchy between free settlers and felons.

One of the pleasures of creating this anthology was bringing together stories that spoke directly to each other across the decades, as is the case with Henry J. Goldsmith's nineteenth-century story and Nicholas Shakespeare's recent tale. In 'The Hermit of the Huon'—which has some of the flavour of Jerome K. Jerome's later *Three Men in a Boat* (1889)—Goldsmith offers his readers a gentle account of a reformed and ultimately respected convict, while also satirising government circumlocution. More than a hundred years later Shakespeare revisits the Huon in a playful retrospective concerning the convict-era arrival of a ship of women.

As writers can usually be relied upon to move around between genres, and in particular between long and short forms of prose fiction, we had a quiet expectation that our searches in the back catalogues of Tasmanian short fiction would turn up a good number of stories by the island's better-known novelists. Sometimes, however, we were surprised by what we did not find. Novelists such as Christopher Koch, Amanda Lohrey, Richard Flanagan, Katherine Scholes and Heather Rose have made only rare, if any, forays into the form.

For Koch, a keen observer of Tasmanian letters, sensitivity to geography is a key characteristic of the island's literature. In his essay 'A Tasmanian Tone' he suggests Tasmanian writers owe much to their landscape and its cool temperate tonality. Isolation, islandness and the coastal environment are important in the stories here by Eberhard, in which a young girl experiences the ecstasy and agony of wearing her first bathing suit to the beach, and by Wood. Similarly, the island and the individual intersect in Rohan Wilson's 'The Needle in the Shoe', in which an ageing author looks back—from his spectacular vantage point on the east coast—on a life in which he has failed to connect with those around him.

Tahune Linah's 'In the River' takes the reader to a time when hardworking men, piners, used the fast-flowing watercourses of the west coast to transport logs of ancient Huon pine. Pining was central to the settlement era of Tasmania's history, as was mining, the industry at the heart of A. J. O.'s 'The Salted Claim'. Also set on Tasmania's west coast, this cautionary tale describes how a group of larrikins separate a naïve and unsuspecting investor from his money during a period of 'mining mania'. The tall tale is taken to greater heights by James Leakey, a brother of the novelist Caroline Leakey, in his wild colonial yarn 'The Tasmanian Devil', in which a hunter travels across the globe in search of the fabled marsupial carnivore.

Side by side in this collection are tales from Tasmania's most prolific writer, Roy Bridges, and its foremost champion and practitioner of the short-story form, Geoffrey Dean. Bridges, whose name is a shortened form of the grand moniker Royal Tasman Bridges, penned thirty-six novels and numerous short stories in his career. Here we have included 'The Magistrate', a swashbuckling story of true love and bushranging in the Tasmanian Midlands. Dean, the author of eight collections, has elsewhere been anthologised alongside internationally renowned writers such as Margaret Atwood and Kurt Vonnegut. From his output we have selected 'The Meat Merchant', an apparently simple tale but one that bears out the critic Giles Hugo's observation that beneath Dean's 'sunny exterior beats the maverick heart of a wry anarchist, laughing and gently mocking' the ways of middle Australia.

One of Tasmania's best-loved writers and public figures is Margaret Scott. Primarily a poet, she also published two novels and a number of short stories, and late in life made an unexpected crossover into television celebrity. The wit and keen observational powers that made her a national treasure are evident in her story 'Preserves'. Set in a rural community reminiscent of Premaydena, the Tasman Peninsula hamlet where Scott lived for many years, 'Preserves' is the tale of the tireless home industrialist Zena Bromyard and the tragedy which forces her to recognise that not even her peerless arsenal of bottled fruits and vegetables can hold back the forces of disorder.

When we came to organise the stories we had selected we knew at once that Joan Wise's feisty 'The Conquest of Emmie' should conclude the collection. Perceiving a literary kinship between Wise's Emmie and the heroine of Rachael Treasure's 'The Mysterious Handbag', we placed the two stories together. When the time came to write the biographical entries, Wise proved elusive. Her life and her achievements are undocumented in the public sphere and her books were published without a hint of personal detail. Imagine, then, our surprise: first, when we discovered that Wise is

Treasure's maternal grandmother; and second, when we found that Treasure, though she knew her grandmother was an author, had no knowledge of this story.

In selecting the stories in this collection we were governed by simple guidelines: to present excellent stories that reflect the island's history and evoke its atmosphere, and that draw on its convict past, its isolation and its environment; not to include more than one story by any writer; to include only writers who were born in Tasmania or who settled, at least for a time, on the island; and to prefer stories with a Tasmanian setting. The only exceptions are James Leakey and A. Werner, whose stories are so quintessentially Tasmanian that they excuse the authors' seemingly limited experience of the island. Our longlist included many fine stories that do not appear in the following pages. As we made the final and most difficult decisions, we tried to maintain some balance between the number of offerings from the three centuries the collection spans, and to keep faith with the palette of the mosaic.

We believe the variety of stories in this book is testament to the dynamic life the short story has had in Tasmania over two hundred years. And, as the pieces chosen from this century affirm, the short story continues to flourish as a literary form on the island. Looking over the contents of this collection we are excited that a new generation of readers will become familiar with these great tales.

Ralph Crane & Danielle Wood
Hobart, 2012

A. Werner • 1886

Black Crows: An Episode of 'Old Van Diemen'

He had never heard of the 'enthusiasm of humanity'—the expression was not in fashion in his day, and, if it had been, I doubt whether he would have understood it; for he was only an Australian stock-rider, a 'Sydney cornstalk' born, who had never read a book in his life except the Bible, and perhaps not very much of that, and was more familiar with bush craft and horsemanship than with abstract principles of any sort. Yet, if actions prove anything, the thing which that famous phrase has come to stand for was not altogether unknown to him.

It was in Van Diemen's Land—we hadn't heard of Tasmania in those days—that I made Jack Hepburn's acquaintance. At that time he was in the employ of my friend Allardyce on the Emu Plains, and had been so for about two years—the only free stockman on the run. Allardyce—himself one of the finest fellows that ever stepped—had unbounded confidence in him, and looked to him as a sort of sheet-anchor in the midst of the endless troubles and annoyances arising out of a supply of convict labour. He was a tough, muscular, black-bearded fellow, a trifle over six feet, and fairly good-looking; active in his movements, but slow and very sparing of his speech, and not particularly remarkable for anything unless it were his scrupulous honesty and strict truthfulness.

I had left the colony when the incident happened which I am about to relate. I heard various accounts of it afterwards, and the substance of them, as nearly as I can give it, is pretty much as follows.

There were four of them up in the bush at the hut known as 'Dicey's', one clear January evening. Dicey, the hut-keeper—a grizzled old sinner, popularly reported to have been one of the first arrivals in Sydney, though I have reason to believe that this is incorrect—was busy cooking inside; Jack Hepburn sat on a stump a little way from the door, plaiting a new lash for his stock whip; and the other two—'hands' both of them, and of a pretty bad type—lounged in the doorway, chewing tobacco and carrying on a low growling conversation.

Now Jack was a good-natured, kindly fellow enough; but he never forgot the difference between himself and these men, and never allowed them to forget it; and, naturally enough, they detested him. No doubt this was scarcely Christian charity, but Jack was not a perfect character—very far from it—and, in justice to him, it must be remembered that, in spite of natural prejudices, in his own phrase 'he never liked to be rough on a hand as wanted to behave himself decently,' which, on the whole, was not the deepest desire of the two specimens before us. But even a worm will turn, and, though they doubtless fully deserved the curt contempt and lordly superciliousness with which he treated them, they didn't like it.

All this by the way. Jack was not paying any particular attention to the dialogue going on in the doorway—it was not his habit to take an interest in the conversation of those gentlemen, which, it must be allowed, showed a certain monotony—when his ear was caught by a much-emphasised assertion as to the shooting of crows. He knew that, in their dialect, this word was applied to bronze-coloured and featherless bipeds oftener than to black and feathered ones; and he was well acquainted with the reckless disregard of life—not confined to convicts either—shown towards the unlucky natives of the island. It was a curious trait in Jack Hepburn's character—considering the universal and deeply rooted prejudice of all colonial Englishmen—that his naturally strong sense of justice suffered no bias or abrogation where 'black fellows' were concerned. Perhaps his experience of convict whites and his sojourn among the wild tribes of the bush (I know his wanderings had been wide and adventurous before he settled on Allardyce's run) had shaken his belief in the comparative worthlessness of the latter. However it may be accounted for—and I am not writing an analytic dissertation on his character; I am only telling his story—such was the fact. And he knew that there was a tribe of natives not very far off; he had seen their tracks in the bush that very day.

So he listened, without seeming to hear, while one of the two—a lowering, sullen-faced creature, with small eyes, a retreating forehead, and cruel jaw—gave a circumstantial statement of a wanton murder committed some months before. Facts of the kind may be found in plenty by those who care to read the cruel record.

Then he looked up and said in his quietest tones:

'Hawk Williams, that might do well enough on the Tamar, but I tell you I won't have it *here*.'

'Hawk' Williams gave a brutal laugh; the other man stared and whistled.

'What —— call hev *you* got to meddle? Who the —— made *you* boss of this here consarn?'

'Call or no call, I *won't—have it*,' said Jack Hepburn, giving a twist to the end of his whip-lash.

'How'll you stop it?' sneered Williams. 'There's no law agin the killin' of black crows, is there? Meredith on the Tamar was glad enough to have 'em picked off, and so will Allardyce be for that matter.'

'I know better'n that,' said Jack Hepburn, and finished his work reflectively, without lifting his eyes, for his soul was stirred within him. He knew that the man's words were on the whole perfectly true—that he had no force of law or public opinion to back him; that he had no authority over these men to compel them to refrain from such a deed should they wish to do it; that Allardyce, who he felt sure would be on his side, was miles away at the station, and that he had heard Allardyce's partner, Kearney, treat such things as the merest trifles. And, as he thought, the slowly smouldering fires of his disgust and indignation burnt through their embers and leapt up into words.

'I don't know,' he said, slowly, looking full in 'Hawk'

Williams' evil face—'I don't know about the law and what folks think; but I *do* know this: that if I saw a chap doin' as you said just now—firin' on them poor helpless critters, women, kids, and all, for pure sport—I'd just shoot that fellow where he stood.'

'I'd like to see you,' laughed Hawk. 'I always knew you were a mean-spirited cuss, but you'd never dare that. I've a good mind to try. Hallo!'

Jack Hepburn turned and followed the direction of his eye. His own, trained to the bush, at once detected the slight movement in the scrub, and knew what caused it. Williams had turned into the hut.

'Look, Hawk!' said Cass, the other convict, who had not as yet spoken, seeing him come out again with a loaded gun in his hand. 'Sh! Over there!'

'So it is,' said Hawk, taking aim.

Jack Hepburn's rifle lay beside him; he took it in his hand and stood up.

'Hawk Williams, I give you fair warning. Put that thing down.'

'Not for you, you cantin' sneak. You darsn't shoot a white man. *That's* a hangin' matter.'

'I know it is. If you fire I'll shoot you dead and swing for it.'

They both stood motionless, with guns cocked, Williams watching the edge of the scrub, Hepburn watching Williams. None of the natives ventured out into the open ground; they had learnt to be cautious in the neighbourhood of white men's huts, and perhaps the bright eyes peering through the branches awhile ago had seen the shining gun-barrels. So perhaps five minutes passed, and then—it might have been a bough stirred by a puff of wind, or a kangaroo rat passing through the underbush; but something moved, and Hawk Williams fired into the scrub.

As the shot snapped there was a shriek, and a brown figure darted into the open, a good way farther off, but still within rifle range, and fled up the hill. Jack Hepburn still stood like a statue. Perhaps Williams thought he was hesitating; anyhow, he fired his second barrel. The brown figure dropped.

Then Jack Hepburn levelled the rifle that had never missed fire yet, and without speaking a word shot Hawk Williams through the heart.

He had taken the dead man up and laid him in his bed-place inside the hut, unhelped by the others, who seemed struck dumb with consternation and perplexity. Old Dicey, the cooler of the two, was fairly puzzled as he vainly searched his memory for a parallel case. Both kept outside the door, stealing uneasy glances every now and then at the silent man who sat, with his head in his hands, beside what had been Hawk Williams, as though they thought he might suddenly rise and kill them too. But he never moved, and as the dusk stole up and the air grew damp and chilly, they were fain to turn in and seek their blankets.

Only once he looked up.

'Mates,' he said, 'when does Allardyce come round? Is it to-morrow?'

It was a point of etiquette with him to mark his status as

a free man by never speaking of 'Mr Allardyce', as they were obliged to do—within hearing of the authorities.

They looked at each other and muttered 'Yes.'

'All right,' he answered, then returned to his brooding watch, and so they found him still seated when they awoke in the morning.

He stayed about the hut all day. 'You chaps might think I wanted to cut an' run,' he remarked, 'and I want to be on hand when he comes. You can tell him what you please.'

It was afternoon when Allardyce arrived. He must have met with Cass on the way and heard something already, for he galloped up in frantic haste and threw himself from his horse, crying 'Hepburn, what's this?'

'It's quite true, sir,' said Jack, quietly. 'Come along,' and he led the way into the hut.

Old Dicey met them in the doorway with a high-pitched and voluble story about a quarrel in which Hawk Williams had not been to blame; but Allardyce pushed past him and stood with Hepburn beside the dead man.

'I shot him, sir, you may see, and I'll show you why. I gave him fair warning, and I told him I was ready to take the consequences. Will you come this way?'

They went down the hill together and into the scrub, and Jack parted the branches and showed him a copper-coloured corpse lying there on its face, the limbs twisted and hands clenched in the terrible death agony, and the hole where the bullet had torn its jagged course from back to breast.

'I shot him straight,' said Jack, as if to himself. 'He didn't have to suffer like *that*.'

But Duncan Allardyce turned his white face away and leaned his hand heavily on Jack's shoulder.

'That's not all,' said Jack, looking at him narrowly. 'But—'

'Go on,' said Allardyce.

They went on to a spot where there was an opossum-skin rug spread out on the grass; and Jack Hepburn lifted it up and showed a dead woman—a slight-limbed creature scarcely more than a girl—with a child in her arms.

'There!' he said, hoarsely. 'He knew that; he could see it well enough from where we stood. And if it were to do over again I'd do it. And if it's hanging—why, I'll hang.'

Duncan Allardyce turned to him and took both his hands.

'God help us both, Jack!' he cried. 'I think you're right.'

It *was* a hanging matter. The trial created rather a sensation at the time, and it ended as might have been expected, seeing that the counsel Allardyce engaged failed to establish the plea of lunacy, the only extenuating circumstance the court would have admitted. Kearney was not inclined to ruin himself in trying to save a fool who would meddle with what was no business of his. He and Allardyce quarrelled and parted over that affair, and the latter spent his money alone and to no purpose. He was with Jack Hepburn the night before he died. They had always liked each other, but those last few weeks had drawn them together strangely, and they parted as dearest friends do.

The time was nearly gone. They had sat side by side, silent, holding each other's hands—how the consciousness of the fast-slipping minutes strikes those dumb who have so much to say!—for the last time; then at last Allardyce said:

'Is anything troubling you, Jack?'

He looked at him with sad, perplexed eyes, and spoke slowly and hesitatingly:

'Maybe—I don't know whether it was wrong; I don't want to say it wasn't.' He laid his head down on Allardyce's shoulder and went on in a hoarse, hurried whisper: 'Parson says I can't get to heaven if I don't repent—and I—I can't say I'm—sorry for a thing—when I know I'd do it again—if it happened so...and I wouldn't like to get in by telling a lie—if such a thing could be. I...oh! I don't know how to tell you what I mean...and that chap just riles me...and I don't want to feel angry with anyone...'

'I think I know,' said Allardyce, and his voice was very low and gentle. 'Dear old lad, I'm not good; I can't talk to you as—as one ought; but I understand what you are feeling. Don't you mind what he tells you. God is just, and He understands, if no one else can. Go straight to Him, and ask Him, if you were wrong, to give you grace to see it...though, as He hears me—I believe you did a right and noble thing...' His voice choked with the sob in his throat, but the loving clasp of his arms said all that words could not.

'He said I had no right...'

'Don't you believe it! God is greater and juster than he! Oh, Jack, my boy!'

'There, they're coming. You'll have to go.'

'Good-night—good-bye. Kiss me—there! good-bye! Don't forget I'm—thinking of you to the last.'

'Don't fret yourself about me—don't! Good-bye, Allardyce. God bless you!'

The key turned in the lock and the door swung on its hinges, letting in a broad band of light from the turnkey's lamp.

'Time's up, sir.'

I do not judge him; I have only told his story.

H. W. Stewart • 1923

Nectar of the Gods

You may date this story ten thousand years ago. It may have been more, it may have been less. I can only say that it was after the sinking of Bass Strait separated the island of Tasmania from the mainland of Australia. That much is certain, as Merriwee's great discovery never reached the continent. Perhaps, on second thoughts, it would be better to date it 'Once Upon a Time'.

Warm rain had melted the last of the belated winter snow on the Western Tiers and the Lake River was in flood. The water had risen over the flats where Merriwee's tribe usually camped for a few weeks before climbing the mountains; so they had built their bark breakwinds under the shelter of the tea-trees in a gully of the foothills. The smoke from their fires rose straight into the clear air, and every peak along the range was plainly outlined against the blue sky.

Merriwee was proud of a new chopping tool that he had just fashioned from a piece of chert. It had a nice hollow for the thumb to get a grip of (no genius had yet arisen to show the tribe how to put a handle to their tools), and its crescent edge was chipped beautifully even and sharp. Parts of it were keen enough to shave the hairs from his arms. More by way of giving it a trial than anything else he was searching the tree-tops for a bee's nest or hollow limb where a brush-'possum might be sleeping.

Twice he had passed thick trees containing the bulky stick-and-leaf nests of the ring-tails. But the ring-tailed 'possum feeds on gum-leaves and is only fit for women to eat; whereas the brush-'possum comes down and feeds on the succulent grass, wherefore its flesh is food for warriors. There were scratches on a tall cider-gum; and a few minutes' examination convinced him that the 'possum was at home in a hollow limb fifty feet up. Three feet from the ground he chipped a notch in the white bark. Then he swung his grass rope round the tree, got inside the loop that it formed, placed his big toe in the notch, and stepped up. With the ends of the rope in one hand, he leant back and chopped a notch for his left toe. Then he pulled the rope until he stood close against the trunk of the tree, jerked the loop three feet higher and stepped up again. He continued chopping and climbing until he reached the first limb. Then he took the loose end of the rope, swung it across the fork, caught both ends and pulled himself astride. From that upwards it was easy climbing until he reached the broken hollow limb where the 'possum had his nest. He hammered until a round-eared, brown-eyed creature came out, blinking at the sunlight. Catching it by the bushy tail he dragged it off the limb, swung it round, dashed its head against the tree, and let it drop to the ground. In a few seconds he was beside it.

He felt well pleased with his new chopping tool. Two or three cuts with it made a beautiful climbing notch. He picked it up and idly chipped at the first notch until it was large enough to put his fist into. Yes, he decided; it would be equally good for cutting out bees' nests.

A piece of honeycomb would be good eating after his 'possum, and he began to look for a hive. The ground was covered with orchids, irises, buttercups and daisies, but there were few bees visiting them. Nearly all had been lured to the tops of the gum-trees, where they were helping the birds rifle the pale yellow flowers. But the tops of the gum-trees were too high for him to be able to see in what direction the bees were going.

In a near-by creek-bed the blackwood and prickly wattle made a patch of gold, and the thick scrub that bordered the creek was covered with lilac blossom. At one of the low bushes he caught a laden bee and stuck a tiny piece of feather fluff to its back with a dab of wattle-gum. Then he released it and followed it as it flew heavily away. Up the hillside it led him, straight as an arrow, to a blue-gum, where the little shiny bees were passing in and out of the knot-holes. To climb up was easy, but the hard, dry wood took a lot of chipping away, in spite of the excellence of his new chopping tool. He had been at work half-an-hour before he was able to put in his hand and draw out three circles of brown comb, oozing golden honey, sweet and aromatic with the scent of gum blossom. Satisfied, he wandered back to the camp-fires in the gully.

Some days afterwards, passing the cider-tree that he had climbed for the 'possum, Merriwee was attracted by the sight of hundreds of moths and butterflies flitting around the hole he had chopped in the trunk. Half-a-pint of pale golden liquid lay in the hollow, and every insect about seemed to have collected there, drinking. When they had drunk their fill they climbed or flew aimlessly, or sat, half stupid, basking in the sun. The day was hot, Merriwee was thirsty, and the liquid looked tempting. He dipped a finger and sucked it. At first he was hardly sure whether he liked the half-sweet, half-sour taste or not; it was so different from anything he had tasted before. Two fingers dipped in for a second taste decided him. He skimmed away the insects that had fallen in, put his mouth to the hole, and sucked up as much of the liquid as he could reach. It was sharp to his tongue, tingled in his throat, and gave him a warm, comforting sensation in his stomach.

He liked it so much that he plucked a straw and drained the last dregs.

Picking up his spear and club he went up the hillside on the look out for a kangaroo. As he walked he began to experience some new and pleasant sensations. He had never noticed before what a beautiful world he lived in, or what a wonderful adventure it was just to be alive; he felt as though he owned the earth, had a mortgage on the sea, and a reasonable chance of inheriting the sky. He wanted to shout, to jump, to sing. When he saw a kangaroo, instead of stalking, he began to run after it, waving his spear and shouting, confident that he was the faster runner of the two. The ground seemed to rise up in front of him, and he tripped and fell; but he got up satisfied that only for the fall he would have been successful. Not only did he feel that he could run as fast as the kangaroo, but he believed he could fly like a bird if only he could get a start. He climbed on to a log and he saw the trees and bushes circling round him and the earth rising and falling like the waves of the sea. The sight made him giddy and he tumbled to the ground; but nothing seemed to matter. As he lay beside the log he felt that it was necessary to hold on to the earth lest he should fall away into space. But even that did not worry him. The sun was comfortably warm, myriads of insects were singing a lullaby and he was sleepy.

When he woke it was getting dusk, and he was obliged to return to the camp empty-handed and be laughed at by the successful hunters. He recounted his experiences to an incredulous audience. In the Happy Hunting Grounds, he assured them, such nectar was drunk by the Immortals. The young men jocularly hinted that he had only invented an excuse for coming back without any game. The old men gravely listened to his tale of the magic liquid that made a man feel like a god, and solemnly shook their heads over the fact that he, a young man, hardly more than a boy, should have presumed to drink what was, doubtless, intended solely for the elders. Their council immediately decided that this new drink, if Merriwee's tale were true, should be taboo to all the women and the young men, as were all the choice bits of food.

Next day Merriwee led several of the elders to the tree, expecting to find a fresh supply of nectar. The hole was full of liquid, but when the old men tasted it it was sour, and none of them afterwards felt the magic that Merriwee had boasted about. After scolding him for leading them on a foolish quest they went back to the camp.

But Merriwee was not satisfied. The liquid appeared the same, and yet there was a difference, but a difference he found it impossible to explain to the scoffers. He decided that the hundreds of moths and butterflies that had been rioting around the tree were in some way responsible. Full of hope he chopped the original hole deeper, and another alongside it.

Early in the morning he visited the tree again. Both holes were full of sap, but there were no moths or butterflies, and when he tasted the liquid there was no magic in it, so he went away disappointed. Next day there was a kangaroo hunt, and Merriwee was obliged to take his place in the line of warriors that speared the animals as the women and children drove them past. Had his experience been ordinary he would have forgotten it, but it was not, and on the morning after the hunt he went across and found the tree surrounded by a halo of fluttering insects.

He only waited to assure himself that the magic had been at work once more, and then went back to the camp for the old men. He found them incredulous; but two, less sceptical than the others, followed him. They tried the liquid and found it pleasant, and the magic sensations that came over them afterwards were like nothing they had ever experienced before. The three of them drank deep of the fermenting sap and then started back to the camp with the good news. By the time they came back in sight of the fires their progress was hilarious and their antics, after they arrived, provided the tribe's dramatist with the material for the most successful corroboree he had ever produced.

The council of the old men considered this strange thing and decided that, as Merriwee had become possessed of a powerful magic, he should be admitted to their circle, although he was only a youth. Dire penalties were promised the other young men and the women if they dared to drink so much as a drop.

For two weeks the tribe stayed in their camp and Merriwee regularly extracted nectar that was fit for drinking every second day: and the old men saw that none of it was wasted. But as summer drew nearer, and the weather grew hotter and drier, the supply of sap diminished, and nothing but a sticky gum would ooze into the holes that Merriwee chopped.

The time came for them to gather up their belongings and follow the spring to the mountains. They camped on the plateau by the shores of the Great Lake, where there were other groves of cider-gum. For several weeks Merriwee was able to produce a regular supply of nectar. Then these trees, too, dried up, or, as the old men affirmed, Merriwee lost his magic.

The matter was long debated round the council fire. Merriwee had a powerful magic and now he had lost it; what was lost must have been stolen; the thief must be one of the Big River tribe. Such logic was irrefutable.

The summer was passed pleasantly on the top of the Tiers, and when autumn came the tribe migrated to the coast. If it had not been that the corroboree of Merriwee's magic was regularly performed most of the tribe would have forgotten the Nectar of the Gods. But not Merriwee: he still went about chopping holes in the trees—in blue-gum, peppermint, myrtle and sassafras trees; in trees on the hills and trees in the gullies—but none yielded anything.

Camped behind the sandbanks on the seashore, the men had an easy time. Prizing limpets and oysters off the rocks, diving for crayfish down amongst the strands of the giant kelp, and digging for edible roots was all women's work. The men took their pick of the food when it was brought to the camp, and threw what they did not care for over their shoulders to the women who had done the collecting. Occasionally, for sport, the men speared stingrays in the shallow hollows of the beach, or for a change of food organised a kangaroo hunt.

While the black swans were moulting they were easily speared, and when they built their nests in the shallow waters of the lagoon the tribe feasted on their eggs. Then it was time to follow the spring towards the mountains. On their way two of the young warriors speared one of the men belonging to the Big River tribe, who was trespassing on their territory. Trespassing was punishable by death; but this doubtless was also the thief of Merriwee's magic. They arrived back at the camp at the foot of the Tiers, and Merriwee chopped a number of holes in the clump of cider-gums where he had first discovered his magic. Next morning the holes were filled with sap, and the day after a halo of winged creatures testified that his magic had again been successful. Great was the rejoicing of the old men; and Merriwee was once more admitted to their council.

Some days later it was the Spring full moon and a great corroboree was held to celebrate the re-discovery of the

Nectar of the Gods. What had been merely an impromptu farce when first performed was expanded into a full night's entertainment. A piece of level ground was cleared and ringed round with fires. The women and children took up positions on one side, the men on the other, the old men in a group slightly apart. The performers, a picked band of the younger men, as naked as they were born, had been well coached by the tribe's dramatist. The orchestral accompaniment was provided by the women hammering sticks together and beating with their hands on rolled-up kangaroo skins.

Merriwee's discovery of the magic liquid was acted; his taking the old men to be disappointed; then his taking of the two old men and their return to the camp after finding that the magic had worked; the young man of the Big River tribe stealing Merriwee's magic while he slept; the spearing of the thief; finally, Merriwee's magic again successful. The intoxicating rhythm grew faster and faster, and the performers leapt higher and higher until their sweat-covered bodies gleamed like polished bronze in the light of the fires. It was midnight when the performance ended with the exhaustion of the last dancer.

Year after year the corroboree of Merriwee's magic was performed at the same place and season. As time passed, what was originally intended as celebration was believed to influence the sap rising and fermenting in the hollows cut in the cider-trees. It became a symbol, a myth, part of the religious ritual of the tribe, the omission of which would in some way prejudice the return of Spring.

James McQueen • 1985

Death of a Ladies' Man

From the cemetery on Vinegar Hill you can see fifty miles on a clear day—past the wharf and sheds and stockyard at the bottom of the hill out over the channel to the first of the islands in the chain and beyond them to the mainland hills, all pale and smoky in the distance.

After it was finally over I went across to where the bearers were standing together by a clump of she-oaks, all solemn and ruddy and uncomfortable in their blue suits, and shook hands with them. They had all been mates of Chris's, had gone to school with him, boozed with him, played football with him. Mannie Boone was there, the one whose sister Claire we thought Chris was going to marry at one time. I wasn't sorry when it blew over, because Mannie is as thick as two planks, and Claire's not much brighter.

Away near the fence there was a little group of boongs, three or four of them. When I looked closer I could see that one of them was the Marsden girl, and I thought, shit, she's got a cheek...

Then I saw that she was crying, and hanging on to one of the others.

They turned away then, and were off out the gate and down the track before I got back to the old man.

'You ready to go?' I said.

You never know these days if he hears you or not. He just looked at me, lifted his chin a bit and turned away, headed for the car, leaning on his stick. Elaine took my arm, and we followed him. Everyone else hung back until we passed.

The old man sat in the back on his own. He used to like to sit up front with Chris when Chris was driving.

We rattled down the track to the road and turned north, away from the harbour. The day was cold and clear and bright as only mid-winter can be on the island. The steering of the old Falcon chattered on the corrugations, and I made a mental note to check the mounts on the steering box.

'That was good of them,' said Elaine.

'Who?'

'Hawthorn—you know, sending the wreath.'

I just grunted. Big city football clubs and wreaths and telegrams of condolence. The truth is that Chris thought they were a bunch of shits, all of them.

I glanced over my shoulder at the old man, but he was just sitting there straight as a ruler, staring in front of him.

I drove in through the gate at Emerald and parked by the front door, let Elaine out. She tried to help the old man, but he brushed her off. He eats the food she cooks, wears the clothes she washes, lives in the house she cleans, but he barely looks at her. He's never forgiven her for not being able to have kids.

I went in and took off my suit and got into my working clobber. Island funerals are like that, there's no wake, no piss-up, just the church and the cemetery, and then home to do the milking or dag the sheep or whatever. When I came out the old man was sitting there on the verandah, his face as hard and expressionless as a hatchet.

'You want a cup of tea, dad?'

He took no notice, so I went off and left him, I thought that by the morning he'd be right, and back to work. He's only seventy-three and spry enough, and hard as an old boot. Always has been. I think he was born tough. When he was only eleven or twelve his family took up five hundred acres, rough acres, in outback New South Wales, and he and my grandfather ringbarked and cleared the lot. They worked from daylight to dusk; and then by moonlight, and if there was no moonlight they lit bonfires to see by. And once when my grandfather gashed his leg with his axe he just walked back to the shanty, stitched it up with black cotton, gave it a dab of Stockholm tar, and went back to work. Anything less than that sort of behaviour the old man thinks is sissy.

I was wrong about him coming back to work, though. For a long time after the funeral he just sat there on the verandah, hour after hour, day after day, staring out at our six hundred acres of clover, at the straggle of sheep, the stunted tea-tree scrub that stretches away to the coast. He did nothing, just sat there, his bony face pointed westward as if he were waiting for something. But he didn't have much to wait for now. All the spark was gone from him, all the life, and in those months he seemed to turn dry and thin and bone-brittle.

It's strange—I found an old photograph the other day, taken at the island show five or six years back. Chris and the old man and me, standing just outside the cattle pavilion. Things were going well that year, I remember, the clover knee-high, the sheep shearing seven kilos, money in the bank, and Chris ready for the big time in Melbourne. And the three of us, all dressed up in our good clothes, alike as three peas in a pod. Except for the difference in ages. And except for that subtle thing that set Chris apart from the old man and me. Oh, you'd never mistake him for anyone but a Barton, one of old Black Jack's brood, but where in me and the old man it's a matter of hard lines and angles and bony noses, in Chris it was different somehow, softer, gentler, with little curves and laughter lines. A sort of innocence to him. Everyone loved him, as far back as I can remember. Not too many loved the old man. Or me, for that matter.

In the first few weeks after the funeral the old man grew into his new habits, and every morning he'd go out after breakfast and sit in the old green armchair on the verandah, locked deep in his deafness and his misery. For a while I tried to jolly him out of it. God knows I didn't feel too jolly, none of us did, what with Chris gone, his absence like a black hole in the day. Still, I tried. But he didn't seem to hear me at all, and most of the time he just looked through me.

The truth is that for him Chris had been the future. Looking back I can see that it all started to change when he found out that Elaine and I weren't going to have any kids, ever. His interest turned slowly to Chris, focused on him, and we felt ourselves, Elaine and me, slowly fading into the background like a pair of ghosts...

The thing about Chris's death that so stunned us, I think, was its appalling triteness, the bloody *silliness* of it. He ran out of cigarettes one night, and took the old ute to drive into town and get some. It was late, and we never thought a thing about it.

When I got up next morning I went to his room to wake him, the way I always did, and he wasn't there, his bed wasn't slept in. Something was badly wrong, and I knew it straight away. I didn't say a word to anyone, just slipped out and drove off down the road, looking for him.

I didn't have far to go. A mile down the road, he'd managed somehow to hit a culvert and up-end the ute into a creek. He was still there, had been all night, crushed and bloody and still, the cold dark water rippling over him through the broken windscreen.

God knows how it had happened—a clear night, a straight road, him as sober as a judge. I don't know, too fast maybe, a wallaby on the track, a sudden distraction...

First I had to get him out, and that took a while. And then I had to go back and tell the old man. And that part of it is something that I just don't want to think about...

It was months after the funeral that I heard about the baby. Coming up to shearing, and we were getting the gear cleaned up and greased, and the boongs were yakking together instead of working and I was just going to shut them up when something made me prick up my ears.

'What did you say? About the Marsden girl?'

Herbie Alberts, who is some sort of cousin of hers—they're all bloody cousins of some sort—just looked sly, and half-grinned, and dropped his eyes.

'She's up the duff, Dick,' said Trevor Murphett. 'In the puddin' club...'

'Better than being in the bludgers' club, like you two,' I said, just to shut them off. I didn't really want to have to think too much about it, to tell the truth. They just grinned at each other and went back to work.

But I told Elaine that night while we were getting ready for bed. She was in front of the mirror, doing those things that women do in front of mirrors, cream all over her face. She was still all of a sudden. 'Do you think it is?'

'Christ knows,' I said.

She was silent then for a minute. She knew that Chris had been going about with the girl. She always gets a bit odd about babies, not being able to have any herself.

After a bit she went back to work on her face. Then: 'Do you think he was...you know?'

'Rooting her? Christ knows.'

But I knew he was, because he'd told me—come in late one night half-pissed, and tried to tell me all about her. Well, he was only twenty-three, and there isn't much on the island for them to do Saturday nights at that age except get pissed, buy a couple of bottles of plonk and drive down the island looking for a bit of black velvet. I know, I've done it myself at that age. And if a girl has a baby, generally she doesn't have a clue who the father is and even to think of a paternity suit would be a joke.

'She's a bright girl,' said Elaine.

'Mmm.'

'I taught her in Grade 4.'

'Ah.' Elaine taught half the bloody island in Grade 4.

We got into bed and I turned out the light.

'Put your arm round me,' she said after a while, and I did.

'Did you ever do that sort of thing? You know, with the black girls?'

'Not me,' I said. 'The old man kept me too busy. Besides, I've never fancied it, you know, the black stuff...' I was glad the light was out and she couldn't see my face.

'She's not really black, only about a quartercaste,' she said. 'And she's very pretty...'

'That a fact?'

It was time to take my arm away and turn over and go to sleep. But tonight was different somehow, and so I didn't move. We just lay there, warm and close. And there was that old pain between us, and I knew that she was thinking about babies again, and kids about the place and Christmas trees and all that, so I just kept my arm round her and we didn't move for a long time.

He never had much time for the boongs, the old man. Coming from the kind of country he did, I suppose it's no wonder. And I suppose it would be a miracle if some of his feeling hadn't rubbed off on me. The thing about them is they're not *steady*, and steady is what farming's all about.

And to give the old man his due, if he doesn't think much of the boongs, he doesn't think much of anyone else, either, outside the family and a few of the locals who are as hard as he is.

Because he never had it easy, coming here late as a soldier-settler, landing with his few belongings, half-frozen from the trip in the cargo hold of a Bristol freighter, no money and a wife who didn't like farming, couldn't stand the island, the people, the wind, the dullness, the *sameness* of the life. She was a city girl and was back in the big smoke within a year. So he was left with not much, and the locals gave him the business straight off. Within the first week on the property they were trying him out to see if he'd let them walk over him. Bennet Kelly, one of the old settlers, an old island family, our next-door neighbour, had his cows grazing on Emerald grass within a fortnight, a fence down, a gate open. All this was before I was born, but it's part of the legend now how old Black Jack started on the island.

He asked Kelly politely to take his cows out. He did, but they were back in a couple of days—a different fence, a different gate. This time the old man was less polite. The cows went again, and were back the next week. The old man took out the old 303 with a couple of clips and shot ten of them, left them lie. No more free grazing, and they all knew that they weren't going to walk over him.

That was a couple of years before he got married again. Realised that he wasn't going to make it on his own, so he took the weekly flight to the mainland. In Melbourne, he walked down to Flinders Street and fronted a copper on the corner, said to him, I've come to Melbourne to find a wife—you got any clues? And the copper, taking him seriously—everyone did, sooner or later—said, Well, there's a place about two blocks along, just past the pub and up the stairs, they do that sort of thing...

So the old man trundled along, up the stairs, into this bureau, and told them about his problem. Within a day they had him suited with a big strong ex-Women's Army girl who came from a Gippsland dairy farm. They were married in a week and back at work the day after. And oddly enough it worked out, the happiest marriage you'd ever see. But they weren't young, and he was pushing forty and she wasn't much younger, and she had a hard time when I was born. Ten years later having Chris killed her. The light seemed to go out of the old man then. Always hard, a hard man; but up to then he'd laughed a bit, just at home between the three of us.

No one said anything to the old man about the girl being in the club. You would have had to shout in his ear, anyway, and no one was about to do that. In fact it was a pretty quiet place, the old house, in those days, we got into the habit of eating our meals in silence, a thing we'd never done before, because meals were the times when you planned work, had a joke, caught up on things. Just silence now, and the chink of crockery. The old man would usually finish first and push back his chair, go out on the verandah, or if it was tea-time, into his room.

'What are we going to do about him?' I said to Elaine one

night when Chris was a month gone. 'He'll just bloody fade away like this...'

She just shook her head.

The truth is that we missed Chris so badly—the bent nose, the incongruous violet-blue eyes, that bloody smile—that we just couldn't seem to make any impression on the future at all.

And I'll bet we weren't the only ones that were missing him. There would be a sad lassie or two on the island. More than one or two. The truth is that I think Chris had screwed nearly every woman of screwable age on the entire island. They just seemed to melt when he smiled at them, he was so bloody lovely. Strange thing to say about a bloke, but he was. And gentle. That's why he came back from the smoke after a single season in the VFL. I asked him about it, of course, why he came back, and he just said: They're too bloody serious about it, mate, they're just a lot of professional butchers. He didn't want that, he wanted to play a game with his mates and get pissed with them afterwards and chase a few girls. It just wasn't important enough to him.

He was a lovely boy, Chris, inside and out. And now he was gone, and the old man was sitting there every day on the verandah looking out at nothing, waiting to die.

'She's got a caravan down at the wharf,' said Elaine one day when I came in for a cup of tea in the afternoon. Warm day, and the kitchen hot from the big AGA, fresh bread smells, scones and home-made jam, and it would have been all right except for the old man still sitting out there, silent, motionless, staring across the flats. Even when you couldn't see him, you *felt* him there.

'Who has?'

'The girl—Lynne, you know.'

'Oh.'

'On her own, Mrs Pearn said.'

Usually they're not on their own when they move into caravans.

I didn't say anymore, but the next time I was down that way I drove past the old Harbour Trust office that hasn't been used in ten years, and there behind it, in the lee of one of the wharf sheds, was this little green plywood caravan. And that was all I saw. No sign of activity, no movement. Just the van.

But somehow it reminded me of the old man on the verandah—I couldn't see her, but I could sense her there. Sense life behind the tatty panels, the dusty panes. Knew that she was there, that she was going to have her baby there, away from the dirt and rubbish of the abo settlement. And from then on I always seemed to be conscious of those two, the old man and the girl, waiting in their own separate silences, just waiting...

At the tag-end of summer I had a blue with one of the local hoons. I'd been in to town to watch the cricket, a break from the place and from the old man, and after the match I went up to the pub with some of the blokes for a drink. We were standing at the long bar, and someone was grizzling about the bowling, and how they missed Chris's leg-breaks, and then one of the yobboes said something about a few wives missing him too, and I hit him harder than I'd intended—it was all right for me to think it, but not for him to say it—and I broke his nose. And that reminded me even more of Chris, and of how I'd tried to set his broken nose after the school match when he broke it, and how I mucked it up and it set crooked, and how he would never do anything about it, get it reset. So I drove too fast on the way home and nearly lost the car on the bend at the end of the long straight, and then had a puncture a mile from home and found that the spare was flat...

That was how I learned that the baby had arrived.

The first car past was a rusty old FC with four young boongs in it, and before they dropped me at the gate one of them told me, nudging his mate, that the Marsden girl had had her baby.

'Dropped her kid,' he said...

'Yeah,' said another, 'and a light-skinned little bugger too...'

Then the driver said, straightfaced: 'How's the old man taking it? About Chris?'

And I couldn't do anything, because they'd given me a lift.

So when I got out at the gate I was in a mood. But when I walked round the corner of the house, there he was, still sitting there, staring out across the patch of she-oak and sand and native heath at the sunset. And I saw him before he saw me, and there was a terrible emptiness in his face, a look of enormous sadness and loss, and he seemed suddenly so old and tired and beaten that it nearly stopped me dead in my tracks. Then he saw me, and his face set into the old lines again, hard and bitter and proud. I wanted to go up and touch him, just put a hand on his shoulder or something. But I didn't, because we'd never been that way.

So instead I went inside and made myself a cup of tea, then got out the account books and started going over them.

Elaine knew, of course, about the baby.

'It's a boy,' she said that night, after the old man had gone to bed.

'What is?'

'Lynne's baby.'

'Oh, that…'

There was an awkward silence while she stacked the dishes. Then: 'Are you going to go down and see her, or anything?'

'Why should I? None of our business.'

'The baby's got blue eyes, they say…'

'All babies have blue eyes when they're born.' And so they have.

She didn't say anymore, and I felt bad about what I'd said. Because really, under it all, that was what I wanted to do, go down and see her, do something, say something. Because I hated to think that Chris's kid—if it was his—might end up crawling round in some abo camp…

But I couldn't bring myself to do anything. Because I just didn't know what to say, how to act, how to ask her…

So I just grumped and growled and refused to talk about it.

It must have been six weeks later, maybe a couple of months, because the autumn winds had started, sweeping in across the Southern Ocean, lashing the tea-trees into wild spasms, laying the clover flat, drifting mist over the granite tops. After a week's blow the wind finally eased, and the clouds got smaller and smaller as they wound their way across the island, and the sun was bright again, and warm, and there was only a hint of frost in the evenings.

I'd come in for morning tea, and as I sat down I heard the old man coming into the house from the verandah, going off down the passage to his room. I frowned a bit, because there was something odd about the sound of his steps. Kind of purposeful, a marching sort of feel to them after all the months of just dragging along. But it went quiet, and I sat there sipping my tea and wondering if we could afford a new tractor this year, and whether the compressor really needed a new set of head gaskets before winter. And the next thing I knew the kitchen door swung open and the old man was standing there, looking at me, dressed in his best blue suit, collar and tie and all, his grey Akubra with the quail feather, and a mean hard look in his eye…

'Get the car out,' he said.

When he has that look to him, that tone in his voice, well, you jump. So I jumped. I went out, checked the oil and water, drove round to the front and parked. He was standing there waiting, rubbing his toecaps on the back of his calves to give them a bit of a shine, face set as hard as concrete.

He climbed in beside me.

'Get going,' he said, staring straight ahead, hands resting on the crook of his stick.

'Where to?'

'Down the wharf.'

Just like that. Deaf as a post, hadn't had a visitor in months, hadn't heard a word from us, but he knew all about it. That's the thing about the old man, what makes us feel the way we do about him—he always seems to know every bloody thing...

I was half tempted to drive him onto the wharf and park in front of the super shed, just to see what he'd say. But the truth is I wasn't game. So I drove very carefully and sedately up the road to the old office where the green caravan stood, and rolled to a nice neat stop, just like a bloody chauffeur. But he didn't seem to notice, just opened the door and got out, stood there a minute looking round him like a bloody general on parade.

It looked different, not what I remembered or expected. She'd tidied up the rubbish, and made a little path to the van's door and bordered it with white stones. And there were a couple of red geraniums planted in paint tins beside the door, and neat white curtains at the windows. Someone had levelled the van up, set it on blocks, and there was a line full of nappies stretched between two she-oaks up the back.

I saw him straighten his back a little, then off he marched up the path to the door. Rapped smartly a couple of times, stood back waiting.

A slight tremor to the van as someone moved inside, shifted the weight a little, light footsteps. The door swung back, and she was standing there, pretty as a picture, white blouse and tight jeans showing off her figure, all slim and clean and neat. High cheekbones, big intelligent eyes, dark wavy hair cut short. Her mouth went a bit thin at the sight of the old man.

'Where's the baby?' he said, before she could open her mouth. I think that's the only way he knows how to go about things. And he moved forward up the steps, crowding her back.

She made the best of it, backed off and smiled a tight furious smile, made a little gesture with one hand, like a hostess, you know, do come in Mr Barton, you're a bloody rude pig, but come in anyway…

I followed him a bit sheepishly, and she didn't even look at me.

The old man was standing by then over the old wicker bassinet at the end of the van. It seemed very crowded with all of us in there. But it was clean, clean as a hound's tooth, neat as a pin. Kettle on the little kero stove, more nappies soaking in a bucket of disinfectant, a little bowl of flowers on the tiny table. She had her head up very high, chin pointed at the old man as he looked around.

Still no one said anything. A bit belatedly the old man took his hat off, kind of bobbed at her once, then leaned down over the bassinet.

I edged up quietly so that I could see over his shoulder. The baby was fast asleep on its back, all pink and plump and shapeless, the way all babies look. Oh, there was a faint dark blush to the skin, all right. But not black, not black by a long way. Then the baby seemed to sense something, maybe the old man's shadow over him, and he opened his eyes, and they were bright soft blue, almost violet, and I got this shivery feeling, and I wanted to move, to do something, but I didn't know what. And I looked very carefully at the baby's face, but the truth is I couldn't really tell if there was a likeness there at all, not with the baby so young and maybe the eyes not their final colour yet...

The old man looked at the baby steadily for what seemed like a long time, and the baby stared back at him. And then the old man turned his head, looked at the girl a moment, very hard and intent, but not unfriendly. Then he sort of relaxed, and there was almost a little smile on his face. And he leaned over, and with the tip of his finger he pressed the baby's nose to one side, and in a flash I saw that it was Chris there, his face, his eyes, his broken nose, everything...

And the old man straightened up and turned to the girl again.

'He's one of ours,' he said. 'Bring him home.'

If you didn't know him well you'd never pick the softness in his voice then, a matter of tone too slight for strangers, and the girl bridled, started to say something. But he leaned forward and touched her lightly on the shoulder. I couldn't see his face, but the girl could, and there must have been something in it, because she started to melt a little, her eyes got very soft and moist, and all the starch went out of her suddenly. And he put his arm round her shoulders and bent down and kissed her lightly on the cheek.

And then I saw his cold grey-blue eye on me over her shoulder.

'Help her pack,' he said.

So I did.

On the way back up to Emerald she sat in the back with the bassinet, the old man beside me in the front seat. She said nothing, just kept her hand on the basket. The old man said nothing either, just sat there staring straight ahead. But occasionally I could see out of the corner of my eye that his lips twitched a little. And that's high good humour for the old man, so I relaxed a bit, and even whistled a bar or two of 'The Stone Outside Dan Murphy's Door', which I know he hates; and he never turned a hair. And as we swung in over the grid it seemed more like a homecoming than it had for a long time.

Well, it wasn't smooth sailing, especially not at first. The two women were a bit cool to each other until they sorted out the running of the house and the looking-after of the baby; and both Lynne and the old man have got sharp tempers and sudden tongues and now and then they let fly at each other; and sometimes Lynne's relatives came to call and sat in the kitchen with her, all fat and black and doggy, and the old man would go out grinding his teeth; and sometimes I would see that look in the girl's eyes, a sudden panic as she realised how alone she was, how cut off from everything that'd been her life before...

But after a while it seemed to calm down. Still, there was a sort of uncertainty in the air, as if none of us was quite sure of our part in the old man's scheme of things.

And then, a month after we brought the baby home, we had visitors. A nice enough couple who owned a property at the other end of the island who came down to look at some ewes. They were well-dressed, middle-aged, old settlers, and their kids had all gone to grammar school. And when they came inside the old man stood there in the living room with his hand on Lynne's shoulder, and he said to them, 'I'd like you to meet my daughter-in-law.'

And—to their credit—they said all the right things and their smiles were just casual enough, their handshakes just friendly enough; and the old man smiled at them like an ancient crocodile, and God knows what he would have done to them if they'd wavered…

But they didn't. And I knew then that somehow things were going to turn out all right.

Hal Porter · 1961

Great-Aunt Fanny's Picnic

On and off through the years, by Otterwells alive and kicking as well as by Otterwells tucked away in the family graveyard, the scandal of Great-Aunt Fanny had been mulled over with conscious dispassion, and repeatedly put aside like a tricky crossword. There was, anyway, always happening, in this or that Otterwell-dominated part of Tasmania, another Otterwell wedding, birth, or birthday. Or Lent began or school holidays or shearing or a vice-regal visit or the racing season or war or...well, tedious external things. No one alive seemed sure how Fanny's prolonged sojourn in foreign territory had started: she herself divulged nothing, but a tattered rumour inclined to some necessary patriotic gesture during the 1914–1918 War. Aunt Ann, being Aunt Ann, had other ideas—unpleasant ones, suggestive of hanky-panky, and diplomatically disregarded. Great-Aunt's legendary predicament was a subject as engaging as a pet tortoise; it often came out, like a snail, at night. It withdrew, pronto, at the merest squeak of new christenings, courtships, or tonsillectomies. Finally, however, explosively out of the blue, Uncle Eustace pronounced a decision: he himself would fetch her back.

In the family, Uncle Eustace was famed and feared for this nineteenth-century forcefulness, this taking-the-bull-by-the-horns Chinese Gordon resolution, as much as he was renowned for being the one Otterwell bachelor, not only for his period but for as far back as records were known. The probity of his bachelordom, with no heart-of-gold barmaid kept in a Battery Point love nest, and certainly no one or nothing else more dubious kept anywhere, added a dignifying halo to the eccentricity of wifelessness. Who knew what forces galore, untapped by wife, child, hidden sorrow, poverty, or unmentionable vice, still occupied him? For example, at seventy-three, he had just given up Royal Tennis.

On Christmas Eve 1960, after performing a Father Christmas as terrifying as Lear, and while reviving himself with Courvoisier, he czarishly shouted them all...even Uncle Hereward who always fidgeted whether to take an umbrella or not, blazing or pouring...into believing that they had inclemently abandoned Great-Aunt Fanny 'among who knows whom,' Eustace blared Ezekielly, 'among tradespeople, shepherds, mercer's counter-jumpers, journalists! And *exactly* where, who knows, eh? Forty years! A disgrace to us all. While Fergus was alive it was wise to keep mum, eh? But he's been dead for twelve years. Best leave it to me, eh? Pour me another, Varley. Leave't to me, eh?'

'Yes, oh yes, Eustace,' they heard themselves cravenly pipe, and would have crossed themselves had they been one of *those*. Eustace was an alarming not-to-be-denied Pied Piper once he got going. They all quickly had another drink. After all, it was Christmas too.

By Candlemas, Uncle Eustace, in Isle of Butte tweeds, point-to-point cap, and pelargonium buttonhole, face pink as sporting paper or baby's, had dominated, sniffling rather and headachy, Fanny's uprooting. It was a chilly day, miles from anywhere respectable. Trees dripped on him as though he were a postman. Her nearest neighbour was a politician with a scruffy Socialist past. She should never, of course, have spent all those years there. She should have been with the family. With the family she would be. Reluctantly, he had to leave her, at the railway station, to travel on, poor lady, in the care of a man with a suspect accent, to Campbell Town where Uncle Eustace proposed to catch up with her next day.

The next day he was unable to keep his appointment because of what he savagely called a summer cold. This so swiftly galloped into danger that on St Valentine's Day he nearly died.

'Completely dying would, in the circumstances, have been absolutely killing,' said Gwendoline, young Mrs Ian Otterwell, who concealed a marshmallow heart under a shocker's exterior.

'And *needlessly* ironic,' said Aunt Ann, fingering her cameo as though she'd said nothing at all.

Not until Whitsunday was he finally out of bath chairs, and his knees out from under afghans, and he fit and pink and loud enough to ask about Great-Aunt Fanny. Silence fell. Time dropped a number of stitches. He asked again, more loudly. Evasion was tried: Hereward offered a cigar. Evasion and cigar were roared at. 'But...' they all began chattering at the same time, disobedient children botching justification, 'but Eustace *dear*, but old boy, but Uncle, while you were so very, *very*...'

In listening to the dangerous wind keening around Eustace, in listening to the wind that never stopped flowing through the garden of Otterwells, tugging off a leaf, a branch, a heart, a life, they had, one and all, utterly forgotten to keep an eye on Great-Aunt Fanny's move.

Not saying they were but unmistakably considering them ninnies, he next day drove fifty-odd miles to see if Fanny were settled in her proper place.

While everybody was telephoning everybody else, there he was, in the family graveyard with its own century-old chapel, peering and poking about, getting cemetery mud on his brogues, trouser cuffs and knees. He returned to the car with the ominous stride of Alexander the Great. He drove back as recklessly as a joy-riding hot-rodder, and held the floor.

The billiard-table-sized Welsh slate slabs roofing the vault, in which Fanny should long ago have circumspectly been, seemed not, he thought, to have been recently moved. She'd certainly—he'd seen to that, eh?—been got out of that other wretched cemetery. Perhaps...per-*h-a-p-s*...he further thought...moss in the crevices *could* have been recently disturbed, could indeed have been replaced with a species of commercial piety. But he'd forgotten to take his spectacles; autumn leaves and a Scotch mist had made pure decision difficult. Curse that summer cold!

A telephone call to the undertaker's revealed that he of odd accent, who had been in charge of Fanny's digging-up, train trip and reinterment, had been a short-time employee since returned to Australia. A Mainlander! Eustace gave a terrible shout, and crashed down the receiver. The earth, that great globe, winced. Varley dropped a sugar bowl, fortunately silver. A Mainlander!...someone from...Carlton was it, eh? Woolloomooloo?

Swiftly as a Terrytoon vegetable, suspicion put on buds, leaves, dire flowers. Uncle Eustace became taller than Abraham Lincoln, and noisier: 'The fellow's a jackanapes. Mortician he calls himself. An employer of criminals. Dabbling in cremation like a blasted Hindu, the silly ass. Phonograph music and foam-rubber lilies! Coffins of xylonite...plastic...whatever the muck is, I suppose, eh? Mortician! Right from the jump I was against his joining the Club. He's like the barber's cat: all...'

'Eustace!' snapped Aunt Ann. 'There are gentlemen present.' She had been a maidenly suffragette with, nevertheless, ears.

In the next few days Eustace occupied himself Napoleonically, very much head-of-the-family, with the minutiae of a grandiose plan. He wrote fiats to everyone, each succinct sentence brutally clear, too specific, too personal to be misunderstood or fobbed off. Intimations of excommunication glittered so ferociously between the lines of his old man's virile copperplate that newer Otterwell wives, the just-read command on Spicer's Deckle still between their finger-tips, switched off spin driers or forsook semi-built Constance Spry flower arrangements, and sped in M.G.s to buy trowels or whatever they were. Otterwell telephones were rung, and rang, constantly. Who, my God, last had the crow-bar from the potting shed of the old Sandy Bay place? What the hell *was* a mattock? Listen, dear, Varley says we'll be expected to picnic, so if you do a double lot of your divine little scones with Gentlemen's Relish, I'll do a double of my special Madeleines and we'll interfeed...

No one cared to let the side down; no one dared scamp Uncle Eustace's mandates.

On the selected Sunday, from every part of Tasmania, cars packed with tools, food, wicker-clad thermos flasks, children, and their Otterwell parents and relations, moved towards the graveyard. Wound up like a clock, generations ago, the family ethos was so well-oiled, had ticked so surely and sturdily for so long, that it would have been useless as well as traitorous for any member to suggest *I should like to be otherwise, someone else*, or *elsewhere today*, as useless as saying *I should like to be an echidna or called Marco Polo*. From faith and habit, non-Otterwells seemed to them as eels must to eagles, however glossy and silver-plated the eel, however like fractured sunshade the eagle. Sheer lunacy this plan of Eustace's, they might think, but ratifiable Otterwell lunacy. We're all in it. So, by ten o'clock, everyone punctual, from Melton Mowbray, St Helen's, Westbury, Huonville, Oatlands, New Norfolk, everywhere, everyone had arrived. It was an autumn day, exquisite for any outing, perfection for one of this nature: nowhere are sunshine, birds, breezes, weeds, more subtly exhilarating to the senses and conceit of the living than in a graveyard.

Fecundity was the first impression—children everywhere; their knowingly uninhabited ink-blue, dead-still Otterwell eyes spotted the air. There seemed double the actual children, for each child had accompanied its own Sunday-go-graveyard self as one extra child simmering unseen to be barbaric and crazed, to flash diabolically aflame past the corner of adult consciousnesses; but, the time early and the occasion touchy, they discreetly simulated severe charm and, speechlessly as nursery rhyme characters on kindergarten friezes, carried buckets, rakes and Dutch hoes. With their tweedy aunts, with wavering aunts, champagne-bottle-legged golfing aunts, tittuping aunts and Burne-Jones aunts, they advanced towards and grouped themselves below Uncle Eustace who had mounted, civic-statue-like, the top of the vault to which, in an orderliness obscured by gorse, periwinkle and pre-Raphaelite Austrian Copper briers, other Otterwell graves lined up.

Even Aunt Ann, inclined to perpetual fractiousness, was momentarily halcyon in the group which, standing mutely as waxworks, chins uplifted, listened to Uncle Eustace. Only the oldest aunt, Aunt Beatrice, sat. She sat in a camp chair, centrally front, her bone fingers burdened with diamonds and rubies. The crowd, accidentally dramatic, of overlapping generations had the impermanent coherence of a combination in whose each mind, as much as in the corporate one, lay no mental reservation like a segment of decaying trevally. At least, on this occasion. First of all, beneath their soles lay the boxed scraps of their own dead. Second, many of their houses had once been these dead's, or contained objects wherein the grimaces or half-smiles of the dead still lingered—in Wainewright portraits, darkening looking-glasses, on the bumlike curves of silver rose-bowls, in photograph albums containing pressed pansies picked last century by fingers that, then, could write *Otterwell* on a will or a love letter. Third, Great-Aunt Fanny, so long a sherry-party joke, now claimed by right of blood this protective picnic, this family prying into her gothic contretemps. Was she here, *now*, below, in her destined niche, filed for reference on the Last Day? That is what the family, through Uncle Eustace, hoped and had jolly well paid for. Or had the Mainland ghoul, obviously with a face caddish as a monkey's, done something too nasty to think of but nevertheless thought of...a council rubbish-tip? a lake bed? a stinky fire in a Midlands' gully once lair for convict bushrangers?

As they listened to Uncle Eustace avoid putting these outraging possibilities into words, they stared remorselessly at him, their thoughts sprinkling salty glints of anger in their eyes. He, too, began to glint—but he was rebuking *them*. 'Moreover,' he was saying, 'moreover, the graveyard, our graveyard, the *Otterwell* graveyard...' He was rubbing it in. '...is in a shocking state. Eh? As you can see.' As they could see. 'Our own people! We are to blame. We! *We!*' They were to blame. 'That's why I wrote you all to come prepared to clean up while the vault is investigated. Except, of course, Aunt Beatrice.' Aunt Beatrice lifted an ancient jewel-knobbed hand with queenly deprecation. Everyone looked at her as at an unbelievable idol but with sufficient affectionate respect. 'There are,' continued Uncle Eustace, 'enough of us, God knows—eh? In my letters you were each allotted a certain task in a certain section. It took some planning.' He paused. He stopped pausing, and made a dangerous remark: 'Any questions?'

Before Aunt Ann could uncurl—he knew his danger—he side-stepped quickly, side-stepped imperatively: '*Good*—no questions. Charles, you have the crow-bars? Mattock, Greg? Pickaxe? Bill-hook? Mallet? Bamboo rakes...Grace? Varley? Ah, I see you've a trowel, Young Christopher!' Everyone had brought everything asked for, and held them up: *sans-culottes* preparing to march on the Tuileries. Everyone except...and Uncle Eustace's eyes narrowed...'Your secateurs, Ann?' Aunt Ann's German secateurs were famous. She had not brought them. She tossed her head; no angel, she did not fear treading. *Her* little indigo eyes also narrowed, and flashed wickedly. Level-toned yet sharp, she said, 'I have brought Fanny's own silver teapot. I felt it fitting.'

To everyone's surprise, Aunt Beatrice said, almost cried as loudly as someone younger, '*No!*' What could she mean? Her old mind wandering, off and away?

Aunt Ann stuck out her chin, whiskery as an as-yet-unshaved youth's, at Eustace. It was a mutinous gesture. Uncle Eustace clenched a fist.

'An unseemly disturbance is imminent,' whispered twelve-year-old Young Christopher who was wicked, sophisticated, and far too handsome. His cousins sycophantically giggled, 'Fie! So early in the day. And before us innocent innocents. Oh, *fie!*'

Then Grace, lanky gentle Grace, said gently, 'Aunt Ann asked me to bring *our* secateurs, Eustace,' and she held them up, high, at the end of her long long long arm, like a symbolic Communist. There secateurs were. Uncle Eustace laughed—oh, quickly and fruitily as a prime minister. 'To work!' he shouted, semaphoring meaninglessly. 'To your posts! To work!'

In a geyser of released conversation, of greetings, of hullabaloo and movement, children bursting like grenades from between adults, the group milled and crumbled and scattered. To work all the women went except old Aunt Beatrice whose lilac-coloured chiffon scarf was rearranged, one after another, by five women. To work all the children seemed to go except the youngest twins with silkworm silk hair who ran about clutching their flies, and squealing, '*We* are to blame. We! We! Wee-wee. Pee-wee. Wee-pee. We pee. We poo. We poo-poo!' Their stately Labrador, its severe head like an heraldic profile or one from an old walking-stick handle, lumbered woodenly as a rocking horse between them. A surfeit of forbidden things to do had lashed them to exaltation.

While the women, garden-gloved or gloveless, worked on paths, headstones, urns, broken columns, sandstone scrolls, granite tombs and cast-iron railings, their unfettered, faultless voices called in the sunlight above the buried, tongueless skulls.

'My dear, how very kind of Eustace to put me on Digby's grave—I shouldn't admit it with his age so clearly stated, but we were childhood sweethearts. Though he once stole my agate marbles.'

'This rose bush must be a cutting from the big Maman Cochet at The Grange.'

'Shall I scrape all this moss away? It looks so fitting and darling. Or just leave aesthetic enough, like the Japanese?'

GREAT-AUNT FANNY'S PICNIC

'I wish I'd brought my old steel kitchen knife. Men don't *know* about steel kitchen knives.'

'What *did* James Frederick *really* die of?'

'I,' said Aunt Ann, 'shall not pretend that I am at all surprised, but Eustace has allotted me the prickliest grave.'

Although these statements seemed merely the trite ones of feckless humans, and utterable by anyone with a tongue, they revealed that the speakers had preserved, throughout their own vicissitudes and those of the world they had been born into, viewpoints and moralities as much of their class as their accents were, and their children. These creatures, in constant motion, had seemingly much multiplied, separating themselves from themselves as amoebae do. They mafficked about with the alacrity of vandals to whom no vandalism was that day permissible. Some, for a while, browbeatenly scratched lichen from headstones, or permitted themselves to be hectored into carrying off pruned brier suckers and Great Mullein stalks. Otherwise they roamed restlessly outside the cage of adult duty, hampered by miles of undulating paddocks and the obvious infinity of a cloudless sky. Aunt Ann kept on capturing some of them with her fish-hook eye and, as other aunts did, mistaking them for their siblings or cousins. Were they, she asked, street arabs or swineherd's waifs crept in through the may hedge? This was surely cryptic humour on her part. Yet, even to aunts and uncles less whimsical than Aunt Ann, there appeared more of these youngsters, who no longer wore sailor suits and knew of *The Windsor Magazine*, than seemed reasonable. The gold-mopped twins, for example, had become a sextuplet, banshee-shrieking by with attendant Cerberus.

Meantime, ponderously and sonorously and warily, the men confronted the paramount mystery of Great-Aunt Fanny. Dedicated and daylight Burkes and Hares, they assessed the vault covering. Under their off-hand dandyism and leather-patched sports coats was the muscular and maternal brutishness of those who worked with animals and their neuroses and needs, and who fought into submission, just as their women in labour fought necessary pain into submission, the seasons and the earth. These Otterwell males, or males chosen as sires by Otterwell women, had weathered youth, injudicious passions, disillusion, the whims of weather, scandals, and boils on the backside, with concealed and tenderized arrogance. Their manners were perfect, and would have remained so while they killed an enemy or stopped a crucifixion. Tenderly their huge hands and shrewd eyes examined the tomb; tenderly they prodded crevices with crow-bars and pick-axes, inviting each other's suggestions to poo-hoo them, before attacking like convinced burglars the vault slabs. With vigour and precision they made the first attempts at prising. These failed. Swearing began. Those who did not smoke pipes offered each other cigarettes, saying, 'Christ, eh! She's going to be bloody tougher than we thought. Christ!'

Young Christopher was, of course, in earshot. He possessed a special sense.

'They are blaspheming,' he said to his entourage of underling cousins.

'They are blaspheming,' echoed the myrmidons and, giggling from trying not to giggle, held hands over mouths, and stuck out their round bellies farther, and rolled inky eyes.

'They are corrupting influences,' Young Christopher continued. 'They are immoral fiends and wicked monsters. We must inform the sheriff! Yippee!' And he galloped off, being, centaurlike, horse and rider; and the smaller centaurs galloped at his pace after him, caracoling like a posse of goodies behind him, and shrilling like Comanches around the church.

The men made a scarecrow of a marble angel with their coats and, thus coatlessly defiant, attacked the slabs again.

Presently, for Otterwell women were deft, most of them had fulfilled Uncle Eustace's behests. On the other side of a raffish rosemary hedge was a handful of humbler graves, not Otterwell. Gwendoline, forthrightly why-notting and dammit-all-let's-do-the-decent-thinging, persuaded others less forthright and more dubious, but amenable to sentimental platitude disguised as decisiveness, to work with her on these alien plots.

With less intensity of feeling they idly toiled, as at an inferior charity, and were so toiling, and placidly deep in obstetrical legend, when a shadow they immediately knew was monitory fell upon their bowed backs, and a fluting astounded voice said:

'Those graves are not *ours*!'

It was Varley, intellectual and perfectionist (her rose garden was a miracle, so were her potted shrimps; she read Elizabeth Bowen), who had just restored Edwin Otterwell's grave almost to the condition it was in 1863 when he had died under a runaway barouche.

'What the hell does it matter, Varley?' said Gwendoline in a contemporary way, softish but boldish, from her kneeling pad. She pushed back a lock of hair to stress barefacedness. 'Dammit, let's be decent!'

'Need you swear?' said Varley, who really didn't mind a scrap. 'I don't think we should interfere.'

'With the *dead*?' said Gwendoline, lighting a suave cigarette.

Varley was not to be caught. She too lit a cigarette—slowly—and blew out—slowly—a vampish cone of smoke.

'With the dead of others. The dead do not belong to themselves. Graves belong to *others*. Those others should tend them with love. They are not *ours*. Your work, however worthy, is…is municipal. There is no love.'

'Bosh!' said Gwendoline and, to show unabashment, '*Dammit*, Varley!' Young Christopher would have cherished this but was being immaculately vile elsewhere. All the children were. The twins and their dog, because they had been forbidden the road, were on the road terrifying a rustic bodgie passer-by who had intended terrifying them.

Gwendoline spoke again: 'Oh, *double* bosh, Varley!' for Varley, towering, had fixed her with a navy-blue look.

Varley said, 'Be that as it may. Gwendoline, you've laddered your stocking—left leg.'

Gwendoline said, 'Damn and *blast*!'

Women said, 'Spit, dear.'

Who said, 'Surely Varley,' yanking out a thistle belonging to an unloved non-Otterwell, '*surely* it's easy to love humanity when it isn't there?'

It sounded a Brontë-ish remark but came, naturally, from

Aunt Ann whose magnanimities even had always a dash of vinegar. Varley, who had once published at her own expense a book of poems (*Roses of Silence and Solitude*), looked away, mysteriously as a poetess vouchsafing nothing, and walked away thinking something nicer.

Nearby aunts, older, some, finding it time to suggest to themselves starting a headache as reason for luncheon but mainly cups of tea, drew from their pockets noon-showing enamelled watches they had had since black *moiré* butterfly bows tied back their then-thick-and-coloured hair.

Varley, drifting, saw in the distance, frailly royal under the big Cedar of Lebanon, Aunt Beatrice. Old old aunt, time-shrivelled aunt, had long ago, restless and fretful, left her camp chair. With a trailing totter, she had moved from group to group in her Queen Alexandra manner—the painted and thickly powdered face also; the gracious word dropped vaguely here and there. Yet she seemed touched by the wind of an intangible bitterness, to be seeking wearily, seeking and seeking. Now that the vault was full—or would soon, they hoped, be proved to be, for Great-Aunt Fanny had been destined for the last unoccupied niche—perhaps Aunt Beatrice, long the widow of a husband buried at sea, sought a place for herself. She tacked; she contemplated spaces; she tacked again. Certainly, certainly, when next the family gathered she would be underground, bereft of her far too many wonderful old-fashioned rings, of her paint, of her Arabian nimbus of scent, even of her scant flesh. Underground where? Oh, where? She had entered the blue shadows of the cedar, uninterested in the housewifely kneeling, the trowelling and grating and hacking and snipping, the chattering, the bonfire the children were prodding into smoke a paler blue than the cedar shadows. 'Joffre Blue,' she whispered. It was a colour of her middle years. Tears suggested themselves to her. 'Joffre Blue,' she was whispering when Varley arrived. 'Fanny spilt Indian ink on my Joffre Blue blouse with the pearl buttons.'

Using a handkerchief almost all lace she blotted a shallow tear before it furrowed her powder.

'Why, Aunt *Beatrice*...' said Varley, coming into the shadow. 'Darling, why not come and sit down again? Or should you like to be in the car? Luncheon'll be soon.'

Old Aunt Beatrice looked haggard above her chiffon pussycat bow of scarf. She spoke with querulous wildness:

'I don't want to be buried *outside*. It's too noisy. Grasshoppers. Omnibuses going past to Hobart. And too much light.' Varley knew that she sat always with her back to it, the blinds three-quarter-down. 'I want to be in the *vault*. With grandmother and mama and Alexander and Galamiel. Fanny always grabbed everything. She spilt ink on my blouse. She gave my lovely scrap-book to the Orphans' Home. *Without* permission. She's in the vault. It's not fair. She doesn't care. Look where she got herself buried the first time...'

Varley was becoming horrified when there was a great calling-out and waving from the men: 'It's open! It's open! We've opened the vault!'

Varley looked *Come on, Aunt Beatrice* and held out a hand. 'Leave me here,' said the ravaged old woman in the cold shadow. 'Leave me. I don't want to see...' She did not say *Fanny* but grew infinitely fragile.

Varley did not know what to do, and felt larger than a land-girl.

'Go away,' said Aunt Beatrice, waspish. 'Go away and leave me, mean selfish Fanny,' said the old woman to Varley.

Within minutes, all of them, husbands, wives, aunts, uncles, children, twins and dog, cynical Young Christopher, flushed Varley, were at the vault.

What ultimately and most and for years impressed the adults was that the name-plates on the coffins were completely untarnished, as though they'd been done with Goddard's Plate Powder the day before; this despite the fact that six inches of strange still water that seemed depthless covered the floor.

What impressed the children first was a frog sitting on Galamiel Otterwell's coffin. That was explicable: water, frog, place for frog to sit when not in water.

What impressed the children most, and nightmarishly until they themselves approached death, were the metallic-green blowflies, fat and important, sulkily muttering as though drunk. Why? Whence? The boys scratched their necks, and did not want to ask questions.

Great-Aunt Fanny was not at home.

As, they all said, they had all along all known.

The last niche was empty.

Rage (quite savage) and horror (sickening) overtook the Otterwells, and they edged more closely together. The rage was clear-cut at good money paid for what amounted to profanation, at being gypped—the *Otterwells*!—by a Mainland spiv. The horror was an atavistic and family horror that, somewhere—and they were responsible, which increased the horror—a section of their heritage and own lives had been lost as carelessly as a tennis racquet. Otterwells had been sunk in oceans, blown to bits in currently fashionable wars, buried in China, in *Père Lachaise* Cemetery near Sarah Bernhardt, in dozens of places, and even Ireland. Those were seemly enough; there was evidence; if tears were to fall they knew which quarter to splash towards. The losing of Great-Aunt Fanny was...was...

The men swore vilely, even Uncle Hereward who could rarely make up his mind. Uncle Eustace seemed to be planning something in the nature of a Royal Commission. The sun grew hotter. One aunt, foreseeing endlessness without tea, considered a fake half-faint on a suitably low tomb.

Meantime, where *was* Great-Aunt Fanny?

Varley, as always, came first to her senses. Precise and romantic and fervid, with her Otterwell-ink-dark but un-Otterwell-protruding eyes, she twined among them and conspiratorially revealed another truth to them. Presently, in silence, they had all turned their eyes towards the Cedar of Lebanon.

Without a word to each other the women started to move, to subtract themselves from the mingled group, to begin walking towards the cedar.

The men, dividing themselves from the children, moved a few paces after the women, and then stopped. The path to the cedar was not for them. They lit pipes and cigarettes, and turned inwards to each other, backs to the women, backs to the children. Life is not for men.

The children looked down their noses: they had been

made to feel like children. They got smaller, starved-looking, even world-weary Young Christopher; they drew together and retreated. There was an impression of walking backwards from an insane world.

The women now began, young and old, to hasten, almost to run stumbling, towards Old Aunt. They had no manly or childish embarrassments; they were female, and of earth. Some began to weep as they hurried but without wiping away the great sweet tears, the soft soft tears, the tears coloured with life and death.

Old Aunt saw them coming, a pack with some appalling information to reveal, and some outrageous deed to do—it must have seemed so to her faded eyes. Yet, for she had been a woman too, she touched her scarf, and moved into the sunlight that was less kind to her painted wrinkles, and advanced towards them, fantastic and beautifully hideous. They were upon her; they surrounded her.

'Oh, Beatrice!' they cried, tears streaming down their smiles. 'Oh, Aunt Beatrice, Great-Aunt isn't there! She's not there! Fanny isn't there! Oh, Aunt Beatrice, where is Aunt Fanny? Lost! Gone! Not there! Empty, the niche is *empty*!'

Aunt Beatrice knew what they were telling, what gift they had run to bring her in their hands stained with graves. She closed her eyes happily against their happiness for her, yet two old tears, and two more, and another two, ran refreshingly as creeks through the drought of powder.

'*Poor* Fanny!' she said in her ecstasy.

Philomena van Rijswijk • 2002

Faith, Hope and Charity

Sometimes I pour myself a glass of port, emptying the bottle, and my wife puts her Sting CD on, and the girls flounce in and out the door, make toast, do yoga from the pictures in a library book…and the feeling of sadness and slowness in me is weird and familiar. It is as if you'd never noticed how the world almost stands still in an agony of ordinariness. And you have spent the last three days tossing and turning as if your life is a set of white linen sheets twisted around your legs and arms.

My New Year's resolution back in 1960 was to find a church that I could go to. At fourteen, I would rather have invented my own, but I decided that would have been too time-consuming. I had come to think that perhaps Jesus was a Jewish boy with too much time on his hands.

Our story was like this: my mother married three brothers. First she married Darcey when she was eighteen years old. He died in a plane crash on the west coast when she was twenty-four. Next she married Darcey's younger brother, Cedric, who was killed by a freak wave, fishing off the rocks at Lufra. Finally, she married Sidney, who died unsensationally of pneumonia. In all those marriages, she produced nine children. I was the youngest. Not quite a change-of-life baby, I still had some obvious handicaps, and my older sister, Dawn, was what in those days was called a mongoloid. I thought it meant she came from another place. Looking back, I think maybe she did.

Dawn was the best friend my mother ever had. Unlike the rest of us, she remained a child, at least until that summer we went to Whitecliffs. Mum dressed Dawn in white bobby socks and lace-up shoes, the compulsory uniform of girls like her in those days. And she and Dawn held hands wherever they went. Although I was younger, and I loved Dawny fiercely, I consciously detached myself from the two of them in public. When we walked down to the fruit or the fish market, I dawdled ten paces behind, pretending to be alone.

Every Saturday Dawn would have to kneel over the bath with her poor flat knees on the cold tiles, and Mum would wash her head, tipping saucepanful after saucepanful of water over Dawn's thin hair, the latter yelping and pressing an old wet towel against her eyes. The last saucepanful caused the biggest yelp: always a couple of quarts of straight cold water right out of the tank. Then she would have her hair rubbed and put into plastic curlers until she looked as though her face was so tight and shiny it might split down the middle.

Since our father died, we'd lived in a semi-detached house right next door to the Diemen's Luck Hotel. Dawn and I looked after five orange cats that had been born under the bottle crates at the back of the pub. On weekends we walked miles, collecting soft-drink bottles from the banks of Waterloo Creek. During the week I was in second form at St Brendan's, and Dawn swept up hair and made cups of cheap coffee at the barber and tobacconist's down the road from our place.

At sixty-one, our mother was still a dressmaker. She worked from a tiny back room in our home and told me once that she had never had the time to earn a living before her husbands died, partly because of us kids, but mainly because she had spent most of her time apologising to the three brothers for their own bad behaviour. Consequently, she had grown into the habit of being angry most of the time. She said it was the only way she could think.

In my dreams, Waterloo Creek is still the same as it was then. Sometimes it was full of mountains of froth like soapsuds. There were rubbishy gum trees and tea-tree right down to the edge, and a track had been worn down from the top to a place where the rough kids got underneath the bridge to smoke. Sometimes Dawn and I would pause for a while in our search for Cascade bottles, and we would talk about fishing. It had always been our mutual fantasy that one day we would go fishing. Sometimes Dawn was allowed to borrow a fishing magazine from the barber's shop and we would leaf through the pages, awed by the complicated equipment, tantalised by readers' stories of the big plump fish they'd caught.

It was the Monday before her big operation that Dawn discovered the sets of tackle in the hardware shop next door to the barber's. She had been sent in for a bottle of metho for the big window, and had taken a minute or two to visit the fishing gear right in the back corner of the shop. Since we had last been in, the bottom shelf had been filled with beginners' kits: nets, handreels, knives, sinkers, lures, and even a little book of information. Dawn was so excited, she almost forgot to worry about going into hospital at the end of the week.

Dawn was twenty-four, I guess. The operation was to take away her womb, Mum said. Since she wouldn't be needing it anyway, and she wasn't discreet. Which meant that she'd never got over the feeling of being proud of something that if you were normal you were meant to be ashamed of. Anyway, the doctor said it would save Mum a lot of fuss and bother, and you never missed what you never knew you had in the first place.

Dawn mightn't be herself, Mum tried to warn me. Doctor Connor said she might rebel for a while after the operation. He said it can affect their brains.

From what I could tell, Dawn didn't have the strength to be rebellious when she came home from the hospital. She seemed bruised and sore and stiff and could feel something missing inside, and spent the first few days wandering around and wondering what it was. Finally, Mum felt so sorry for her she asked Dawn what she would like that would cheer her up.

'One of them fishing kits for me, and one for Sonny,' she said, 'and a holiday at the beach.'

We had never had a holiday before, but Mum had been saving for new carpet to replace the old green Feltex in the lounge room. That afternoon she rang and booked the cottage at Whitecliffs.

We caught the bus to Whitecliffs, and walked from the town. Mum had shown us a black-and-white photo of Cuttleshell in the book, but it wasn't what we had expected. For one thing, there was another house out the front where the owner and his family lived, and there was a big vacant field between the cottage and the corner of the street.

'Look at the curtains!' Mum laughed, when we were close enough to see them. They were mostly hanging in red strips. At one time they had been red and white stripes, but the red parts had perished with sunlight and age. Other than that, I suppose it was just a normal holiday house, with the musty smell of old kapok pillows and thin grey Army Surplus blankets, and the gritty feel of unpolished boards underfoot and the surface stickiness of being near the sea. That night Mum dressed for bed with the light off, and told Dawn to do the same. She could feel someone watching her from the vacant paddock. Also, from that first night, she slept with the big kitchen knife under her pillow.

When Dawn was a kid, she would never do anything that would get her hands dirty. On the beach the next morning, she was terrified of the sand. Still, Mum insisted, and when we walked across the dunes the white-hot sand squeaked underfoot and sent Dawn off, crying in terror. She said later that she thought she could hear voices under the sand. It was on that first day of our holiday that I discovered that Dawn wanted to be saved from Mum, and that I would have to be the one to do it.

It was because Dawn had been so miserable on the beach that I asked the next day if I could take her fishing. For once,

Mum was pleased to let us go. She had an old friend, Beryl, whom she'd known since they were girls. Beryl's husband had died when her two children were only babies, and since then she had devoted her life to the church and the RSL club. Over the years, Mum and Beryl had more or less lost contact, but Beryl lived near Whitecliffs, and Mum had looked her up. For the first time in her life, Dawn was free to fill the day in as she pleased.

We went down to the breakwater. There were two fishing trawlers just in, and there were cranes lifting the big crates of fish onto the wharf. Dawn held my hand and we watched until the boats had been emptied and the decks hosed down. I watched Dawn close her eyes and breathe in the stink of fish and salt and sticky blood. We left the trawlers and followed a ribbon of seaweed along the rocks, stepping over the skeletons of a couple of big fish. We could see where someone had lit a fire on the rocks. We found a spot for ourselves and I showed Dawn how to thread the bait onto the hook. I had only been fishing once before, with my mother's brother. I tried to cast my line out but it just loped and flopped in the shallows. We persisted with our handlines, but every time we cast them we lost our bait. We had bought it at the service station, where the man told us it was called bluebait. They were tiny fish, blue on top, silver underneath, with flat eyes and delicate, gaping mouths. Dawn liked the smell of them on her fingers.

The tide was on its way out, but we persisted with the handlines and they kept snagging on the rocks. I tried some snail-type things as bait, pushing the muscular part inside the shell onto the hook. The waves bubbled and shoved at our feet. Two white seagulls came from across the bay and slow-motioned over the rock where we had our bait, then a big pacific gull came squarking down, and they disappeared.

'This is what you do!' called one of the fishermen from further up the breakwater. He picked up a handreel and swung the line in a circle above his head, letting it spin out into the deep water beyond the rocks. He turned and grinned at us. He had one long tooth sticking up out of his bottom gum, and peppery hair. I decided he could have been thirty or sixty.

'I'm Dawn,' my sister laughed, and I could tell straightaway that she had fallen in love.

Turned out his name was Captain Hodge, but Dawn delighted us by calling him Cap'em 'Odge. The captain moved his gear and a battered fishing stool down next to us and showed us how to thread the bait onto our hooks. He told us how he had once got a fishhook in the palm of his hand, and how he had had to push it through to the other side and pull it out with a pair of pliers. I watched Dawn thoughtfully stroking her belly, and knew he had reminded her of the operation. The captain showed Dawn how to cast off with his willow rod, and I watched her standing beside him, her face open and happy under the big straw hat that Mum had made her wear.

Under Captain Hodge's instruction, I saw my sister become a fisherman. Her broad flat hands, usually so clumsy with fiddly things, spliced and knotted with the precision of a lacemaker. I watched as she bit her lip before taking a wide stance and casting her line out exactly the way the captain had shown her, while mine still lay slack and uninviting in the seaweed at the foot of the breakwater.

'You're a natural, for sure,' the captain said, putting a weathered hand on my sister's sloping shoulder. It was the first time I had seen someone touch her when it wasn't in order to boss her around.

'What's them humps out there?' Dawn asked, pointing to a couple of small islands spread out across the bay.

'They're the islands called Faith, Hope and Charity,' the captain explained. 'If a sailor can find his way between those three reefs, well he's just about home and hosed.'

Suddenly Dawn was cackling and jumping up and down on the spot. 'I got one!' she called out, the rod in her hands whipping and arching.

'Bring 'er in then,' the captain said calmly. 'You'll be havin' some Whitecliffs bream for yer dinner tonight!'

'Take them outside,' Mum said, when we arrived at the back door with three fat silver fish. 'You catch 'em, you clean 'em!'

At first Dawn looked disappointed, but outside she brightened up. Cap'em 'Odge had already shown her how to clean and fillet the fish. 'He said come back tomorrer,' she whispered, happily scraping the scales onto a piece of newspaper.

That was the first Saturday night that Dawn refused to have her hair put in curlers. She stamped her plump and flat foot (I had never really noticed her feet before) and said that she wanted to wear her hair straight from now on.

'It's good for her,' I reassured my mother the next morning. 'She likes bringing something home for dinner, and she's really good at it.'

'Be that as it may...' Mum argued.

Dawn was calm and businesslike on the way down to the breakwater the next day.

'There he is,' she remarked calmly. 'He said he would come today.'

That was when I first started to worry. At fourteen, I was old enough to know that blind faith inevitably led to disappointment.

'He won't be able to come every day, though, Dawny,' I cautioned. But she wasn't listening. Already she had sped up and was intent on getting to the captain first.

That holiday at Whitecliffs was three weeks long. Every day after that first day we went down to the breakwater. It was the first time I had ever seen Dawn keep something a secret from Mum, and the first time Mum had not been intent on finding out.

Every night after tea Dawn and I walked and walked, feeling safe in the dark and cool. I can't remember what Mum did, but in my memories she is never there, but always at her friend Beryl's, drinking cheap sherry by the tumblerful, listening to the details of Beryl's relationship with the parish priest.

Meanwhile, Dawn and I would walk the streets of Whitecliffs. Blue television lights would shrink and swell in lounge rooms with lime-green carpet and orange lamps. Someone would be standing at a kitchen window tilting a glass of water in the light from a bare globe. The front windows of children's rooms would be dark: those little boys who had sworn and grimaced at us in the daytime, those girls who had sung 'Puppet on a String' into the handle of a skipping rope, now breathing inaudibly, their mouths pressed open like moist petals, their hands warm and salt-swelling with sleep. And babies, their curls defined with sweat, their fat bottoms poking up towards nylon mosquito nets, the corners of their pillows wet with milk-sucking dreams.

Oleander bushes in those front yards became black hollows, garden hoses and Aborigine statues took on strange and sinister meanings. We would walk and walk and eventually come to the last house before the paddocks of long grass that gave way to the sand and the sea. Listen! If you stood still you could hear the night-waves making angry sounds on the beach. The drag and then the dump and fizz. And while you stood there, smelling the deadish smell of the sea so close, those paddocks of dry grass that in daytime were merely a hot dry nuisance before you got to the business of the beach became a quiet, watchful place. A place that said Go Back! So you turned back and went into the shop with the purple V sign out the front. Inside V's there were fluorescent strips that made the things on the shelves look unreal. You chose a Barrett's Sherbet Fountain or a Big Charlie Bubble Gum and savoured the smell: the holiday smell of lollies under glass. You turned the postcard rack and fiddled with a knob on the pinball machine.

Then it was back out into the dark where more lights had been turned off. Behind those front windows the people of Whitecliffs were conceiving wayward children, soaking dentures, reading folded old letters, biting nails, wetting beds. We walked back and were glad when we were home, because even though it wasn't home, but a holiday cottage rented from strangers, it had become home. We crawled between heavy cold sheets with our feet sandy, and in the distance could hear the sea keeping its lonely vigil over the sleep-breathing world.

Early one morning we went down to the rocks to meet the captain. He took a kitchen knife from his pocket and prised oysters off the rocks, tipping the pearly shells to let them slide onto our tongues. They were big in our mouths, and every one tasted surprising, stinging the backs of our throats and nostrils with salt. When they had gone down we ground the fragments of shell between our teeth.

'Holiday-makers like you are the lifeblood of a place like this,' the captain told us. 'You lot keep reminding us that we're still alive. That Brigadoon's awake for another day, so to speak.'

Our last whole day at Whitecliffs arrived. I got up at six o'clock. It had been raining all night, and it was still semi-dark outside. A rooster in the next street had started its lonely crowing in the drizzle. The shadows of the kitchen chairs were long and warped on the floor. The fridge was humming. Mum's travel clock ticked. Fat drops were randomly drumming their fingers on the roof. Tonight was the night that Dawn had decided to run away with the captain.

All that day it rained and rained. Mum had gone to bed with a migraine. The rain hit the house in waves. The toilet floor flooded. The towels had fallen off the line onto the grass. It was not until after dinner that the rain stopped. Dawn and I ran outside to look at the light. It was about nine o'clock and the sky was a yellow grey. The gums and the grass were sulphur-green, like when you look through a piece of yellow cellophane.

There is nothing like walking on cool sand in the dark. The beach is blue and the grasses on the dunes are black and scary. A headland could be a dark and endless hole in the universe. The sea humps on wet sand. There is a glow just above the horizon. If your thong falls off you have to get down on your hands and knees and feel for it. A piece of driftwood could be a dead seal. A scrap of seaweed could be the remains of a pelican. A man in dark clothes at the far end of the beach could be the captain, but is not.

Three men brought their runabout in from across the bay. One stood and pissed off the side of the boat. Another finished the dregs of a can of beer and threw it into the water. I stared at them, warning them off, but they came in closer and followed us up the beach, talking about Dawny and laughing. One of them called out, over and over: 'Fishface! Don't go, Fishface!' Dawn was frightened, but she knew not to hurry. We continued along the beach. 'Fishface!' the man was still calling.

Early the next morning, Captain Hodge came to the back door. He was dressed tidy and clean. He said he needed me to do something for him.

The ferry left from Constitution Dock at five every Sunday evening. That first Sunday back in Hobart I took Dawny down there. We walked around the wharves, up past a grey navy boat to the end of the wharf where a motley group of people were fishing. A couple of Chinese fathers were there with their sons, and a man with galls on his face like a gumleaf, and an Englishwoman with a coarse accent. Each group had a bucket of blotched fish. Dawn said they were Australian salmon. They writhed in buckets of dirty water. There were smears of scales and wipes of blood on the concrete. A boy sat scaling a fish he had just caught, though it hadn't yet stopped twitching. We walked past sailing boats, fishing boats, a police boat, all jostling together in noxious fluid. The fish launches had plumes of scum coming out of their rear ends; the navy boat filled our lungs with fumes.

I paid for both of us to have a cruise on the ferry. From the water, Hobart looked like an unreal city, like something you would see in *National Geographic*. The trees were algae-green and lush, the buildings placed neatly like little toy railway houses. That cruise up the river could almost have been a trip around the world. There were mountains, a castle, gardens, even a desert. Victorian blocks of flats looked like pop-up pictures from a children's picture-book in front of a prehistoric mountain and an abalone-shell sky. You could see the road out of Hobart disappearing between the hills, like the secret way the children went when they followed the Pied Piper.

'It's like a toy town and only half-a-dozen people are allowed to play in it,' I said to Dawn. The lights came on like fairy-lights and I wondered: are those people sitting at their tables eating marzipan food? Do their children pick up the oak leaves in Salamanca and call them tree stars?

'I have to tell you something, Dawny,' I said. She smiled at me, only half-listening. 'It's about Captain Hodge.' Her head jerked up. 'He asked me to tell you he's sorry he can't marry you. He's got a wife of his own already.'

She wrapped her arms around herself and rocked from

side to side with the motion of the boat. 'Dun't matter Sonny. Dun't matter!' My sister put her arm around me, then, while I cried.

I have sent the three girls to bed, and have opened the window on my wife's side of the room. Please God let me have some peace and quiet! The air is cool under my bare legs. How long since I lay on a bed next to an open window? We used to leave the windows and even the doors open on hot nights in Waterloo Street. During the night you'd usually wake and close them. By then the street lamps would even be looking cooler. All the lights would be off in all the narrow houses down the street. You could have tiptoed and peeped in at windows, heard people snoring, children whimpering softly, women rolling in dreams of unfamiliar embraces. In the light from the street lamps the gum trees in tiny front yards made shadows on still-warm footpaths. The crickets in side alleys would have been lulled to silence by the dew. Orange toms that had spent the hot part of the night screaming blue murder had minced off somewhere else. A breeze might rattle the three shrubs in front of the Olsons' and a glass windchime might tinkle on a verandah. If you walked out on the grass in the back yard, your feet would be wet and cold with dew. The moon would no longer be fat and pulsing, but flat and cool, the stars cold enough to peel a finger.

This night is cool and fat and wide. I pull myself down under the blankets. It is a sweet weight on my shoulders and the back of my neck. My face already feels flaccid with sleep.

That holiday at Whitecliffs was the first time we ever

saw lights on the water. The harbour was black and oily and the lights smeared and viscous and corrugated. We had never seen anything like it before: purple street lights and white mast beacons and green and red channel-markers all made fluid by the night. But Dawny is gone now. The narrow house where she lived alone for so long in Waterloo Street will be sold.

When I stick my head out the window, I can hear the creek and I can hear a possum in the pear tree. What am I doing in this room with its grey timbers and brown photos and striped curtains? How did my life bring me here? Was I asleep? All I can think of is this...how that summer in 1960 I told Dawn that the captain didn't want her, and it was a lie.

Carmel Bird • 1987

The Woodpecker Toy Fact

The magpie is the scandalmonger of the woods.
The verb 'to mag' meaning 'to gossip' derives from magpie.

My mother was a magger.

A paling fence divided our garden from the garden next door and over the back fence lived Mrs Back-Fence. My mother and Mrs Back-Fence might have been posing for a cartoonist as they stood on either side of the fence, magging. Behind each woman was a rotary clothes line. We had striped tea-towels, white sheets, woollen singlets, pink pants and knitted socks all hanging from dolly pegs. Some things were patched and darned, the mending being more obvious when the clothes were wet. It was unsafe to hang anything damaged but unmended on the line, for this would be noted by other maggers as a sign of degeneration in the family. And once, when a torn, unmended nightdress had got through the washing and as far as the line, our rabbit attacked it and shredded it so that it had to be thrown out. My mother and Mrs Back-Fence had floral aprons, and often their hair was set with metal butterfly clips, covered by a chiffon scarf knotted at the front. They did not wear fluffy slippers. Instead, they nearly always wore rather thick stockings and brown lace-up shoes, like nurses.

Over the back fence these maggers passed hot scones wrapped in tea-towels, cups of sugar, bowls of stewed plums, and a continuous ribbon of talk. They sifted through the details of everything they heard and saw and thought, and arranged them into art. Children under the age of ten, considered to lack the ability to understand the narrative, were allowed to listen, provided they were still and quiet. (Today, magging usually takes place on the telephone, I think, and so a child listener becomes restless because there is only one side to the conversation.) The Crusaders took from the Arabian Desert the seeds of the wild flowers, which later became the glory of English gardens. The maggers scoured the lives of their relations and neighbours, and sometimes the lives of famous people, to shake out the seeds from which would grow undulating plains of exotic grasses and flowers giving colour and perfume.

One of the most hypnotic habits of the maggers was the constant use of possessive pronouns and parentheses. They constructed sentences which could go on all day in dizzy convolutions, as one relative clause after another was added.

'Edna and Joe (his brother was Colin who married Betty Trethewey who later divorced him which was when he had his breakdown over the Kelly girl so that it was no wonder business went downhill) were having their twenty-fifth anniversary which was just before Easter which was early that year, and Pam (she's the daughter, you realise) was there with her fiancé who was Bruce French (his father had the hardware next to the Royal Park) when it turned out that Joe was electrocuted in the cellar which was where he kept the wine (they drank a terrible lot of wine in those days) and it wasn't long after that that Edna turned round and married Bruce, and Pam went and lived next door to them (this was fifteen years ago now) and she hasn't spoken to them since which is very hard on the daughter, Susan, who doesn't even know that Bruce is her father, not that Bruce can be certain himself really, but of course Edna knows and she has never forgiven Pam for not telling her she was going to have Susan when she was engaged to Bruce.'

As a child I never saw any Marx Brothers films. When I did see them, I was surprised to hear Groucho Marx using my mother's phrases. Trapped in her language, like fish in a net, were snatches and snippets from the Marx Brothers' scripts. Inserted into the magging of two women in a Tasmanian coastal town of the 1940s, the expressions of Groucho Marx had a curious lifelessness, and their meaning was elusive. But I, as a child, accepted the words at face value, in faith, expecting to have their meaning revealed in good time. It took many years for things to fall into place. Perhaps the child who called his bear Gladly after Gladly the cross-eyed bear is an apocryphal child, but the story has a nice ring of truth. Harold be thy name. I applied the same unblinking acceptance to the name of the local toyshop. The end of the sign had fallen off and so it was called 'The Woodpecker Toy Fact'. I even accepted the name of the toymaker as an ordinary name, and now I don't know whether it was his real name or not. He was called Jack Frost. At Christmas, he used to make wooden peepshows of the crib. You closed one eye and looked through a hole in a box. Inside, in an unearthly light, were first the shepherds, then the animals, and, further back, the baby like a sugar mouse in his mother's arms. The angels were in the far distance; wings sharp like the wings of swallows. And Jack Frost carved our rocking horse. Even the name of the horse, Dapple Grey, I failed to see as descriptive, and thought of as Christian name and surname. I must have existed in a blurry blue mist where I waited for the words to acquire meaning. Something that I always connected with the verb 'to mag' was some stuff called 'Milk of Mag'. This was a thick, white, slightly aniseed, shudderingly horrible laxative medicine, the 'Mag' being short for magnesia.

I tried to join in some magging once. I made the mistake of thinking that if I introduced some fabulous fact, I would be included in the discussion. So I said that Jack Frost had told me he had made the original statue of the Infant Jesus of Prague. Nobody took any notice of me at all. Or so I thought. But after a while I realised that terribly silly lies were being referred to as woodpecker toy facts.

'And then she tried to tell me the baby was premature. A woodpecker toy fact if ever I heard one. It is no mystery to me that he weighed nine-and-a-half pounds. Nine-and-a-half pounds! I ask you.'

There was a special quality to a toy fact. There was a desperation—either to attract or to deflect attention. And a toy fact only became a toy fact after it had passed through the special sifting process of the maggers, and had received from them a blessing.

I had generated a term, which had drifted into the net of the maggers. Little did I know (as a magger would say) that the spirit of my words was being given the same weight as that accorded the words of Groucho Marx.

Over the years, the concept of the woodpecker toy fact has become very important and dear to me. I have lived here in Woodpecker Point, on the northwest coast of Tasmania, all my life. My parents have died and my sisters have all married and left the island. I live alone in the house with the rotary clothes line and the paling fence. Mrs Back-Fence is in a nursing home in Burnie, and I have never seen the wife of the Turkish man who now lives in the house. They have a baby daughter who sings *Baa-baa-black-sheep* sadly and endlessly in the garden. It is a very boring and irritating song, after a while. Jack Frost has disappeared. One of my nephews took Dapple Grey to the beach and left him there and he was washed out to sea. As these and many other things have changed, so the idea of the toy fact has changed and developed. The quest for the toy fact has gradually come to dominate my life.

Once when I was at the beach, years before the toy fact was named, I captured a starfish in my tin bucket. The tide was out and there was a cold breeze coming in across the shiny wet sand. I was sitting on the pebbles, which were shaped like eggs, and smooth, and all different kinds of white. I had the bucket between my legs so that I could stare down into it at the starfish, and I was given the ability to understand the shape of everything.

The moment passed, and yet it has never left me. Five minutes later, the sky went darker, and a red-haired girl in a green dress came up behind me and grabbed the bucket. She ran off across the pebbles with the starfish. My second-oldest sister chased the girl, and the girl defended herself with the spike of a beach umbrella. She drove the spike into my sister's lip, ran off with the bucket, and disappeared.

I think my quest began with the starfish. Perhaps if that girl had not stolen it when she did, had not injured my sister as she did, I might never have undertaken the quest. Then, when the toy fact was named and its nature defined in a rudimentary way, I sensed that there was a system of knowing things that could, if handled in the right way, lead to understanding, the idea of which dazzled me. The simplicity and complexity of the starfish, punctuated in time by my sister's blood, and coupled with the glorious lie (which might not have been a lie) about Jack Frost and the Infant of Prague, suggested to me that if I assembled facts in a special way every minute of every day for years and years and years, I would eventually see something more beautiful and more wonderful than anything I could have imagined. It was as though I had a golden thread which I wove to make a net in which I caught the toy facts, trapping them, bright birds in flight, planets in amber. I have collected and assembled the toy facts in my brain, and I am still uncertain as to whether I will ultimately discover The Toy Fact and so complete the pattern, or whether, by placing the final fact I will produce The Toy Fact. The quest itself is, however, absorbing, and has, as I said, come to dominate my life.

It is not only a matter of discovering things, but of manufacturing from those things the toy facts in all their fullness and beauty. I sometimes think my golden net of facts is like a fabulous story I am writing in my head. Once, when I was studying poetry at school, I used to think that everything was a metaphor, and said 'metaphor' in answer to every question.

'If we took a slice off the top of her head,' said the teacher, and I thought she was going to pay me a compliment, 'we would find that the only thing in there was a metaphor.' She meant to be insulting but had stumbled on the beautiful truth. It was this remark of hers that set me on my final course. From then on, I did not have to pass any exams or do anything much at all. I have spent my time since that day listening to people, reading encyclopaedias, browsing in the library, sitting on the beach, and generally pursuing one toy fact after another. I cared for my parents when they were ill, and I have worked in the Morning Glory cake shop for the past ten years.

One day, I am going to know everything about everything. I will know what makes a Cox's Orange Pippin different from a Granny Smith. I will know what it is that stops hydrangeas from having any scent. I will see the pyramids being built and survive the Hundred Years War. I will understand the nature of fire, and know the depth to which the longest tree-root goes down into the earth. I will know what sorrow is made from, what constitutes joy. I will have conversations with the sage of Zurich; afternoon tea with Chagall in his garden; speak to Polycrates the King before his crucifixion in Magnesia. There are bound to be times when I can think in Chinese.

Meanwhile, I live here in Woodpecker Point, not far from the ruins of the park where the deer and the peacocks used to roam. I prune the roses and the fruit trees and I talk to my finches.

I have a large collection of feathers, and am making a study of their colours. At present, I am particularly interested in the iridescent colours, which ripple and change on the necks of pigeons. They are formed when the light is refracted from the surfaces of the tiny scales that make up the feathers. I suppose some colours of reptiles and butterflies work on the same principle. I have spent a lot of time with butterflies, and can here, quite naturally, in the course, as it were, of the conversation, mention a very high-class toy fact. This is the fact that the Cabbage White Butterfly arrived in Tasmania on the feast of St Teresa in 1940, which was the day that I was born. We both arrived in Devonport at the same time, and have been constant observers of each other from the beginning. It is possible that the Cabbage White knows more about me than I know about it. I have a photograph of myself with a cloud of Cabbage Whites. I am three and I am standing among the cabbages in my maternal grandmother's garden, wearing the blue dress with the white edges that my grandmother knitted for me for Christmas. As these were the days before colour photography, the blue of my dress and the blue-green of the cabbages are tinted with inks. My hair is the colour of butter, and my shoes are magical red. The butterflies are untouched by the tinter's brush so that they possess a quality of ethereal purity, which is lacking in the coloured areas of the picture. I have always been pleased that I had a grandmother who had Cabbage Butterflies in her cabbages. And I have the photograph to prove it. It was taken the day before Christmas, and on Christmas Day my grandmother died.

The night before they buried her, she came to me as I lay sleeping. She had taken by then the form of the smallest British butterfly, the Small Blue, so often found near warm and sunny grass slopes and in hollows. She was like a forget-me-not. She alighted on my quilt and smiled at me, sweetly, as she always smiled. All she said was one word. This almost shocked me at the time, because she was a magger, like my mother. She had no doubt trained my mother. She smiled at me and she said:

'Listen.'

Barney Roberts • 1987

A Jar of Raspberry Jam

For the time of year it was warm. A dry spell, Bern's father had said, peering at a cloud, a big, shining, white one, which had slid quietly over Bassett's hill on its flat bottom, its top, dollops of mashed potato. Another fine day.

Bern wasn't interested in the weather, just then, although it was always easier in fine weather, you weren't stuck in the house or a shed.

He sneaked off without anyone seeing him except Vic who watched from under the quince tree to see if he was only going to the lavatory, saw he wasn't and followed him down past the calfshed, past the cowshed, along the hedge and over the railway to the bank, which looked north over the river to Ridge's and Edward's.

Bern sat on the grass amongst the ferns, which would make him hard to see by anyone over the river. The spaniel lay beside him, on his belly with his head resting on flat paws. His ears were touching the ground, his eyes were soft and dull, but followed the boy's slightest movement.

Bern reached a hand to lay it on the dog's shoulder. Only the eyes moved. If there was a problem, they would share it.

But there was no problem; not one you could write down or talk about. It wasn't as simple as that. An unease, an ache, that he couldn't describe; yet alleviated in a way just by sitting there, where he was, alone with the dog and everything familiar about him; like the relief of a poultice on a boil. But this was not something you could put your finger on, like you would touch a boil with the tips of your fingers and feel the core of hurt, an electric contact with the brain.

As he stared blankly across the river he began to focus on a vague something that caused his brows to lower and glower, and his mouth to pucker; an unattractive face, scowling and angry-looking. If you reminded him he could tell you how Mrs Webster had mistaken this look of deep concentration and stopped in mid-sentence to stare at him and say: Wipe that scowl off your face! And he had been amazed and said belligerently: I wasn't scowling. Don't dare answer me back, she had said. I wasn't scowling! (more belligerently) How dare you! Give me that cane! (pointing to the boy in the front desk). And Bern had jumped to his feet: I'll get it. And hurried down the aisle past the teacher, grabbed the cane from behind the piano and handed it to her, almost poked it at her, standing there angry and temporarily nonplussed. He could tell how she vented her anger by slashing at his hand and sending him out to the sheltershed to wait until she told him to come back: how when school had finished and the others had gone home and she had imagined he had gone with them, he had stayed, still angry and pigheaded, in the sheltershed for an hour, until he had attracted her attention by dropping a board: how she had come out to the shed amazed and shocked to find him and ask him why he hadn't gone home when the others had left. And the culmination—his victory—You told me to stay until you called me.

If Mrs Webster had come across him sitting there on the bank with the dog she would have recognized that same ugly frown but it is possible that in his eyes she would have been just another nebulous object like the willows, the white gums and Ridge's barn on the hill (stuck there like an oversized dunny).

It was to do with the Cullens. For all of Bern's twelve years the Cullens had been neighbours at the end of the road. And now the property had been purchased by the Shekletons.

Cullens! Mum, can we go up to Cullen's? Dad, do you want us to take that fork back to Cullen's? Or they had a fish to drop in. Or their mother, realizing the boys liked to see the Cullens, would ask them to take some little thing to them.

There was always a welcome there, perhaps because their only son, Frank, had been tragically drowned, and unmarried Stella was no longer living at home; perhaps, because the boys had no grandparents, they had adopted this old couple. Tom, who forever seemed to be singing tunelessly his deedle-um-de-de, and was apparently never busy, at least never too busy to stop and talk with the boys; and Clare, whose short, thick body was always clothed in a black and sombre dress, which contrasted markedly to the warm smile of welcome. 'Don't go far away, boys, and I'll have some scones out of the oven in two shakes,' or, 'Would you like to pick yourselves some mulberries? Or cherries? The starlings'll get them if you don't.'

There was the time when they were close to the house and the boys heard Mrs Cullen call: 'Tom! Tom! What do you think. The old goose has hatched out her goslings—nine of them.' 'Nine, did you say, Clare? Well, well, well, I'll go to beggery. I'll go to beggery.' It was another Cullen contribution to add to the boy's store of mimicry, as well as: 'Come and have a cuppa-tea, Tom.' 'O.K. Clare, deedle-um-de-de, deedle-um-de-de.'

The Cullens were poor, as every farmer in the district was poor, except for Mr Norton Smith, the manager of the Van Diemens Land Company, who owned 'Amberley', a beautiful and fertile property on Roberts's eastern boundary.

But Cullen's property was small and hilly and mostly covered with ferns and scrub. Mr Cullen grew a few potatoes, and oats for the horses, and turnips, and milked several cows, but since Frank's death he had little heart for the extra work required to halt the yearly advance of bracken, and rushes on the flats.

What little money they earned was barely enough to buy the few necessary items of food, and to allow the two old people to hold their heads erect on Sundays when the congregation's donations were read from the pulpit. Their Sunday clothes were used sparingly and with extreme care; they were the same they had been wearing for twenty years or more.

Their clothes, like the house, the sheds, the horses' harness, and the water tank (which sprouted countless bits of rag and tarred wooden plugs) in spite of constant care and attention, were deteriorating to the point where they were becoming gradually unserviceable.

Notwithstanding all these problems, the Cullens were able to take pity on Old Jim, who they found destitute and sick, lying on the side of the road, to take him home with them, where he lived for years in Cullen's hut.

Yes, Bern knew, it was to do with the Cullens. There had been deaths in the district, plenty of them: old people, babies, a young man he hardly knew had pulled his gun through a fence and shot himself. None of these deaths had caused him pain. Old Jim had died. But then Mr Cullen. It was Bern's first real feeling of sadness, of loss—much more (although he would never admit it) than the sadness he had felt when his aunt, his mother's sister, had died. The aunt who had painted the picture hanging in the hall, and who had carved the breadboard and the breadknife handle, but who he had barely known.

'Poor Mr Cullen has died,' his mother had told them one afternoon, when they came home from school. And he had gone down to the stable and climbed up to the loft. It was the first time he had cried over someone's death. He thought how Mr Cullen, a few weeks earlier, had taken him and Harry into the house to show them something that someone (was it Stella?) had given them: an His Master's Voice gramophone, which he had wound up and played for them.

The record was an old one which scratched, and went from loud to soft, a man who talked and sang and finished a monologue with the line: Yours to the last drop, George. Several times it was played for them and each time the old people kept their eyes fixed upon those of the boys, revelling in their attention and their smiling appreciation. It was a gift, even bigger and better than the scones and mulberries. 'Come back and hear it, any time,' they had said as the boys ran off to tell their family.

Then Mr Cullen had died. Simply and suddenly. The farm was sold and Mrs Cullen had gone to Wynyard to live.

Now, she too was dead. His mother had told him, told them all. She had died four days ago. And his father didn't know and had missed the funeral.

Only a few days before she died, on the Saturday, Bern and his mother had driven, with Star in the jinker, in to Wynyard to see her and to take her some eggs and vegetables. She was living in a tiny two-roomed cottage near the brickworks by the racecourse. Mrs Cullen was upset because she only had an open fire and wasn't able to bake scones for them. 'A man is coming next week,' she said, 'to put a camp-oven in for me.' She played the gramophone for them but only one record: 'Take a pair of sparkling eyes'. The other one, which the boys liked, had been broken in the move.

When they were leaving Mrs Cullen asked them to wait. She hobbled back up the dirt track and into the house and came out with a jar of raspberry jam. Bern's mother had kissed her wrinkled old cheek and as they drove off Bern noticed his mother had tears on her cheek, which she didn't wipe off.

Now Mrs Cullen was dead. There was only Stella left. And she was ten years older than Bern. He hardly knew her, apart from seeing her often on the road with Florence Smyth, riding double-dinked and bare-back on the piebald pony or cantering down the road with sox on her hands, in the winter, for gloves.

Bern stood up. Immediately Vic stood too and looked up at the boy as if to say: what will we do now? Bern scratched behind the floppy ear, 'Do you remember when Rover died, Vic?' he said. 'Of course you don't, you weren't even alive then.'

Price Warung · 1890

How Muster-Master Stoneman Earned His Breakfast

I

An unpretentious building of rough-hewn stone standing in the middle of a small, stockaded enclosure. A doorway in the wall of the building facing the entrance-gate to the yard. To the left of the doorway, a glazed window of the ordinary size. To its right a paneless aperture, so low and narrow that were the four upright and two transverse bars which grate it doubled in thickness no interstice would be left for the admission of light or air to the interior. Behind the bars—a face.

Sixteen hours hence that face will look its last upon the world which has stricken it countless cruel blows. In a corner of the enclosure the executioner's hand is even now busy stitching into a shapeless cap, a square of grey serge. To-morrow the same hand will use the cap to hood the face, as one of the few simple preliminaries to swinging the carcase to which the face is attached from the rude platform now in course of erection against the stockade fence and barely twenty yards in front of the stone building.

The building is the gaol—locally known as the 'cage'—of Oatlands, a small township in the midlands of Van Diemen's Land, which has gradually grown up round a convict 'muster-station', established by Governor Davey. The time is five o'clock on a September evening, fifty-five years ago. At nine o'clock on the following morning, Convict Glancy, No. 17,927, transportee ex ship *Pestonjee Bomanjee* (second trip), originally under sentence for seven years for the theft of a silk handkerchief from a London 'swell', will suffer the extreme penalty of the law for having, in an intemperate moment, objected to the mild discipline with which a genial and loving motherland had sought to correct his criminal tendencies. In other words, Convict Glancy, metaphorically goaded by the wordy insults and literally by the bayonet-tip of one of his motherland's reformatory agents—to wit, Road-gang Overseer James Jones—had scattered J.J.'s brains over a good six square yards of metalled roadway. The deed had been rapturously applauded by Glancy's fellow-gangers, all of whom had the inclination, but lacked the courage, to wield the crowbar that has been the means of erasing this particular tyrant's name from the pay-sheets of His Britannic Majesty's Colonial Penal Establishment. Nevertheless and notwithstanding such tribute of appreciation, H.B.M.'s Colonial representatives, police, judicial and gubernatorial, have thought it rather one to be censured and have, accordingly, left Convict Glancy for execution.

This decision of the duly constituted authorities Convict Glancy has somewhat irrelevantly (as it will seem to us at this enlightened day) acknowledged by a fervent 'Thank God!'— an ejaculation rendered the more remarkable by the fact that never before in his convict history had he linked the name of the Deity with any expression of gratitude for the many blessings enjoyed by him in that state of penal servitude to which it had pleased the same Deity to call him. On the contrary, he had constantly indulged in maledictions on his fate and on his Maker. He had resolutely cursed the benignant forces with which the System and the King's Regulations had surrounded him, and he had failed to reverence as he ought the triangles, the gang-chains, the hominy, the prodding bayonet, and the other things which would have conduced to his reformation had he but manifested a more humble and obedient spirit. No wonder, therefore, as Chaplain Ford said, that it has come about that he has qualified for the capital doom.

Upon this doom, in so far as it could be represented by the gallows, Convict Glancy was now gazing with an unflinching eye. On this September evening he stands at his cell-window looking on half-a-dozen brown-clothed figures handling saw, and square, and hammer, as they fix in the earth two sturdy uprights, and to those a projecting cross-beam; as they bind the two with a solid tie-piece of knotless hardwood; as they build a narrow platform of planks around the gallows-tree; as they fasten a rope to the notched end of the cross-beam; and as they slope to the edge of the planks, ten feet from the ground, a rude ladder. All the drowsy afternoon he had watched the working party, though Chaplain Ford had stood by his side droning of the grace which had been withheld from him in life, but might still be his in death. He had felt interested, had Convict Glancy, in these preparations for the event in which he was to act such a prominent part on the morrow. He had even laughed at the grim humour of one of the brown-garbed workers who, when the warder's eye was off him, had gone through the pantomime of noosing the rope end round his own neck—a little joke which contributed much to the (necessarily noiseless) delight of the rest of the gang.

Altogether, Convict Glancy reflected as dusk fell, and the working party gathered up their tools, and the setting sun tipped the bayonets of the guard with a diamond iridescence, that he had spent many a duller afternoon. If the Chaplain had only held his tongue, the time would have passed with real pleasantness. He said as much to the good man as the latter remarked to the warder on duty in the cell that he would look in again after supper.

'You may save yourself the trouble, sir,' quoth, respectfully enough, Convict Glancy. 'You have spoilt my last afternoon. Don't spoil my last night!'

Chaplain Ford winced at the words. He was still comparatively new to the work of spiritually superintending a hundred or so monsters who looked upon the orthodox hell as a place where residence would be pleasantly recreative after Port Arthur Settlement and Norfolk Island; and the time lay still in the future when, being completely embruted, he would come to regard it as a very curious circumstance indeed that Christ had omitted eulogistic reference to the

System from the Sermon on the Mount. Consequently, he winced and sighed, not so much—to do him justice—at the utter depravity of Convict Glancy as at his own inability to reach the reprobate's heart. But he took the hint; he mournfully said he would not return that evening, but would be with the prisoner by half-past five o'clock in the morning.

II

When Chaplain Ford entered the enclosure immediately before the hour he had named, he at once understood, from the excitement manifested by a group assembled in front of the 'cage', that something was amiss. Voices were uttering fearful words, impetuously, almost shriekingly, and hands swung lanterns—the grey dawn had not yet driven the darkness from the stockade—and brandished muskets furiously. A very brief space of time served to inform the reverend functionary what had gone wrong.

Convict Glancy had made his escape, having previously murdered, with the victim's own bayonet, the warder who had been told-off to watch him during the night. This latter circumstance was, of course, unfortunate, but alone it would not have created the excitement, for the murder of prison-officials was a common enough occurrence. It was the other thing that galled the gesticulating and blaspheming group. That a prisoner, fettered with ten-pound irons, should have broken out of gaol on the very eve of his execution—why, it was calculated to shake the confidence of the Comptroller-General himself in the infallibility and perfect righteousness of the System. And, popular and authoritative belief in the System once shattered, where would they be?

The murdered man had gone on duty at ten o'clock, and very shortly afterwards he must have met with his fate. How Glancy had obtained possession of the bayonet could only be conjectured. As was the custom during the day or two preceding a convict's execution, he had been left unmanacled, and ironed with double leg-chains only. Thus his hands were free to perpetrate the deed once he grasped the weapon. Glancy, on his escape, had taken the instrument with him, but there was no doubt that he had inflicted death with it, the wound in the dead man's breast being obviously caused by the regulation bayonet. Possibly the sentinel had nodded, and then a violent wrench of the prisoner's wrist and a sudden stab had extended his momentary slumber into an eternal sleep. The bayonet had also been used by Glancy to prise up a flooring-flag, and to scoop out an aperture under the wall, the base-stones of which, following the slipshod architecture of the time, rested on the surface and were not sunk into the ground.

The work of excavation must have taken the convict several hours, and must have been conducted as noiselessly as the manner of committing the crime itself. A solitary warder occupied the outer guard-room, but he asserted that he had heard no sound except the exchange of whistle-signals between the dormitory guard at the convict-barracks (a quarter-of-mile away at the rear of the gaol stockade) and the military patrol. The night routine of the 'cage' did not insist upon the whistle-signal between the men on duty, but they passed a simple 'All's well' every hour. And this the guardroom-warder maintained he had done with the officer inside the condemned cell, the response being given in a low tone, from consideration, so the former thought, for the sleeping convict so soon to die. Of course, if this man was to be believed, Glancy must have uttered the words. It was not the first time the signal which should have been given by a prison officer had been made by his convict murderer.

The murder was discovered on the arrival of the relief watch at five o'clock. The last 'All's well' was exchanged at four. Consequently the escapee had less than an hour's start. The scaling of the stockade would not be difficult even for a man in irons, and once in the bush an experienced hand would soon find a method of fracturing the links.

It must be admitted that this contumacious proceeding of Convict Glancy was most vexatious. Under-Sheriff Ropewell, now soundly reposing at the township inn, would be forthcoming at nine o'clock with his Excellency's warrant in his hands to demand from Muster-Master Stoneman the body of one James Glancy, and Muster-Master Stoneman would have to apologise for his inability to produce the said body. The difficulty was quite unprecedented, and Stoneman, as he stood in the midst of his minions, groaned audibly at the prospect of having to do the thing most abhorrent to the official mind—establish a precedent.

'Such a thing was never heard of!' he cried. 'A man to bolt just when he was to be turned off! And the d——d hypocrite tried to make his Honour and all of us think that he was only too happy to be scragged. It's too d——d bad!'

It certainly did seem peculiar that Glancy, who had apparently much rejoiced at the contemplation of his early decease, should give leg-bail just when he was to realise his wishes. He had told the judge that 'he was —— glad they were going to kill him right off instead of by inches', and yet he had voluntarily thrown off the noose when it was virtually round his neck. Was it the mere contrariness of the convict nature that prompted the escape? Or, was it the innate love of life that becomes stronger as the benefits of living become fewer and fewer? Had the craving for existence and for freedom surged over his despair and recklessness at the eleventh hour?

Such were the inquiries which Chaplain Ford put to himself as, horrified, he took in the particulars of No. 17,927's crowning enormities from the hubbub of the group.

'Damn it!' said the Muster-Master at last, 'we are losing time. The devil can't have gone far with those ten-pounders on him. We'll have to put the regulars on the track as well as our own men. Warder Briggs, report to Captain White at the barracks, and—'

Muster-Master Stoneman stopped short. Through the foggy air there came the familiar sound as of a convict dragging his irons. What could it be? No prisoners had been as yet loosed from the dormitory. Whence could the noise proceed?

Clink—clank—s-sh—dr-g-g—clink—clank—dr-g-g. The sound drew nearer, and Convict Glancy turned in at the enclosure gateway—unescorted. He had severed the leg-chain at the link which connected with the basil of the left anklet, but had not taken the trouble to remove the other part of the chain. Thus, while he could take his natural pace with his left foot, he dragged the fetters behind his right leg.

A moment of hushed surprise, and then three or four men rushed towards him. The first who touched him he felled with a blow.

'Not yet,' said he, grimly. 'I give myself up, Mr. Stoneman—you don't take me! I give myself up—you ain't going to get ten quid for taking me.' And then Convict Glancy laughed, and held out his hands for the handcuffs. He laughed more heartily as the subordinate hirelings of the System threw themselves upon him like hounds on their prey.

'No need to turn out the sodgers now, Muster-Master—not till nine o'clock.' Once more his hideous laugh rang through the yards. 'You had an easier job than you expected, hadn't you, Stoneman, old cove?'

Muster-Master Stoneman had been surprised into silence and into an unusual abstinence from blasphemy by the reappearance—quite unprecedented under the circumstances!—of the doomed wretch. But the desperado's jeering tones whipped him into speech.

'Curse you!' he yelled, 'I'll teach you to laugh on the other side of your mouth presently. You'd better have kept away.' He literally foamed in his mad anger.

'Do you think I couldn't have stopped away if I'd wanted to, having got clear?' A lofty scorn rang out in the words. 'But do you think I was going to run away when I was so near Freedom as that?' And the wretch jerked his manacled hands in the direction of the gallows. 'You d—d fool!'

No one spoke for a full half-minute. Then: 'Why did you break gaol then?' asked the Muster-Master.

'Because I wanted to spit on Jones' grave!' was the reply.

III

Muster-Master Stoneman was as good as his word. Death couldn't drive the smile from Glancy's face. That could only be done by one thing—the lash.

When next the Muster-Master spoke it was to order the prisoner a double ration of cocoa and bread. And, 'Briggs,' he continued, 'while he is getting it, see that the triangles are rigged.'

'The triangles, sir!' exclaimed Officer Briggs and Convict Glancy together.

'I said the triangles, and I mean the triangles. No. 17,927 has broken gaol, and as Muster-Master of this station, and governor of this gaol, and as a magistrate of the territory, I can give him 750 lashes for escaping. But as he has to go through another little ceremony this morning I'll let him off with a "canary"—(a hundred lashes).'

'You surely cannot mean it, sir!' exclaimed Parson Ford.

'Mean it, sir! By G—, I'll show you I mean it,' replied the M.M., whose blaspheming no presence restrained save that of his official superiors. 'Give him the cocoa, Warder Tuff, give the doctor my compliments, and tell him his attendance is required here. Tell him he'd better bring his smelling salts—they may be wanted,' he sneered in conclusion.

'You devil!' cried Glancy. The reckless grin passed away, and his face faded to the pallor of the death he was so soon to die.

As Muster-Master Stoneman turned on his heel to prepare the warrant for the flogging, he looked at his watch. It was half-past six.

At seven o'clock the first lash from the cat-o'-nine-tails fell upon Convict Glancy's back.

At seven thirty his groaning and bleeding body, which had received the full hundred of flaying stripes, lay on the pallet of the cell where he had murdered the night-guard but a few hours before.

At eight o'clock Executioner Johnson entered the cell. 'I've brought yer sumthink to 'arden yer, Glancy, ol' man. I'll rub it in, an' it'll help yer to keep up.' So tender a sympathy inspired Mr. Johnson's words that anyone not knowing him would have thought he was the bearer of some priceless balsam. But Convict Glancy knew him; and, maddened by pain though he was, had still sensibility enough left to make a shuddering resistance to the hangman as he proceeded to rub into the gashed flesh a handful of coarse salt. 'By the Muster-Master's orders, sonny,' soothingly remarked Johnson. 'To 'arden yer.'

At eight fifteen Under-Sheriff Ropewell, who had been apprised while at breakfast of the murder and escape, appeared on the scene escorted by his javelin-men. This gentleman, too, had been greatly perplexed by Convict Glancy's proceedings. 'Really it was most inconsiderate of the man,' he said to the Muster-Master. 'I do not know whether I ought to proceed to execution, pending his trial for this second murder.'

'Oh,' said the latter functionary—flicking with his handkerchief from his coat-sleeve as he spoke a drop of Convict Glancy's blood that had fallen there from a reflex swirl of the lash, 'I think your duty is clear. You must hang him at nine o'clock, and try him afterwards for the last crime.'

And as Convict Glancy, per *Pestonjee Bomanjee* (second), No. 17,927, was punctually hanged at five past nine, it is to be presumed that the Under-Sheriff had accepted this solution of the difficulty.

At ten fifteen a mass of carrion having been huddled into a shell, and certain formalities, which in the estimation of the System served as efficiently as a coroner's inquest, having been duly attended to, Muster-Master Stoneman bethought himself that he had not breakfasted.

'I'll see you later, Mr. Ropewell,' he said, as the latter was endorsing the Governor's warrant with the sham verdict; 'I'm going to breakfast. I think I've earned it this morning.'

Theresa Tasmania • 1869

A 'Model' Dream

I thought I had long wished to behold a particular locality, whose beauties had been often and glowingly described to me. Such terms as 'Garden of the Earth', 'Second Paradise', and 'Another Eden' excited my curiosity and longing to visit so fair a spot. Yet, strange as it may sound, small was the number of those who of their own accord sought this paradisaical region, and, though I would willingly have added one to its visitors, for a long period access to it was denied me.

At length accident threw an unexpected opportunity my way, and I found myself wafted on a favouring breeze, and in agreeable company, to the region of anticipated delights.

I dreamt, then, that I was there at last, or, at all events, within half an hour (as the foreigners say) of this happy territory, and, looking round on all sides, I was bound to confess too much praise had not been bestowed on the beauties that already surrounded me.

I thought the harbour we entered was apparently landlocked; behind us we had left pillars and peaks, island rocks and stern promontories, but the hills that extended their ranges to support these, would not let us out of their sight; they stood, in patriarchal grandeur, flanking us still, and their brown rugged tops put on a smile of welcome in the brilliant noonday sunshine. Before us gleamed the great white walls, the tower-like guardhouse, and the closely-huddled habitations, whose mysteries I so wished to penetrate, with gardens and trees and verdure shooting up from every crevice where a living plant could grow; on our right extended a charming walk under an avenue of gum trees, whose shade looked quite refreshing in the fervid heat, with pretty cottages and gardens dotting the banks of the bay; and on the left, a long sharp promontory, with white glittering beaches, shot out to meet us, as if to ask what right we had to invade the peaceful solitude it guarded. Its point was high, steep, perpendicular, and rocky, bearing a strong resemblance to the side of a quarry after picks and spades have cut many feet through the rock, and the waves rolled up to the perpendicular wall without let or obstruction; a row of heavy cannon pointed seaward was all that was needed to complete the warlike garniture of this grim promontory.

But, with greater delight than ever, my eyes rested on a small but most lovely islet, that stood out half a mile or so from its stern neighbour, the fortress-point. Some said the two had joined at one time—being no geologist, I leave that to wiser heads to determine; but, undoubtedly, a greater contrast between point and island could not exist. The latter was about a mile in circumference, oval in form, shaped like a mound, with the outer edges sloping gently and roundly to the sea; and, instead of the sterile desolate front of its neighbour, it presented a luxuriance of vegetation charming the eye. Tall trees of every description waved their feathery branches leisurely in the breeze, and creeping plants and variegated blossoms drooped to the water's edge. White stones glanced here and there from the luxuriant foliage, and added the finishing touch of beauty to the picture.

'The Island of the Dead!' said the friend whose hand had guided me into this Paradise; and I felt the appellation most appropriate, and the taste faultless that had chosen so exquisite a spot for the last resting place of the departed.

But we turned our backs on that, and landed. Yet I saw the island still in my dream; and, indeed, into so small a compass were compressed all the features of scenery I have described, that, go where I would, I never lost sight of one of them, unless when diving into the recesses of some dewy valley. The protecting hills, the shaded promenade, the bristling promontory, the romantic island, the glancing waters, and the white gleaming houses, were always present to my sight, with many an inland height and verdurous field beside; and I exclaimed with rapture, 'Beautiful! Beautiful beyond all that my fancy painted!'

Dreaming still, and dreaming pleasantly, I was taken into a fine garden, a public place of resort, at the head of which was built a pretty verandahed house, called Government Cottage. The indigenous floral beauties of this garden were such as tempted one constantly to break through the prohibition to pluck them; the winding brook that flowed, fringed by weeping willows, through the lower end, and the latticed octagon summerhouse built round a monster willow, where a dancing party had been held, with variegated lamps hanging from the tree and musicians seated among its branches—all this was like fairyland. Imagination conjured up the romantic scene the garden must have presented on such a night, when the principal walks were all illuminated, and the octagon summerhouse was the centre of light and music and gaiety. How the light-hearted dancers must have revelled in the scene as in a dream of enchantment, and almost expected to find it all vanish if they rubbed their eyes!

Then, in my dream, it seemed that it was Sunday, and I was taken to the large, old-fashioned, but picturesque church, which, as well as Government Cottage, overlooked this pleasant garden, and was approached by a long avenue of handsome trees—acacia, mimosa and wattle, all in bloom, and breathing ambrosial fragrance. The long, feathery, delicately-coloured blossoms of an uncommon species of mimosa, enchanted me most; they drooped over the road, and their scent was delicious. The ground beneath the tree was planted with beautiful indigenous flowering shrubs in admirable variety, many of them very rare, amongst which may be named the splendid native laurel, which shoots up its branches, tufted at the points with a rich circle of green leaves, within which grows the white waxy blossom in clusters of two or three dozen.

From all this outward beauty and glorious sunshine, I stepped into the lofty, cold, stone church, and was shut up in the quaintest of old-fashioned square pews, smothered with drawn scarlet curtains, and forced to creak my neck to look up to the antiquated pulpit, that towered, tier upon tier, three parts of the way to the arched roof. First and lowest stood the desk, where the hymns were given out; above that rose the reading-desk, as high and as large as any pulpit I had ever seen; and beyond again, some six feet higher, the real pulpit, with its immense sounding-board threatening the preacher's life. The echo in that great half-empty church was tremendous, and the ascent of the stairs to the pulpit quite a task, as I found when curiosity led me to mount them.

Scarce was I seated, when I thought the service commenced, and so great was the shock my nerves received, that I was almost startled out of my dream. A sound as of a hundred heavy chains suddenly rattling and clanking together close to me, surrounding me, yet unseen, marred the quaint solemnity of the place, and scared all pleasurable emotions away. It was so sudden, so unexpected, that it needed all my self-command to recollect it was human beings, and not wild beasts, that had risen up to worship God, side by side, but parted off and screened from the sight of the free-limbed worshippers such as I. Some dim recollection memory conjured up, of scenes such as this long ago, of sounds of clanking chains on the limbs of a man who chanted holy hymns every Sabbath; and some faint remembrance I had of pity for the shackled unfortunates, whose cold heavy irons disturbed the solemn service in a church as old-fashioned and as out of date as this. But now the once familiar sound was a sound of horror! it was as if an ugly skeleton, that had been buried for years, and was all but forgotten, had sprung into light again, and rattled its bones in my face.

My sensations of alarm were not lulled by finding that a guard, or escort, with loaded revolvers under their belts, marched these criminals to and fro, and paraded outside the church door; but I was reassured by being told this was a mere form, an old custom, quite unnecessary, but which had never been countermanded. At one time far greater precaution was found advisable, and a large troop of soldiers occupied a portion of the church, a long file being told off to sit facing the fettered convicts during divine service, *with loaded muskets between their knees*.

My horror, and struggles to escape from these hideous sounds, these unseen clanking phantoms, nearly awoke me, when a hand drew me gently away from all this disquietude, and led me along a woodland path, where flowers and shrubs and clustering parasitical plants festooned the trunks of the trees, whose tops formed evergreen arches overhead.

So deep was the shade and humid the air, that from every branch and twig dropped heavy beads of moisture; and on either side of the road trickled tiny rivulets with a pleasant chattering murmur, while ever and anon a rustic bridge had to be crossed, the creek that flowed underneath being usually pretty well blockaded by huge trunks of trees that had fallen in tempestuous weather, and lain there till their timbers were hoary with age and slippery with the greenest of moss.

'A most delightful road!' said I, charmed with its refreshing sylvan beauty.

'Fine!' answered my guide; 'especially when it blows three gales at once, and pours like a deluge, and you have to ride some dozen miles or so on a pitch dark night, with the trees falling round you and across your path with startling crashes, and the comfortable conviction that if one of them struck you or your horse there would be small prospect of reaching home alive. A most delightful road at such a moment, I cannot deny.'

'How do you manage, then, to escape injury?' I asked, my enthusiasm somewhat dampened by this description.

'Lay my head on the horse's mane, clasp my hands round his neck, and let him go full drive. He never slackens his gallop till he reaches his own gate, I can assure you.'

Again the scene changed, and I was made to traverse a narrow bush path, so densely bordered with tall interlaced trees that sunlight never ventured there, and a duskiness as of evening obscured the vision. The air was heavy with fragrance, and cool even to chilliness, and a continuous drip, drip, followed our steps as we picked our way in single file.

Wondering much where this dark passage would lead, and too busy with my footing to look about me, I was agreeably surprised—nay, enchanted, on stepping out suddenly into broad sunshine, to find myself in a fairy nook that might have served Queen Mab and her train for a picnic.

A small irregular square, hedged in, so to speak, on three sides by lofty stone walls, quarried out in time gone by and abandoned, even with the tools rusting in the open air, and on the fourth by the still loftier umbrageous trees, standing still and solemn in a dense mass, only opening to indicate dimly the path which we had traversed. A low rustic hut, half in ruins, and almost buried beneath a heavy growth of Macquarie Harbour vine, immense masses of tangled climbing plants clothing, with a motley veil of tapestry, the greater part of the ragged walls; a group of fine specimens of mimosa—among which was conspicuous the pale tassels of my favourite—in one corner, and a small pond in another, completed the picture. Nothing else could be seen from this secluded spot but the blue sky, and no sound broke the stillness but the joyous warble of birds.

Here was a nook so completely shut out from the world that one could not believe a few minutes' walk would carry one again into the busy haunts of men.

'Oh!' said I, thinking aloud, rather than speaking in my rapture, 'what a delicious place for a picnic on a hot day! How overjoyed some of those unhappy beings, who are frizzling on the other side of the Straits, would be, to feast their eyes on this perpetual greenness! If I could only transplant a few of them here, even for half-an-hour! How I wish I had Aladdin's lamp, with power to use it as I liked! Wouldn't I pick up a friend here, and another there, from the hottest towns, and blind their eyes, all aching with the heat and glare, and set them down just here, take off the bandage, and wait to hear what they had to say? Would they ever forget this fairy scene? Wouldn't they sigh for its refreshing coolness and picturesque beauty ever afterwards, when a hot wind blew and scorched up the blood in their veins? And wouldn't that continual trickle, trickle, be the sweetest music to their ears? Where does that water drip from? I believe there's a spring high up that wall, in that lovely corner behind the mimosa. I shall try and find it out.'

'You'd better not,' said a warning voice. 'The wisest thing you can do, is to keep out of "that lovely corner." It's as likely a place as I know of for snakes.'

Alas! 'The trail of the serpent was over it all.' I relinquished my investigation of Queen Mab's own retreat, and considerably more prosaic in spirit, plodded back again through the dim avenue (it was a region of avenues), which after all had a suspicion of neuralgia and rheumatism about it.

My dream, which was a long one, carried me on to a day when I was taken to see 'the lions', a process which was not accomplished without some diplomatic negotiation with the higher powers. These had to be officially 'requisitioned' to issue an order permitting my important self to visit various buildings, to which the politest of answers was returned, commending me to the guidance of sundry official personages, whose duty it was to guard these lions. Then orders went round in all quarters to prepare for the proposed visit, and finally I found myself admitted into the mysterious precincts, whose doors closed upon me with a harsh grating noise that suggested the thought of that terrible one where those who entered were advised to leave Hope behind.

Well, it wasn't anything very novel. Upstairs and downstairs, and long corridors and narrow cells, very cold and chill, and everywhere spotless cleanliness and a glaring naked whiteness, rather painful than otherwise; then, set off by a very pretty garden, a handsome new building, with stylish octagon hall leading off in various directions to noble apartments, and so arranged that it could be metamorphosed into a commodious and elegant theatre, with all the appurtenances of stage drop scenes and musical instruments. The hall, rooms, and garden swarming with crankies, in different stages of modified lunacy; then a plainer—more unpretending—edifice set apart for the outrageous crankies, whose shouts and wails often fill the air. Lastly, the peculiar institution and pride of the place, which presented only a high blank circular whitewashed wall to public view, and was known as 'The Model'. Ah! that Model!—the thought of it haunts me still. Dreaming, I entered it, and dreaming, I came out; yet it looms up before my eye with a vivid distinctness as I think of it now, and so strange, awful, and unlooked for was the impression it made, that years will not efface the horror of the silent spectacle.

I was ushered into a fine spacious hall, also octagon, and the heavy sullen bolts were drawn immediately. The spotlessly white stone floor was ornamented with long strips of pretty brown matting, of 'Model' manufacture, which met in the centre and diverged into eight different directions. The effect was striking, added to the loftiness of the apartment, lit by a glass dome above by day, and handsome hanging kerosene lamps by night. The perfect cleanliness and beauty of the design drew forth an exclamation of surprise and pleasure, which was quickly checked by a subdued murmur of expostulation from the soft-mannered keeper, to the effect that one mustn't speak loud in 'The Model'.

'Why not?' said I, speaking low in spite of myself, awed a little by his noiseless manner.

A 'MODEL' DREAM

'Silent system,' was the reply; and, listening for an instant, the explanation needed not to be repeated. The silence of the long corridors, leading away like dusky avenues, where watchful constables walked with stealthy tread, and the grave-like stillness of the cells, indicated by the many closed and heavily bolted doors, was simply awful. I looked at the keeper, a pale melancholic man, who had lost all elasticity of spirit as well as the use of his voice, and to whom the solitude of the building had imparted much of its gloom. Awe-struck, and as silent as could be desired, I followed where he chose to lead.

We went, with echoless steps, into an empty cell, painfully white, and saw the scanty accommodations, and the cloth mask which the wretched occupant had to wear whenever he quitted his dreary cell for his dreary monotonous hour's walk every day, or his still drearier hour in chapel; observed the number hung outside the door of the cell, by which only the criminal was known, for he lost such trifling things as name and identity when these pitiless doors closed on him; a number that was made to spring out from the wall with a resounding click whenever the prisoner needed anything, and which was his only allowable method of making his wants known besides writing on a slate that hung inside the cell; were shown three small yards—nearly triangular in shape—whose grated iron gates were placed side by side and formed an angle in each, while the other two angles extended to the circumference of the outer wall. The three yards were divided by walls as high and blank as that outside, and into these yards three solitary sufferers were marched, one at a time, masked and guarded, and obliged to walk smartly about for an hour under the eye of the constable who, posted at the gratings, could watch all three at once; and visited the refractory cell, closed in by four massive doors of double thickness, black as midnight, and silent and chill as the grave, where one human creature had remained seventeen days without touching the bread thrust in to him daily, and yet lived, and was still living, a hopeless inmate of a solitary cell. And, as we walked to and fro, there was not a sound in the building. Yes! one occasionally; the clank of heavy fetters, which resounded with startling distinctness through the oppressive silence.

Then we stole quietly up a short staircase, covered with matting, leading from the hall into a chapel, whose silent horrors were more effectually depressing than all the rest. At the door stood two sentry boxes with seats, where two armed constables guarded the entrance to each aisle at the time of divine service. Steps, each lower than the other, led down the aisles, and at the door of each pew, if pews they could be called, that were five feet in height in front and seven behind, and which were divided by high thick doors at about two foot distances, into each of which a man was bolted and made to stand the whole time of the service, sat the constable who locked them in. These pews held six or seven solitary wretches, all masked, who could neither see behind nor sideways, only over the high partition in front. The prospect comprehended a flat square, on which stood a plain box pulpit, whence issued the only words that reached the ears of these men from year's end to year's end, and close in front of the pulpit was a tall stand containing a revolving box of numbers, which signalled to the prisoners in what order they were to leave their chapel cells. Thus, No. 1 being shown in the stand, informed the unhappy being answering to that number, that he should leave his place silently, singly, and guarded as he entered; No. 2 followed, and so on, till the chapel was emptied and left to solitude, scarcely more desolate than when full of human beings.

Methought I shuddered at this, and not being allowed to give vent to my excited feelings, longed for fresh air, and the *right* side of these terrible walls, to overcome the sense of oppression produced by this whited sepulchre. What was all its spotless cleanliness, its commodious design, and its elegant vestibule, for one destined to wear out a long life within its hopeless environs? Darkness, and the most unattractive plainness, would better have suited his despair.

Bolts and bars gave way happily at a wish, and my friends and I stood once more under the broad free heavens, and began to breathe again. Does Bunyan say, 'Stone walls do not a prison make?' I should think these stone walls made a very real and dismal prison, even to the superintendent of it, and the children reared under its shadow.

It was some moments ere speech could be recovered, and then our voices sounded strange to us. No wonder the keep always bore that subdued and melancholy mien, walked gingerly, and spoke, even outside the walls, in low toned whispers. The superintendents of the other departments were jolly and outspoken enough, like men who did their duty and were kindly inclined towards it in spite of its onerousness; even the penitentiary gaoler waxed garrulous in praise of his domain, and officiously dilated on its management and regulations; but the low spirited keeper of 'The Model', had almost become a silent member himself.

'I wouldn't be that man for a thousand-a-year,' said I. 'What can compensate for the sorrowful restraint of such a post? Ah! the horrors of it! I wish I hadn't gone in. It's like a waking nightmare! The utter solitude and staring blank whiteness is enough to drive the inmates mad.'

'Exactly so,' answered my guide. 'Drink has filled the Insane Departments; but this "Model" will help to keep them going. Look, here's the cage.'

We were then underneath the 'Model' walls, and close to a high circular iron structure, which contained a covered seat placed in the centre. Into this, upon fine afternoons, a few well-behaved criminals from the 'Model' were permitted, singly, to take an hour's exercise. The masked prisoner was brought out, guarded by a constable and the keeper, and marched into this enclosure, and locked in, and obliged to walk round and round, like a caged beast, under the watchful eye of the constable, who patrolled outside it.

The 'Model' and its cage were stationed on a fine mound exactly opposite, and within earshot of my temporary abode; and having now explored the mysteries of the silent tomb-like building, I began to take a mournful interest in the daily walks of these unfortunates, and to look for their appearance in the enclosure; which, miserably suggestive of a menagerie as it was, must have been to them a break in the wretched monotony of their existence. Doubtless they looked forward to their promenade in it as *the* event of the day.

But my cup of enjoyment was poisoned. What mattered it that I was free, to go whither my fancy chose to lead, to utter my thoughts in the loudest key; to laugh and gambol on the broad verandah with happy babyhood, or plan pleasure excursions with attentive friends? One glance cast towards the opposite hill showed me the dismal circular walls of the 'Model', and the iron cage where the solitary criminal was taking his airing, within sight of life and freedom, and bustle and happiness, but debarred from it all; and the laughter faded sadly away, and the jest died on one's lips.

Alas! alas! that 'trail of the serpent'; it was everywhere.

So—growing almost weary of the monotony of prison sights, diversified only by dresses all yellow, or part yellow and part grey, or all grey, and longing for some more cheery music than the perpetual clank, clank, of noisy fetters—I wondered not at—nay, half felt inclined to endorse—an expression that often fell from the lips of one wearied to death with the wretched unvarying round of this existence, 'A Paradise do they call it? An Eden, indeed! There is but one place in the whole length and breadth of creation that can be worse, and that is—*down below!*'

One spot only retained its romance, and bore no disappointment in its train. Dead Island. Beautiful inexpressibly was its situation and its surroundings; and solitude did not detract from its charm. Even the burial of a criminal could not derogate from its fascination; the man was unfettered at last, and the boat that carried him softly and slowly over the waters, the ivy-grown arbour above the little jetty where his body was placed for a few minutes; the lonely guardian of the island, who came forward to receive, and, as it were, to welcome, the dead, and help to lay him in the grave, beneath waving branches and singing birds, was a fairer termination to his miseries than his life could have anticipated. That trail of the serpent, which had left its indelible mark everywhere around, touched indeed here, but then faded, having no more power to terrify.

Altogether, when the hour came to part from this fair nest of gardens, I was not unwilling to say,

> 'Fare thee well! and if for ever,
> Still, for ever fare thee well!'

The latter part of my dream was rough, decidedly. Methought I was tossed upon truly unromantic waves, and distressed by sickness that felt miserably real. Hours of groaning misery were followed by a welcome lull, and I struggled to the crowded deck, and saw the fair round moon, shining on quiet wharves and ghostly houses, with the dark looming form of Mount Wellington guarding the sleepy city. The clock of St. David's just then struck midnight, and thoroughly dissipated the spell that had bound me, and a voice congratulated me on having 'done my sentence.'

Then I knew I had been at Port Arthur.

Tasma • 1891

An Old-Time Episode in Tasmania

The gig was waiting upon the narrow gravel drive in front of the fuchsia-wreathed porch of Cowa Cottage. Perched upon the seat, holding the whip in two small, plump, ungloved hands, sat Trucaninny, Mr Paton's youngest daughter, whose straw-coloured, sun-steeped hair, and clear, sky-reflecting eyes, seemed to protest against the name of a black gin that some 'clay-brained cleric' had bestowed upon her irresponsible little person at the baptismal font some eight or nine years ago. The scene of this outrage was Old St. David's Cathedral, Hobart,— or, as it was then called, Hobart *Town*,— chief city of the Arcadian island of Tasmania; and just at this moment, eight o'clock on a November morning, the said cathedral tower, round and ungainly, coated with a surface of dingy white plaster, reflected back the purest, brightest light in the world. From Trucaninny's perch—she had taken the driver's seat—she could see, not only the cathedral, but a considerable portion of the town, which took the form of a capital S as it followed the windings of the coast. Beyond the wharves, against which a few whalers and fishing-boats were lying idle, the middle distance was represented by the broad waters of the Derwent, radiantly blue, and glittering with silver sparkles; while the far-off background showed a long stretch of yellow sand, and the hazy, undulating outline of low-lying purple hills. Behind her the aspect was different. Tiers of hills rose one above the other in grand confusion, until they culminated in the towering height of Mount Wellington, keeping guard in majestic silence over the lonely little city that encircled its base. This portion of the view, however, was hidden from Trucaninny's gaze by the weatherboard cottage in front of which the gig was standing,—though I doubt whether in any case she would have turned her head to look at it; the faculty of enjoying a beautiful landscape being an acquisition of later years than she had attained since the perpetration of the afore-mentioned outrage of her christening. Conversely, as Herbert Spencer says, the young man who was holding the horse's head until such time as the owner of the gig should emerge from the fuchsia-wreathed porch, fastened his eyes upon the beautiful scene before him with more than an artist's appreciation in their gaze. He was dressed in the rough clothes of a working gardener, and so much of his head as could be seen beneath the old felt wide-awake that covered it, bore ominous evidence of having been recently shaved. I use the word ominous advisedly, for a shaven head in connection with a working suit had nothing priestly in its suggestion, and could bear, indeed, only one interpretation in the wicked old times in Tasmania. The young man keeping watch over the gig had clearly come into that fair scene for his country's good; and the explanation of the absence of a prison suit was doubtless due to the fact he was out on a ticket-of-leave. What the landscape had to say to him under these circumstances was not precisely clear. Perhaps all his soul was going out towards the white-sailed wool-ship tacking down the Bay on the first stage of a journey of most uncertain length; or possibly the wondrous beauty of the scene, contrasted with the unspeakable horror of the one he had left, brought the vague impression that it was merely some exquisite vision. That a place so appalling as his old prison should exist in the heart of all this peace and loveliness, seemed too strange an anomaly. Either that was a nightmare and this was real, or this was a fantastic dream and that was the revolting truth; but then which was which, and how had he, Richard Cole, late No. 213, come to be mixed up with either?

As though to give a practical answer to his melancholy question, the sharp tingle of a whip's lash made itself felt at this instant across his cheek. In aiming the cumbersome driving-whip at the persistent flies exploring the mare's back, Trucaninny had brought it down in a direction she had not intended it to take. For a moment she stood aghast. Richard's face was white with passion. He turned fiercely round; his flaming eyes seemed literally to send out sparks of anger. 'Oh, please, I didn't mean it,' cried the child penitently. 'I wanted to hit the flies. I did indeed. I hope I didn't hurt you?'

The *amende honorable* brought about an immediate reaction. The change in the young man's face was wonderful to behold. As he smiled back full reassurance at the offender, it might be seen that his eyes could express the extremes of contrary feeling at the very shortest notice. For all answer, he raised his old felt wide-awake in a half-mocking though entirely courtly fashion, like some nineteenth century Don César de Bazan, and made a graceful bow.

'Are *you* talking to the man, Truca?' cried a querulous voice at this moment from the porch, with a stress on the you that made the little girl lower her head, shame-faced. 'What do you mean by disobeying orders, miss?'

The lady who swept out upon the verandah at the close of this tirade was in entire accord with her voice. 'British matron' would have been the complete description of Miss Paton, if fate had not willed that she should be only a British spinster. The inflexibility that comes of finality of opinion regarding what is proper and what is the reverse,— a rule of conduct that is of universal application for the true British matron,— expressed itself in every line of her face and in every fold of her gown. That she was relentlessly respectable and unyielding might be read at the first glance; that she had been handsome, in the same hard way, a great many years before Truca was maltreated at the baptismal font, might also have been guessed at from present indications. But that she should be the 'own sister' of the good-looking, military-moustached, debonair man (I use the word debonair here in the French sense) who now followed her out of the porch, was less easy to divine. The character of the features as well as of the expression spoke of two widely differing temperaments. Indeed, save for a curious dent between the eyebrows, and a something in the nostrils that seemed to say he was not to be trifled with, Mr Paton might have sat for the portrait of one of those jolly good fellows who reiterate so tunefully that they 'won't go home till morning', and who are as good as their word afterwards.

Yet 'jolly good fellow' as he showed himself in card-rooms and among so-called boon companions, he could reveal himself in a very different light to the convicts who fell under his rule. Forming part of a system for the crushing down of the unhappy prisoners, in accordance with the principle of 'Woe be to him through whom the offence cometh,' he could return with a light heart to his breakfast or his dinner, after seeing some score of his fellow-men abjectly writhing under the lash, or pinioned in a ghastly row upon the hideous gallows. 'Use,' says Shakespeare, 'can almost change the stamp of Nature.' In Mr Paton's case it had warped as well as changed it. Like the people who live in the atmosphere of Courts, and come to regard all outsiders as another and inferior race, he had come to look upon humanity as divisible into two classes— namely, those who were convicts, and those who were not. For the latter, he had still some ready drops of the milk of human kindness at his disposal. For the former, he had no more feeling than we have for snakes or sharks, as the typical and popular embodiments of evil.

Miss Paton had speedily adopted her brother's views in this respect. Summoned from England to keep house for him at the death of Trucaninny's mother, she showed an aptitude for introducing prison discipline into her domestic rule. From constant association with the severe *régime* that she was accustomed to see exercised upon the convicts, she had ended by regarding disobedience to orders, whether in children or in servants, as the unpardonable sin. One of her laws, as of the Medes and Persians, was that the young people in the Paton household should never exchange a word with the convict servants in their father's employ. It was hard to observe the letter of the law in the case of the indoor servants, above all for Truca, who was by nature a garrulous little girl. Being a truthful little girl as well, she was often obliged to confess to having had a talk with the latest importation from the gaol,—an avowal which signified, as she well knew, the immediate forfeiture of all her week's pocket-money.

On the present occasion her apologies to the gardener were the latest infringement of the rule. She looked timidly towards her aunt as the latter advanced austerely in the direction of the gig, but, to her relief, Miss Paton hardly seemed to notice her.

'I suppose you will bring the creature back with you, Wilfrid?' she said, half-questioningly, half-authoritatively, as her brother mounted into the gig and took the reins from Truca's chubby hands. 'Last time we had a drunkard *and* a thief. The time before, a thief, and—and a—really I don't know which was worse. It is frightful to be reduced to such a choice of evils, but I would almost suggest your looking among the—you know—the—*in-fan-ti-cide* cases this time.'

She mouthed the word in separate syllables at her brother, fearful of pronouncing it openly before Truca and the convict gardener.

Mr Paton nodded. It was not the first time he had been sent upon the delicate mission of choosing a maid for his sister from the female prison, politely called the Factory, at the foot of Mount Wellington. For some reason it would be difficult to explain, his selections were generally rather more successful than hers. Besides which, it was a satisfaction to have some one upon whom to throw the responsibility of the inevitable catastrophe that terminated the career of every successive ticket-of-leave in turn.

The morning, as we have seen, was beautiful. The gig bowled smoothly over the macadamized length of Macquarie Street. Truca was allowed to drive; and so deftly did her little fingers guide the mare, that her father lighted his cigar, and allowed himself to ruminate upon a thousand things that it would have been better perhaps to leave alone. In certain moods he was apt to deplore the fate that had landed—or stranded—him in this God-forsaken corner of the world. Talk of prisoners, indeed! What was he himself but a prisoner, since the day when he had madly passed sentence of transportation on himself and his family, because the pay of a Government clerk in England did not increase in the same ratio as the income-tax. As a matter of fact, he did not wear a canary-coloured livery, and his prison was as near an approach, people said, to an earthly Paradise as could well be conceived. With its encircling chains of mountains, folded one around the other, it was like a mighty rose, tossed from the Creator's hand into the desolate Southern Ocean. Here to his right towered purple Mount Wellington, with rugged cliffs gleaming forth from a purple background. To his left the wide Derwent shone and sparkled in blue robe and silver spangles, like the Bay of Naples, he had been told. Well, he had never seen the Bay of Naples, but there were times when he would have given all the beauty here, and as much more to spare, for a strip of London pavement in front of his old club. Mr Paton's world, indeed, was out of joint. Perhaps twelve years of unthinking acquiescence in the flogging and hanging of convicts had distorted his mental focus. As for the joys of home-life, he told himself that those which had fallen to his share brought him but cold comfort. His sister was a Puritan, and she was making his children hypocrites, with the exception, perhaps, of Truca. Another disagreeable subject of reflection was the one that his groom Richard was about to leave him. In a month's time, Richard, like his royal namesake, would be himself again. For the past five years he had been only No. 213, expiating in that capacity a righteous blow aimed at a cowardly ruffian who had sworn to marry his sister—by fair means or by foul. The blow had been only too well aimed. Richard was convicted of manslaughter, and sentenced to seven years' transportation beyond the seas. His sister, who had sought to screen him, was tried and condemned for perjury. Of the latter, nothing was known. Of the former, Mr Paton only knew that he would be extremely loth to part with so good a servant. Silent as the Slave of the Lamp, exact as any machine, performing the least of his duties with the same intelligent scrupulousness, his very presence in the household was a safeguard and a reassurance. It was like his luck, Mr Paton reflected in his present pessimistic mood, to have chanced upon such a fellow, just as by his d——d good conduct he had managed to obtain a curtailment of his sentence. If Richard had been justly dealt with, he would have had two good years left to devote to the service of his employer. As to keeping him after he was a free man, that was not to be hoped for. Besides which, Mr Paton was not sure that he should feel at all at his ease in dealing with a free man. The slave-making instinct, which is always inherent in the human race, whatever civilisation may have done to repress it, had become his sole rule of conduct in his relations with those who served him.

There was one means perhaps of keeping the young man in bondage, but it was a means that even Mr Paton himself hesitated to employ. By an almost superhuman adherence to impossible rules, Richard had escaped hitherto the humiliation of the lash; but if a flogging could be laid to his charge, his time of probation would be of necessity prolonged, and he might continue to groom the mare and tend the garden for an indefinite space of time, with the ever intelligent thoroughness that distinguished him. A slip of paper in a sealed envelope, which the victim would carry himself to the nearest justice of the peace, would effect the desired object. The etiquette of the proceeding did not require that any explanation should be given.

Richard would be fastened to the triangles, and any subsequent revolt on his part could only involve him more deeply than before. Mr Paton had no wish to hurt him; but he was after all an invaluable servant, and perhaps he would be intelligent enough to understand that the disagreeable formality to which he was subjected was in reality only a striking mark of his master's esteem for him.

Truca's father had arrived thus far in his meditations when the gig pulled up before the Factory gate. It was a large bare building, with white unshaded walls, but the landscape which framed it gave it a magnificent setting. The little girl was allowed to accompany her father indoors, while a man in a grey prison suit, under the immediate surveillance of an armed warder, stood at the mare's head.

Mr Paton's mission was a delicate one. To gently scan his brother man, and still gentler sister woman, did not apply to his treatment of convicts. He brought his sternest official expression to bear upon the aspirants who defiled past him at the matron's bidding, in their disfiguring prison livery. One or two, who thought they detected a likely looking man behind the Government official, threw him equivocal glances as they went by. Of these he took no notice. His choice seemed to lie in the end between a sullen-looking elderly woman, whom the superintendent qualified as a 'sour jade', and a half-imbecile girl, when his attention was suddenly attracted to a new arrival, who stood out in such marked contrast with the rest that she looked like a dove in the midst of a flock of vultures.

'Who is that?' he asked the matron in a peremptory aside.

'That, sir,'—the woman's lips assumed a tight expression as she spoke,—'she's No. 27—Amelia Clare—she came out with the last batch.'

'Call her up, will you?' was the short rejoinder, and the matron reluctantly obeyed.

In his early days Truca's father had been a great lover of Italian opera. There was hardly an air of Bellini's or Donizetti's that he did not know by heart. As No. 27 came slowly towards him, something in her manner of walking, coupled with the half-abstracted, half-fixed expression in her beautiful grey eyes, reminded him of Amina in the *Sonnambula*. So strong, indeed, was the impression, that he would hardly have been surprised to see No. 27 take off her unbecoming prison cap and jacket, and disclose two round white arms to match her face, or to hear her sing '*Ah! non giunge*' in soft dreamy tones. He could have hummed or whistled a tuneful second himself at a moment's notice, for the matter of that. However, save in the market scene in *Martha*, there is no precedent for warbling a duet with the young person you are about to engage as a domestic servant. Mr Paton remembered this in time, and confined himself to what the French call *le stricte nécessaire*. He inquired of Amelia whether she could do fine sewing, and whether she could clear-starch. His sister had impressed these questions upon him, and he was pleased with himself for remembering them.

Amelia, or Amina (she was really very like Amina), did not reply at once. She had to bring her mind back from the far-away sphere to which it had wandered, or, in other words, to pull herself together first. When the reply did come, it was uttered in just the low, melodious tones one might have expected. She expressed her willingness to attempt whatever was required of her, but seemed very diffident as regarded her power of execution. 'I have forgotten so many things,' she concluded, with a profound sigh.

'*Sir*, you impertinent minx,' corrected the matron.

Amelia did not seem to hear, and her new employer hastened to interpose.

'We will give you a trial,' he said, in a curiously modified tone, 'and I hope you won't give me any occasion to regret it.'

The necessary formalities were hurried through. Mr Paton disregarded the deferential disclaimers of the matron, but experienced, nevertheless, something of a shock when he saw Amelia divested of her prison garb. She had a thoroughbred air that discomfited him. Worse still, she was undeniably pretty. The scissors that had clipped her fair locks had left a number of short rings that clung like tendrils round her shapely little head. She wore a black stuff jacket of extreme simplicity and faultless cut, and a little black bonnet that might have been worn by a Nursing Sister or a *'grande dame'* with equal appropriateness. Thus attired, her appearance was so effective, that Mr Paton asked himself whether he was not doing an unpardonably rash thing in driving No. 27 down Macquarie Street in his gig, and introducing her into his household afterwards.

It was not Truca, for she had 'driven and lived' that morning, whose *mauvais quart-d'heure* was now to come. It was her father's turn to fall under its influence, as he sat, stern and rigid, on the driver's seat, with his little girl nestling up to him as close as she was able, and that strange, fair, mysterious presence on the other side, towards which he had the annoyance of seeing all the heads of the passers-by turn as he drove on towards home.

Arrived at Cowa Cottage, the young gardener ran forward to open the gate; and here an unexpected incident occurred. As Richard's eyes rested upon the new arrival, he uttered an exclamation that caused her to look round. Their eyes met, a flash of instant recognition was visible in both. Then, like the night that follows a sudden discharge of electricity, the gloom that was habitual to both faces settled down upon them once more. Richard shut the gate with his accustomed machine-like precision. Amelia looked at the intangible something in the clouds that had power to fix her gaze upon itself. Yet the emotion she had betrayed was not lost upon her employer. Who could say? As No. 213 and No. 27, these two might have crossed each other's paths before. That the convicts had wonderful and incomprehensible means of communicating with each other, was well known to Mr Paton. That young men and young women have an equal facility for understanding each other, was also a fact he did not ignore. But which of these two explanations might account for the signs of mutual recognition and sympathy he had just witnessed? Curiously enough, he felt, as he pondered over the mystery later in the day, that he should prefer the former solution. An offensive and defensive alliance was well known to exist among the convicts, and he told himself that he could meet and deal with the difficulties arising from such a cause as he had met and dealt with them before. That was a matter which came within his province, but the taking into account of any sentimental kind of rubbish did not come within his province. For some unaccountable reason, the thought of having Richard flogged presented itself anew at this junction to his mind. He put it away, as he had done before, angered with himself for having harboured it. But it returned at intervals during the succeeding week, and was never stronger than one afternoon, when his little girl ran out to him as he sat smoking in the verandah, with an illustrated volume of *Grimm's Tales* in her hands.

'Oh, papa, look! I've found some one just like Amelia in my book of Grimm. It's the picture of Snow-White. Only look, papa! Isn't it the very living image of Amelia?'

'Nonsense!' said her father; but he looked at the page nevertheless. Truca was right. The snow-maiden in the woodcut had the very eyes and mouth of Amelia Clare—frozen through some mysterious influence into beautiful, unyielding rigidity. Mr Paton wished sometimes he had never brought the girl into his house. Not that there was any kind of fault to be found with her. Even his sister, who might have passed for 'She-who-must-be-obeyed', if Rider Haggard's books had existed at that time, could not complain of want of docile obedience to orders on the part of the new maid. Nevertheless, her presence was oppressive to the master of the house. Two lines of Byron's haunted him constantly in connection with her—

> 'So coldly sweet, so deadly fair,
> We start—for life is wanting there.'

If Richard worked like an automaton, then she worked like a spirit; and when she moved noiselessly about the room where he happened to be sitting, he could not help following her uneasily with his eyes.

The days wore on, succeeding each other and resembling each other, as the French proverb has it, with desperate monotony. Christmas, replete with roses and strawberries, had come and gone. Mr Paton was alternately swayed by two demons, one of which whispered in his ear, 'Richard Cole is in love with No. 27. The time for him to regain his freedom is at hand. The first use he will make of it will be to leave you, and the next to marry Amelia Clare. You will thus be deprived of everything at one blow. You will lose the best man-servant you have ever known, and your sister, the best maid. And more than this, you will lose an interest in life that gives it a stimulating flavour it has not had for many a long year. Whatever may be the impulse that prompts you to wonder what that ice-bound face and form hide, it is an impulse that makes your heart beat and your blood course warmly through your veins. When this fair, uncanny presence is removed from your home, your life will become stagnant as it was before.' To this demon Mr Paton would reply energetically, 'I won't give the fellow the chance of marrying No. 27. As soon as he has his freedom, I will give him the sack, and forbid him the premises. As for Amelia, she is my prisoner, and I would send her back to gaol to-morrow if I thought there were any nonsense up between her and him.'

At this point demon No. 2 would intervene: 'There is a better way of arranging matters. You have it in your power to degrade the fellow in his own eyes and in those of the girl he is after. There is more covert insolence in that impenetrable exterior of his than you have yet found out. Only give him proper provocation, and you will have ample justification for bringing him down. A good flogging would put everything upon its proper footing,—you would keep your servant and you would put a stop to the nonsense that is very probably going on. But don't lose too much time; for if you wait until the last moment, you will betray your hand. The fellow is useful to him, they will say of Richard, but it is rather rough upon him to be made aware of it in such a way as that.'

One evening in January, Mr Paton was supposed to be at his club. In reality he was seated upon a bench in a bushy part of the garden, known as the shrubbery—in parley with the demons. The night had come down upon him almost without his being aware of it—a night heavy with heat and blackness, and noisy with the cracking and whirring of the locusts entombed in the dry soil. All at once he heard a slight rustling in the branches behind him. There was a light pressure of hands on his shoulders, and a face that felt like velvet to the touch was laid against his cheeks. Two firm, warm feminine lips pressed themselves upon his, and a voice that he recognised as Amelia's said in caressing tones, 'Dearest Dick, have I kept you waiting?'

Had it been proposed to our hero some time ago that he should change places with No. 213, he would have declared that he would rather die first. But at this instant the convict's identity seemed so preferable to his own, that he hardly ventured to breathe lest he should betray the fact that he was only his own forlorn self. His silence disconcerted the intruder.

'Why don't you answer, Dick?' she asked impatiently.

'Answer? What am I to say?' responded her master. 'I am not in the secret.'

Amelia did not give him time to say more. With a cry of terror she turned and fled, disappearing as swiftly and mysteriously as she had come. The words 'Dearest Dick' continued to ring in Mr Paton's ears long after she had gone; and the more persistently the refrain was repeated, the more he felt tempted to give Richard a taste of his quality. He had tried to provoke him to some act of overt insolence in vain. He had worried and harried and insulted him all he could. The convict's constancy had never once deserted him. That his employer should have no pretext whereby he might have him degraded and imprisoned, he had acted upon the scriptural precept of turning his left cheek when he was smitten on the right. There were times when his master felt something of a persecutor's impotent rage against him. But now at least he felt he had entire justification for making an example of him. He would teach the fellow to play Romeo and Juliet with a fellow-convict behind his back. So thoroughly did the demon indoctrinate Mr Paton with these ideas, that he felt next morning as though he were doing the most righteous action in the world, when he called Richard to him after breakfast, and said in a tone which he tried to render as careless as of custom, 'Here, you! Just take this note over to Mr Merton with my compliments, and *wait for the answer.*'

There was nothing in this command to cause the person who received it to grow suddenly livid. Richard had received such an order at least a score of times before, and had carried messages to and fro between his master and the justice of the peace with no more emotion than the occasion was worth. But on this particular morning, as he took the fatal note into his hands, he turned deadly pale. Instead of retreating with it in his customary automatic fashion, he fixed his eyes upon his employer's face, and something in their expression actually constrained Mr Paton to lower his own.

'May I speak a word with you, sir?' he said, in low, uncertain tones.

It was the first time such a thing had happened, and it seemed to Richard's master that the best way of meeting it would be to 'damn' the man and send him about his business.

But Richard did not go. He stood for an instant with his head thrown back, and the desperate look of an animal at bay in his eyes. At this critical moment a woman's form suddenly interposed itself between Mr Paton and his victim. Amelia was there, looking like Amina after she had awoken from her trance. She came close to her master,—she had never addressed him before,—and raised her liquid eyes to his.

'You will not be hard on—my brother, sir, for the mistake I made last night?'

'Who said I was going to be hard on him?' retorted Mr Paton, too much taken aback to find any more dignified form of rejoinder. 'And if he is your brother, why do you wait until it is dark to indulge in your family effusions?'

The question was accompanied by a through and through look, before which Amelia did not quail.

'Have I your permission to speak to him in the day-time, sir?' she said submissively.

'I will institute an inquiry,' interrupted her master. 'Here, go about your business,' he added, turning to Richard; 'fetch out the mare, and hand me back that note. I'll ride over with it myself.'

Three weeks later Richard Cole was a free man, and within four months from the date upon which Mr Paton had driven Amelia Clare down Macquarie Street in his gig, she came to take respectful leave of him, dressed in the identical close-fitting jacket and demure little bonnet he remembered. Thenceforth she was nobody's bondswoman. He had a small heap of coin in readiness to hand over to her, with the payment of which, and a few gratuitous words of counsel on his part, the leave-taking would have been definitely and decorously accomplished. To tell her that he was more loth than ever to part with her, did not enter into the official programme. She was her own mistress now, as much or more so than the Queen of England herself, and it was hardly to be wondered at if the first use she made of her freedom was to shake the dust of Cowa Cottage off her feet. Still, if she had only known—if she had only known. It seemed too hard to let her go with the certainty that she never did or could know. Was it not for her sake that he had been swayed by all the conflicting impulses that had made him a changed man of late? For her that he had so narrowly escaped being a criminal awhile ago, and for her that he was appearing in the novel *rôle* of a reformer of the convict system now? He never doubted that she would have understood him if she *had* known. But to explain was out of the question. He must avow either all or nothing, and the all meant more than he dared to admit even to himself.

This was the reason why Amelia Clare departed sphinx-like as she had come. A fortnight after she had gone, as Mr Paton was gloomily smoking by his library fire in the early dark of a wintry August evening, a letter bearing the N. S. Wales postmark was handed to him. The handwriting, very small and fine, had something familiar in its aspect. He broke open the seal,—letters were still habitually sealed in those days,—and read as follows:—

> 'SIR,—I am prompted to make you a confession—why, I cannot say, for I shall probably never cross your path again. I was married last week to Richard Cole, who was not my brother, as I led you to suppose, but my affianced husband, in whose behalf I would willingly suffer again to be unjustly condemned and transported. I have the warrant of Scripture for having assumed, like Sarah, the *rôle* of sister in preference to that of wife; besides which, it is hard to divest myself of an instinctive belief that the deceit was useful to Richard on one occasion. I trust you will pardon me.—Yours respectfully,
>
> 'AMELIA COLE.'

The kindly phase Mr Paton had passed through with regard to his convict victims came to an abrupt termination. The reaction was terrible. His name is inscribed among those 'who foremost shall be damn'd to Fame' in Tasmania.

Marcus Clarke · 1870

The Seizure of the *Cyprus*

On the 9th of August, 1829, the *Cyprus*, a vessel which was employed by the Government of Van Diemen's Land to carry prisoners from Hobart Town to Macquarie Harbour, was seized by the convicts and carried into the South Seas.

The story is a romantic one, and if it does not equal in interest the story of the capture of the *Frederick*, of which I shall by-and-by have occasion to speak, it is remarkable as showing the condition of convict discipline in the early days of the colony.

Macquarie Harbour—abandoned in 1833—was in these days the Ultima Thule of convict settlement. Established in 1821 by Governor Sorrell as a station for the most irreclaimable of the desperadoes who were sent in shiploads from England, the discipline had gradually increased in severity until it became a hideous terrorism, which often drove its victims to seek death as a means of escape. The picture of the place, as drawn by Mr Backhouse, the missionary who visited it in 1832, is most dismal. The scenery is wild and barren, the scrub and undergrowth impenetrable, and from the swampy ground around the settlement arises noisome and death-dealing exhalations. The surf beating with violence on the rocky shore renders approach difficult; and the westerly winds blowing with fury into the harbour, opposes sometimes for days the departure of the convict vessels.

This place was the last home—but one—of the felon. Once sent to 'the Hell', as the abode of doom was termed by the prisoners, return was all but hopeless. The ironbound coast, the dismal and impassable swamps, the barren and rugged mountain ranges, combined to render escape impossible. Of the many unfortunates who made the attempt to regain their freedom, all save some eight or nine died or were retaken. The life of a convict at this hideous place of punishment was one continual agony. In those times, the notion of reclaiming human creatures by reason and kindness was unknown. Condemned for life to the settlement—often for small offences against discipline—the miserable beings were cut off from the world forever. The commandant—usually some worthy officer selected from the regiment then in Van Diemen's Land for his severity or strength of will—dealt with the men under his charge as the humour took him. The guard was always under arms, and had orders to fire on any man who attempted to escape. The lash was the punishment most in vogue, but those wretches whose hardened hides the cat had cut into insensibility were marooned on rocks within view of the prison barracks. The work was constant and exhausting. Robbers, murderers, and forgers, told off into gangs, felled the gigantic trees which grew in the neighbourhood of the harbour. Chained together like beasts, and kept in activity by the rarely idle lash, they bore the logs to the water-side on their backs. Every now and then some feebler ruffian would fall from exhaustion, and the chain would drag him after the main body until he rose again. A visitor to the place in 1831 says that he saw 'something which he took for a gigantic centipede, which moved forward through the bush to the clanking of chains and the cracking of the overseer's whip.' This was a log borne by a convict gang. Treated like beasts, the men lived the life of beasts. All the atrocities that men could commit were committed there. Suicide was frequent. Men drowned themselves to be rid of the burden of their existence. Three wretches once drew lots as to who should get a sight of Hobart Town. One was to murder the other, and the third was to volunteer his evidence. The lottery was drawn, the doomed man laughed ere his companion beat out his brains, and the two survivors congratulated each other on their holiday on the scaffold of Hobart Town gaol.

To this place Lieutenant Carew, with ten soldiers, set out to convey thirty-one prisoners. As not infrequently happened, the weather proved unfavourable, and the vessel put into Recherche Bay for shelter. The prisoners were all desperate men. Two of them had been before at 'Hell's Gates', and detailed the horrors of the place to their companions. In the semi-darkness of the lower deck, where, chained in gangs of four, the miserable wretches speculated on their doom, it was proposed to seize the ship. A prisoner named Fergusson was the ringleader. 'At the worst,' said he, 'it is but death; and which of us wishes to live?' But the others were not so bold. Degraded by the chain and the lash, they yet clung to life as the one thing the law had not yet taken from them. There were wooden bars studded with nails fastened across their prison, and two sentinels with loaded arms kept watch at the hatchway. How could they—unarmed, weak, and chained—hope to succeed? But with Fergusson was a man named Walker, who had been a sailor, and he urged them on. 'Once free, he could navigate the ship to China!' Six times did the trembling wretches essay the struggle with the soldiers, and six times did their courage fail them. At last a favourable opportunity presented itself.

Lying at anchor in the channel, with the land in sight, life on board the ship became tedious even to the officers. Lieutenant Carew, confident in his soldiers and their muskets, thought he would take a little fishing excursion. His wife was on board, but, for some reason or other, refused to accompany him. The surgeon, however, was eager for some amusement, and taking with them a soldier and convict, the two lowered a boat and went into the bay.

It was the custom to bring the men on deck by sixes and sevens for exercise, and it so happened that on this morning it was the turn of Fergusson and Walker's gang. Fergusson, Walker, Pennell, M'Kan, Jones, and another, came up in their double irons, and clanked up and down under the supervision of the loaded muskets. Fergusson saw his chance—if ever he was to get it—had come now. 'Now is your time, lads,' he cried; 'the captain's away; there are but the two men on deck.'

Sulkily eyeing the muskets, Pennell and M'Kan refused. 'You have failed me six times,' cried Fergusson with an oath. 'If you don't join me now, I'll inform of your former plots.' This threat terrified them into compliance. A rush was made. The two soldiers idly staring over the bulwarks were knocked down before they could fire their muskets. The hatchway was secured, and knocking off their irons, the six were masters of the ship.

But the captain and soldiers below did not intend to surrender without a struggle. They fired up the hatchway, but without effect, and the other prisoners burst their nailed bars and joined their companions. A parley now ensued, the convicts promising to spare the lives of the soldiers if they gave up their arms. A volley was the only answer, and then two prisoners, by Fergusson's directions, got buckets of boiling water from the galley and poured them down the hatchway. Panic-stricken by the knowledge that thirty desperate men were at liberty on the deck, and that the seizure of the vessel was only a matter of time, the scalded soldiers surrendered and passed up their arms.

Carew and the surgeon heard the firing, and came back with all speed to the vessel. Standing in the stern-sheets, as the two rowers ran the boat alongside, he commanded the mutineers to return to their prison. A gun presented at his head was the not unnatural reply. Fergusson, however, had ordered the priming of the soldiers' pieces to be wetted before they were handed up, and the gun missed fire. Now began another parley. Carew, anxious, doubtless, for the safety of his wife, promised that if the men would give up the ship he would say nothing of their conduct to the authorities at Hell's Gates; but the easily-won liberty was too sweet to be resigned so easily. Confident in his own power, Fergusson told the mutineers that he could navigate the vessel to some foreign port, where they could defy the wrath of the Governor and the commandant. The prospect of the sheds and the cat, as contrasted with freedom and China, was not too tempting. As might have been expected, they refused.

A muster was now held upon the deck, and Fergusson formally called upon the convicts to join him. All but thirteen consented, and one of the sailors, possibly an ex-convict himself, threw in his lot with the mutineers. Boats were lowered, and the soldiers and the thirteen were landed by the now armed convicts on the barren coast. With a generosity which to those acquainted with convict customs will seem somewhat strange, Mrs Carew, with her children, was restored to her husband unharmed. Secure of safety, Fergusson ordered rations to be given to his late masters, and recommended them to make overland for Hobart Town. 'The land party,' says Mr Bonwick, 'received sixty pounds of biscuit, twenty pounds of flour, twenty pounds of sugar, four pounds of tea, and six gallons of rum.' The boats were taken back to the ship and hauled on board, and returning to their vessel the mutineers gave three cheers for their bloodless victory.

After a hearty supper and a pannikin of rum apiece, the seventeen set to work to organise their future plans. Some were for China, some for India, and two men proposed to go to one of the islands of the South Seas, sink the ship, and settle among the friendly islanders. After some talk, however, it was resolved to make for the Friendly Isles, where those who chose could remain.

With provisions for six months for four hundred men, arms, ammunition, and a sailor captain, the mutineers felt that fortune had befriended them at last. Amid one knows not what wild thoughts of future liberty, the night passed rapidly away, and at daylight the next morning the marooned Carew and his companions saw the *Cyprus* spread her sails, and move slowly out of the harbour.

Then began the sufferings of the conquered party. They were on a desolate part of the coast; impenetrable scrub and impassable mountain ranges lay, for many a weary mile, between them and Hobart Town. It was impossible to communicate with the settlement at Macquarie Harbour; the country on that side was even more desolate and barren than on the other. Communication between the two places was most rare, and effected by that very ship which was now bearing the escaped party in safety to the South Seas. The only hope was that some passing vessel, either driven by stress of weather or urged by want of water, would put into the channel and take them off. The party in all consisted of more than forty souls, and their slender stock of provision melted away like snow in the sun. Mr Carew showed his courage. He apportioned out the victuals in equal shares, keeping the rum as a last resource. The soldiers were divided into watches, and he himself took his turn with the rest. Day after day passed with the same monotony of silence. The allowance of provisions was decreased, and despair began to sit heavily on their hearts. From east to west, from north to south, their haggard eyes turned in vain.

> 'The blaze upon the waters to the east,
> The blaze upon the island overhead,
> The blaze upon the waters to the west,
> Then the great stars that globed themselves in heaven,
> The hollower-bellowing ocean, and again
> The scarlet shafts of sunrise, but no sail.'

At last hunger broke through discipline. Two men set off overland for Hobart Town, but, frightened at the perils before them, and menaced by hostile natives, returned. Five more attempted to head the Huon, and after coming near to death, were rescued. The others remained waiting for death.

Desperate, and with but two days' provisions left, Popjoy, a convict, determined to try and make a boat. Assisted by a man named Morgan, he framed a sort of coracle of young wattle trees, and covered it with sailcloth. Over this a mixture of soap and resin was poured, to keep out the water. After many failures, the thing floated. It was twelve feet long, and propelled by paddles. During the last two days of its construction the party were without food. In this rude craft Carew embarked the remnant of his party, and, hoping against hope, got out to sea. Luckily, at a distance of twenty miles, they fell in with the *Oxelia*, and the poor fellows were brought safely to Hobart Town. Carew was tried by court martial, and honourably acquitted. Popjoy, who had been transported when eleven years old for stealing a hare, received a free pardon, and returned to England.

In the meantime the *Cyprus* was running for the Friendly Islands. The mutineers had chosen officers for themselves. Walker was captain; Fergusson, 'dressed up in Carew's best uniform', lieutenant; and Jones mate. The days passed quickly by, liberty seemed before them, and all were in high spirits. Getting out of their course, however, they came to Japan. Here, in spite of Fergusson's orders, seven deserted, and cast in their lot with the natives of that lovely spot. Fergusson went on, but seems to have begun to lose his *prestige* among the men. One Swallow, a seaman and convict, now appears to have assumed the command. This fellow seems to have been both powerful and intelligent. He was originally transported from England for rioting, but on the way out saved the ship at the hazard of his life. Allowed to roam the deck and assist the sailors, he contrived to enlist their sympathies, and when the transport arrived in Hobart Town they hid him in the lower deck and the vessel sailed away with him. The crew gave him rations. Despite a rigorous search, he was not found until after some weeks. The captain landed him at Rio, and he was soon again in London. There an old companion 'peached' upon him, and he was sent back to Van Diemen's Land. Half way to Hell's Gates, the mutiny restored him once more to freedom.

To this man was the charge of the vessel entrusted, and he took her to China. On the way a boat with the name of *Edward* on its stern was seized, and Swallow, knowing that he could not account for the *Cyprus*, determined to try a new plan. There was a sextant in the cabin which had on it the name 'Waldron', and with that and the boat Swallow laid his plot. Abandoning the vessel, he appeared, with three others, as 'shipwrecked sailors'. Swallow affected to be Captain Waldron, and exhibited his sextant as a proof of his story. The English merchants in Canton got up a subscription for them, and paid their passage home. Suspicion, however, was excited by the appearance of four more of the party, who did not know the captain's name, but said 'Wilson' for 'Waldron'. Swallow, trapped again, was at his wit's end. Arrived in London, the party were brought before the Thames Police Court, where a few days before a curious incident occurred.

Popjoy, having been landed by the mercy of the Crown in London, was cast upon the streets to find his way to gaol or starvation. Imprisoned from eleven years old, and knowing nothing save how to roll logs and cringe to the lash, the returned convict had taken to begging round about the docks. Begging, like stealing, was a crime, and he was brought before the Thames Police Court. There he told the story of the mutiny and the boat-building.

Though there was not criminating evidence, the appearance of 'Captain Waldron' was somewhat strange, and the story of poor Popjoy—who had been honoured with several paragraphs in the newspaper town-talk—recurred to the mind of the bench. The suspected men were remanded.

This remand cost three of them their lives.

Strangely enough, a Mr Capon, who had been gaoler at Hobart Town, was in London, and, attracted by the report of the case, he strolled down to the police court. One glance was enough; Swallow, Watt, and Davis were detected at once, and the whole party committed for trial.

Watt and Davis, tried as pirates and escaped felons, were hung in London. Swallow and the rest were sent back to Hobart Town. One was hung at the gaol, and the rest sent back to Hell's Gates for life. Swallow managed to escape the death penalty, and went back to the chain. Twice more he tried to escape, but in vain. At last the weight of his doom broke his spirit, and he submitted to his fate. He worked in his irons for life, and died—still in yellow livery—at Port Arthur, a melancholy instance of a brave man crushed into brutality by a senseless system of punishment.

Five years later Popjoy died also. He made some endeavour to procure a pension from the Government, and only waited the arrival of documents from Hobart Town, formally attesting his services to Lieutenant Carew, to obtain it. In the meantime he obtained a seaman's berth in a merchant-vessel, married, and seemed to have lived respectably. Coming from Quebec in a timber ship, however, he was wrecked off Boulogne. Taking to the boats, the crew made for the shore, but the sea was running with great violence, and Popjoy, with another, was washed overboard and drowned, and so never got his 'pension' after all.

Henry J. Goldsmith • 1875

The Hermit of the Huon

In the olden times, when Tasmania was only known by the dread name of Van Diemen's Land, and was groaning under the weight of imported crime, that made it a by-word and a proverb in every mouth; in the olden times, when Sir John Franklin held the reins of government, before he started on his expedition to discover the North-west Passage, before his ever-strengthening desire to further the cause of science led him to rough it among the Polar bears at Beechy Island, and to abandon the *Erebus* and *Terror* in those dreary ice regions, which have never yet told the tale of his fate; in the olden times, when the good old gentleman, stimulated by the same desire of discovery, started on an overland tour from Hobart Town to Hell's Gates, as the convict settlement at Macquarie Harbour was euphoniously termed, and lost himself for several days in the thick bush scrub, leaving the island without any ostensible head of Government until he was hunted out by a search party that was sent out to skirmish around for him; in the olden times, when Lady Franklin, always kind and hospitable, and beloved by all, in spite of the seeming sternness of her manner, in a well-meant endeavour to emulate the virtues of Saint Patrick, who 'banished all the snakes and toads and other kinds of varmin' from Ireland, proclaimed a reward of a penny a head for every snake killed in the island, and a ton of snake's heads—cheerful article of commerce!—were brought into Hobart Town within a week, the destroyers claiming a good round sum out of the good lady's private purse by way of royalty on the indiscriminate slaughter; when convicts, breaking out of their prison fastnesses, took to the bush, and plundered and rioted, and robbed and murdered, until they were hunted into some obscure corner, where they were secure from pursuit, and where they were forced to turn cannibals or die of starvation, or to give themselves back to their keepers, only to undergo again the terrors of the slavery they knew so well; when man murdered his fellow-man to escape by the noose from the world he was tired of living in, and to see Hobart Town again before he died, even though that sight was obtained from the scaffold. A rough and troublous time, my masters.

Hobart Town was a very small place then, chiefly comprising the necessary accommodation for the administration of the Government, the remaining population subsisting mostly on the profits of the whaling expeditions to the southern seas. It was too early for farming, or, in fact, for civilisation, and society was kept in check with an iron hand. Half the population were 'lifers', and perhaps the fertile district of New Norfolk, with a portion of Sorell, were the only agricultural districts known. The prominent buildings were the gaol and the offices of the Government. Money was scarce, and silver was at a remarkable premium. Dollar pieces—the coin mostly in use—had the centres cut out of them, the latter serving for a half-dollar, and the outer ring for an entire coin; while shillings were represented by a dozen copper tokens neatly wrapped in brown paper, and perhaps never untied or opened for a twelvemonth. Ingenious individuals, ever awake to the main chance, often manufactured these lumbersome shillings by compounding a parcel of clay of the necessary size, wrapping it in brown paper, and placing a copper token at each end; and these articles of barter passed from hand to hand, much as bad coins do now, no one thinking of opening them to see what was inside, but always taking the first opportunity to pass them on to some one else.

I was in the Comptroller-General's office, with a dozen or so of fellow-clerks. The situation was not a very munificent one, as far as salary went, but I did much what I liked with myself, and being 'under Government', a certain amount of deference was paid to me as one of the mainsprings of the rising young constitution. This made things bearable. It was more like an eternal holiday than anything else I can think of; we always had free use of the Department boats, and our absence for a few days was scarcely noticed. If inquiries were made, we were 'down at Port Arthur on service', or 'taking supplies to the Neck', or something of that kind, and no complaint was ever made when we came back. Circumlocution had reached us even in that remote corner of the globe.

We used to be sent out on expeditions in reality sometimes, and then we went in for enjoying ourselves to the top of our bent. I think we might have been upset by a squall and drowned, or have been driven out to sea and landed at the South Pole, or have been wrecked in Storm Bay and died of cold and starvation, and no one would have troubled to make more than a passing inquiry about us or to wonder why we hadn't turned up; such was the normal lassitude of our Government. Our actual work might be expressed in one word—despatches. Occasionally some other kind of red tape would creep in, but not often. A certain staff of men looked after the prisoners, and we looked after *them*. If a man was refractory in gaol he was put in solitary confinement, and we made a note of that; if he escaped from his bondage and was retaken, he was treated to a flogging and a position in the chain gang, and we made a note of that; if he committed murder, he was fetched up to town and hanged, and we made a note of that. It was all a matter of business with us; a few men hanged occasionally comprised an entry as if a few bags of sugar had been sold, and there our duty ended. Use soon became second nature with us.

One day towards the end of a beautiful spring I was told off with some others to make an indefinite expedition 'down the river' to Port Esperance—or, as it was lovingly termed by the genial whalers, the Port o' France,—it being the intention of the Government to establish a penal settlement at Hope Island, and to disseminate the convict element over the length and breadth of the land. I didn't known then, and I have never found out yet, what I was sent there for;

whether they wanted my opinion on the salubrity of the climate, or whether they wished me to take the soundings or to make a coast survey, or to take charge of a band of desperadoes, never troubled me. I was perfectly indifferent to the motive. I saw the chance of taking command of an exploring expedition which might with judicious care be prolonged for several weeks, and I was jubilant over it. I didn't know where the Port o' France was, and I didn't want to know; it would form part of an expedition to find out. They, I mean the Government, wanted to send a boat's crew with me, but I said I could manage better with two friends, as we could sail all the way down the river, and if we had more than three on board provisions might run short before we had time to explore the unknown country.

My request was complied with, a boat was fitted out for us with rather 'rough tack' in the way of provisions, and Cowper and Perkins were told off to accompany me. I received my despatches, took them to my lodgings and read them carefully over once, but failing to make any definite instructions out of the dense conglomeration of adjectives and participles, I put them aside and never looked at them again. Cowper and Perkins were at the wharf—we called the beach the wharf then—before me next morning, and in five minutes our pretty white whaleboat was pushed off from the jetty and we were flying goosewing out of the harbour.

It was a beautiful calm day, with just sufficient of a light, rustling breeze to fill our sails, and we lay in the bottom of the boat and enjoyed it—at least Cowper and Perkins did. I lounged on the gunwale, and rested my arms comfortably on the large oar with which I was making a poor show of steering. It was the supreme intensity of delightful indolence. We did not even speak much; we lay back and watched the white sails and the blue sky, and listened to the plash and ripple of the water against the bows of our boat. We had passed Brown's River before Cowper brought into action a large plug of compholleis tobacco, and we lit our pipes and scudded on over the bright sea and past the beautiful headlands that mark the entrance to the harbour, in an ecstacy of delight in our freedom. Then we sank to rest again. I prevailed on Perkins to take the steer oar, and I sat in the stern sheets and watched him, while Cowper got up in the bows and paddled his hands about in the little rippling breakers that dashed against the boat as she cut through the water. It was a benign laziness that took us all that day, and let any man who boasts his hard-working propensities put himself in our position and see if he won't be as lazy as we were.

Turning a point nearly opposite the rock which was afterwards known as the Iron Pot, we lost the fair wind, and had to tack. This gave us a little more work, but the pleasure was by no means diminished. I could have spent a lifetime at this kind of thing; I thought so then. We passed Peppermint Bay and Oyster Cove, and, by the evening, had reached the boundary of the known country—known, at least, to us—a low, jutting promontory, which we called Tree Out Point, from the strange appearance of a solitary sheoak, which seemed to spring from the end of the point and to droop over the water. The name was afterwards corrupted into Three Hut Point, by which name it is known to this day.

We ran in to shore here and camped for the night. The air grew cold as the evening advanced, and we found use for all the blankets we had with us. The sea air had made us all drowsy, and the low, dull roar of the breakers rushing up D'Entrecastreaux Channel into Storm Bay, on the other side of Bruni, lulled us to sleep in spite of their chilly breeze. When we woke in the morning the wind had freshened, and we deemed it advisable to take our own time and go steadily. We had no idea in which direction Port o' France lay—even we called it Port o' France from custom—and at this point our search expedition really commenced. We rounded Three Hut Point in face of the stiff sea breeze, and found ourselves in an open estuary, studded with small islands, into which the wild sea wind was lashing the water up to a long, sandy beach on the mainland. It was a magnificent scene, but we had not much time to pay attention to it, as all our efforts were now required in the management of the boat, and the excitement, coupled with the danger, was glorious. We passed close by a small volcanic rock, comprising less than a hundred square yards of surface, standing in seventy feet of water, a mile away from the shore, and pierced by what seemed to be a tunnel through the rock. As we passed we could see imprints of fossilised shells on the rock, over which the spray was flying and beating furiously; but we could not venture near enough to land, and we left the rock for examination on our homeward voyage. A few miles further on was a pretty little thickly-timbered island of about a hundred acres, and we steered our course under the lee of this for shelter.

But the wind seemed to gather strength as we scudded along, and I think Perkins was beginning to get a little frightened. However, we reached the lee end of the island with no further disaster than shipping several heavy seas, and hove to for a time. We did not land, but anchored about fifty yards from the shore, took down the sails, and fell into our old positions at the bottom of the boat.

'Where's Port o' France from here, George?' asked Cowper, after a very lengthened cogitation. He was doubled up in what appeared to be a most uncomfortable position in the fore sheets, and seemed to be languid and sleepy.

I told him I didn't know.

'Let's go ashore here,' he said, 'and do the Robinson Crusoe business for a bit; we could knock out a month very comfortably here, and we could let Port o' France go to the deuce. You can report on it just as well without going there.'

Perkins examined the locker and said it wouldn't do—we couldn't hold out for a month without more provisions, and there didn't seem to be much game on the island. Cowper grunted in languid indifference, and the gentle rocking and swaying of the boat riding at anchor soon made Perkins and myself feel as languid and sleepy as he was, and we all fell quietly off to sleep.

It was afternoon when Perkins awoke and roused us. The breeze had sunk, and we prepared to get under way again. In our ignorance of the geographical position of Port o' France, we headed in a wrong direction altogether, but that was of no consequence to us. If we had known where Port o' France was, I don't think we should have cared to face the open estuary to get at it—and we should not have known the place if we had seen it. Cowper ingeniously suggested that the land-locked bay we were in was in all probability the real Port o' France, and that the island under whose lee we had anchored was Hope Island.

But we could not allow this to interfere with our expedition, even if it were true. We were free and untrammelled, and we resolved to make the most of it. We reached Flight's Bay—it had no name then—that evening, and camped there for the night. This was a change from our Camp at Three Hut Point. We were shut out from the open sea, and could only get a view up the long vista of the river terminating at Bruni, with the islands dotted about it; and above us rose a tall hill like an amphitheatre, covered with dull pines, peppermint and stringybark, seeming to spring from the water's edge.

We were up betimes next morning and proceeded on our voyage; but we soon discovered that we had entered another river which we rightly guessed to be the Huon, and by two o'clock the wind had failed us, and we had to take to the oars. We didn't enjoy this half so much as lounging in the stern sheets watching the bellying sails, and Cowper suggested returning to the Port o' France. Somebody—it must have been Perkins, who was nearly asleep—said he was lazy, and Cowper rejoiced at the opportunity, pretended to be in a rage and unshipped his oar. But a light puffy wind sprang up and we hoisted sail again, Cowper's temper soon recovering its equanimity.

We seemed to be getting deeper into the dense wilderness

every minute, but I had made up my mind to go up the river as far as it was navigable, trusting to luck to get back. Just as we passed a low, flat, swampy island in the middle of the river, from which the wild duck arose in clouds at the unwonted appearance of a boat in full sail, Cowper startled us all with an exclamation from his place in the bows.

'Hallo! smoke ahead, by jingo!'

We looked up the river, and there, sure enough, was a thin stream of blue smoke curling up from the river bank and bending down gracefully before the light breeze. We sat gazing at it for some minutes when Cowper again disturbed the silence with an ungrammatical ejaculation,

'That's savages!'

We looked to our fire arms. We did not fear savages much while we were in the boat—even if they were savages. But another suggestion flashed through Cowper's fertile brain, and he shouted,

'It's not savages, boys; it's bushrangers, by the Lord!'

This was a more serious matter. If our boat and store of provisions were taken from us, we should be in a sorry plight, and should have to walk back to Hobart Town the best way we could; and the boat would certainly be the first thing the bushrangers would look for. We ran in-shore, stranded the boat among the scrub, and waited till morning.

There was no sign of human presence next morning, and we resolved to get out while we had a chance. We launched the boat and prepared to pull down the river in the teeth of the strong breeze that was coming against us; but in spite of our efforts the boat drifted up while we were preparing, and, turning a small, sharp point, we came on the cause of the smoke almost before we knew it.

Beside the river was a small log hut, with a large clay chimney at one end, and a door looking out on the river. Between the hut and the water was a small patch of ground comprising scarcely two acres, sown with grain. Not a soul seemed to be about—not a sound disturbed the silence of the scene. We were struck dumb with astonishment, and sat long staring at the phenomenon of a bush hut in a spot where it was thought no white man had trod. Perkins was the first to give vent to his feelings.

'By Jove, here's a rum go!'

We landed and went to the hut, hoping to find the occupier, but we could see nothing of him. The door of the hut was composed of matted rushes hung from the wall-plate, and there was no window. We entered and surveyed the place. There were a few cooking utensils, one or two rough shelves in a corner, a slab-table—whose legs were driven firmly into the ground, and a bush bunk, made of the same kind of matting which composed the door. The implements of husbandry of the occupier consisted of a couple of worn-out spades and a clumsy rake made of saplings and iron spike-nails. The plot of ground was fenced in with saplings, and the small crop looked clean and promising; and down by the river side was a log, on which the occupant of the hut had evidently been lately busy with an axe which lay beside it, in an attempt to shape out a rough canoe.

Perkins suggested that the owner of this 'desirable river frontage', as he called it, was probably at work in the bush, and we waited patiently for his return. But no one came. We moored the boat to our mysterious friend's rough jetty, and waited through the day with the same result. Not a sign of anyone. Cowper began to get annoyed with him for not turning up, and swore he'd stop for a week but he'd find him; and the curiosity of all of us was sufficiently aroused to wait for a solution of the mystery. We got no sign of him that night, and camped down in the boat, Perkins nominally keeping watch, and falling asleep quietly as soon as he found we were fast moored in dreamland. I awoke at daybreak and looked around for any signs of life, but all was still as ever. No one had been about in the night. Presently, something at a distance on the slope of a hill caught my attention. I thought I saw the bush move. I lay down in the boat, seized my gun, and watched that bush for half-an-hour.

After a long watch, it moved again, and presently I saw a face peering out from among the leaves. I made no movement, and a man stepped out into the open, and made his way cautiously towards the hut. He was a man of about fifty years of age, well built and healthy, but with a scared, hunted look in his face which I shall never forget. He watched the boat earnestly for some minutes, to make sure that we were asleep, and kept under cover of the scrub as well as he could. Both Cowper and Perkins were snoring vigorously, and this seemed to reassure our mysterious friend, who crept stealthily towards us. I allowed him to come within twenty yards of the hut, when I jumped up with a shout, and, gun in hand, made after him.

He was off towards the bush the moment he heard my shout and ran swiftly up the gentle incline, but he was weak and evidently tired, and I soon overtook him. He seized a huge stick, and, placing his back against a tree, glared defiance at me, but said nothing. His look was sufficient; that showed his intention of never yielding while he had life.

'Throw down that stick or I'll fire at you!' I cried, levelling the gun.

He said nothing in reply, but lowered the stick to the ground. I approached him, but at the first step the stick was whirling in the air again, and defiance and hatred were flashing from his eyes. Then he spoke his first words, deep and husky,

'I've never committed murder yet. Don't tempt me!'

I stopped and parleyed with him; told him that we had come here by accident, and only wanted to see who lived in the hut. But he would not allow me to come near him.

'Who are you? Not one of the Government bloodhounds?'

'I belong to the comptroller's office,' I said.

A frightful passion came into his face, hate and fear combined, and he grasped his stick firmly as I spoke the words.

'Don't come near me!' he cried, huskily. 'Don't come within my reach, or, as sure as I stand here now, one of us will go to death! Look to your life! I am reckless of mine, but I warn you. Don't come near me!'

It struck me then that he was an escaped convict. I hastened to inform him that I was only acting under my despatches, which were instructions to find and report upon Port o' France, and did not give me authority to arrest him, and that he stood in no danger from any of us. He seemed to doubt me, and I called Cowper and Perkins, who came up in a state of utter bewilderment at the prize I had taken. The man seemed satisfied after a long parley that we were not Government spies, and threw down his stick. As he did so, I held out my hand to him, and he seized it eagerly. We entered the hut, and he sat on his bunk eyeing us curiously for a long time in silence.

He explained that he had seen us the day before, and recognising the Government boat, had taken to the bush at once, neglecting to provide himself with any food, and that he had been since yesterday morning without a mouthful. We fetched him some meat from the boat, which he accepted eagerly, and sat on the bunk munching it ravenously, as he watched us out of the corners of his eyes. His scrutiny seemed to be satisfactory, for after finishing his meal, he said, abruptly,

'You're friends, ain't you?'

'Yes.'

'You want to know who I am?'

'We can guess *what* you are,' I replied, 'though we can't guess how you came here, or how you live.'

'Are you to be trusted?'

'I think so.'

'Well, give me your promise as friends, not as Government officers, but as gentlemen, to leave me alone here, and not to say a word to anyone that you found me? Can I rely on you for that?'

We all promised faithfully, if he wished it, but we thought if the matter was laid before Government—

'Never mention that word to me!' he cried, fiercely. 'Government! A lot of cowardly tyrants, who grind down an unfortunate man until he dare not call his soul his own; who keep him on for years in a lingering death, and punish any attempt he may make to relieve himself of life's burden! Don't talk to me of Government! You'll keep your promise!'

We said we would.

'Then, I'll tell you who I am,' he said.

Cowper hit on the idea of lighting his pipe, and we all followed suit. The wild man looked so eagerly at us as we did so that I felt compelled to offer him my pipe, but he put it aside and held out his hand for the plug of tobacco, from which he cut a piece and put it in his mouth. Then, sitting on his rough bunk in the heart of the forest, where he had lived so long, he told us his story.

'Never mind what I was sent out for,' he commenced, 'that's nothing to do with you. I was sent out; that's enough. I was a lifer. I came out over ten years ago, and was transferred from Norfolk Island to here. I was put in the chain gang on my arrival, because I had been ill on the voyage. For nothing else, as I am alive. Then I was sent away to Hell's Gates. You know that place? But you have never been there. If there is one desolate place on this earth, it is that. Nothing but sea in front of you—nothing but thick impenetrable wood and jungle behind. And they formed a station for us there—for us who had been sent out to do penance for crimes which, in many cases, were committed unknowingly. Why, I've seen men in hundreds—Irishmen—shipped out for wearing rosettes on their coats; they were told that they were O'Connell rioters, and would have to serve the rest of their lives in places like Hell's Gates.

'Think of it, you who have never known what the inside of a prison is like! Think of an innocent man—not that I was innocent—being herded with a crowd of the world's greatest ruffians, and forced to wear out a life more wretched and more degrading than any dog could lead. They made us cut timber at Hell's Gates, and carry it in to the settlement. They made us into what they jokingly called 'centipedes'; gave forty or fifty of us a log to carry by placing bars across it to carry it on. We were worse than slaves; our lives were in their hands. A fierce look was a fortnight in the solitary cell, and a muttered complaint of harshness was a flogging at the triangles. Yes. They flogged us. Lashed us to the triangles, and beat out our lives that way. They flogged us if we grew tired and sank beneath the weight of our burden. If we resisted, we were put in the chain gang for twelve months.

'They were not afraid that we should escape. They knew the country too well. And they knew that many a man who had tried for his freedom had sunk down and died in the bush, from which there seemed to be no outpath, and that many had returned and delivered themselves up, preferring a life in the chain gang to the horrors of starvation in that terrible forest.

'They flogged me one day. I was out on the hills with the gang cutting timber, and one of us—a weakly, handsome boy, whose only crime had been the wearing of the O'Connell badge, for which he was transported for life—sank down beside the rest of us in the centipede. He was roughly ordered to get up and work, but he had fainted, and they flogged and kicked him as he lay there. He staggered to his feet, and one of the Government devils struck him down with a piece of timber. He never rose again. His body was thrown on one side for the crows and eagles to feed on; he was denied even a decent burial. I called God to witness that that boy was murdered. I said so; and I was flogged for saying it.

'I escaped. I fled from the place, and would have faced anything, death, starvation, any suffering under heaven, rather than live in a terrible den like that. I was not followed. They reckoned that I would return or die in the bush; they did not care which. They used to boast that we dared not run away.

'I need not tell you what I suffered in the bush. By luck rather than knowledge of the country, I made towards Hobart Town. I climbed up a steep mountain, which I did not then know was Mount Wellington, and was going down the other side, when, on a sudden, the scrub and undergrowth in front of me seemed to be cleared away, and I obtained a view of the scene before me. Down below, by the river side, was the township I had thought never to see again; and at my feet was a precipice, falling sheer five hundred feet.

'I drew back in horror. It never struck me that I could not be seen; I only thought that I was near the dreaded spot again, and that I must keep clear of civilisation. I descended the other side of the mount, and came to this river. Here I stayed for some months, living on fish and what birds I could snare. No human being came near me, and I determined to stop here. I snared wild game and preserved the skins, living a hand to mouth existence for over twelve months. I built this hut. Then I mustered up courage to venture into Hobart Town, and with a bundle of skins I tramped along the river till I reached the town. I was not recognised as an escaped convict. The report had already died out that I had escaped from Hell's Gates, and had perished in the bush. With the money I got for the skins, I bought a few bushels of wheat and an axe, and returned to my forest home, where I have lived since in seclusion, seeing no one, and at peace, except for the dread of one day meeting those terrible Government bloodhounds.

'I have been in Hobart Town twice since I came here. I only go for absolute necessaries; and I can live now with the little grain I raise on that patch. That is all my story. I put faith in your promise not to betray me, for I believe you will think that I have gone through enough hardship now. So now leave me. I can get on well enough for the rest of my days, or until I am hunted down. Then, perhaps, you may hear of me again.'

'Isn't there anything we can do?' I asked. 'We could bring a cargo of rations down some time or other, when we're out exploring, and no one would be any the wiser.'

'No! Leave me a bit of tobacco. That's all I want.'

We gave him half our stock, and the next morning, at his urgent request, we left him alone in the forest. We returned down the river and keeping along the Flight's Bay shore, tacked down to the Port Esperance whaling station one day, in the face of a strong sea breeze. We stayed there a day or two, and returned to Hobart Town, where I prepared an elaborate report of the appearance and suitableness of Port Esperance and Hope Island, and sent it in to the authorities. None of us breathed a word about the old man we had met on the Huon.

But he was not destined to remain long in his seclusion. The population was spreading daily, and the back settlements of the Huon were not left unnoticed. The old man was unearthed, and was taken to Hobart Town as an escaped convict; but the matter was brought before the Government, and urgent appeals were made on his behalf, resulting in a grant of his freedom and a free gift of the farm he had taken up and lived on so long.

As a curious coincidence, I may mention that some time afterwards I lived for upwards of twelve years on the island under which we had then sought shelter, and I then became well acquainted with the man whom we had discovered on the Huon, at the very spot where now stands the flourishing agricultural settlement of the Franklin. As settlement became more general he throve considerably, and at last became the proprietor of a river barge, and went into the timber and firewood business. No man was better known or better liked on the river, and every old settler now residing there will tell you how he bears in kindly remembrance the hale and hearty veteran, long since dead, who was only known by the name of Old Martin.

Nicholas Shakespeare · 2009

The Castle Morton Jerry

We called it the Castle Morton Jerry, though I never knew why. Ever since a child I remembered that band of cold thick fog suspended above the river opposite our cove, sometimes all morning until the sun burned it off. When the jerry rolled in like that, you couldn't see anything. Walking home, you'd reach out your hand and you'd feel a hard object and you'd have to decode what it was, whether it was a gum tree or a fence post or the leathery, nearly round face of Old Stan who jerked awake as he did on that day.

'Hey!'

'Sorry, mate,' when I saw that I'd blundered onto his deck. And when he'd seen who it was and relaxed, at least enough to stop hollering at me for poking him out of his sleep, I said: 'This jerry—I really do loathe it, you know.'

Old Stan must still have been half asleep because he stared at me almost like he was seeing himself at my age, fourteen, and then he said in a careful voice, 'You shouldn't hate it, boy.

That's the same thing as hating what you come out of.'

'Come out of this horrid fog? Sorry, Stan, I don't follow you.'

He looked at me in a thoughtful way. 'Granny Gordon never told you about the jerry?'

'Reckon the only thing Granny Gordon told me was not to pick my nose.'

'She didn't hum you this song?' and his cracked voice warbled through the mist, thinning it a little: *'So I hauled her into bed and I covered up her head, just to keep her from the foggy, foggy dew.'*

'Granny Gordon wasn't the humming type,' I said. 'And I don't recall her telling me no stories.'

'Well, maybe she had enough on her hands bringing you up without wanting to go spading about in the past. But if it wasn't for the jerry you wouldn't have a nose to pick, none of us would,' and that's when Old Stan told me about the *Castle Morton* and the story his grandfather Ralph told him, who ran the ferry service at Two Mile Creek.

'You grew up knowing Huonville, but before it became "Hoonville" it was Victoria and before that it had no name that I'm aware of. You've got to remember how remote Tasmania was then, before it was woodchip heaven. Believe you me, boy, this place was re-mote. It wasn't even called Tasmania, it was Van Diemen's Land. And this valley was one of the re-moter valleys in Van Diemen's Land. Why, there wouldn't have been more than three bluestone houses and eleven men in a hundred square miles of thick bush. Mr Gordon—your great-granddad—and his four convict workers; Mr Hacking and his four workers, and my granddad Ralph. All single men of notorious and immoral character, as the Governor in Hobart liked to put it. And in the whole district just one solitary female—Granny Lawrence, a noisy, irritable woman who was lame in one leg and had a fleshy mole on the side of her chin, and a scar on the tip of her crooked nose and over her right eyebrow, and whose rare grin opened on a row of missing teeth. Oh, and sheep. You sure your own Gran never told you anything about this?'

'I already said.'

'Personally speaking, I never believed the stories about Mr Gordon's riding boots and Granny Lawrence's soreness at finding traces of a ewe's back leg in one of them. All I do know, the situation was pretty desperate for a lusty and profligate man. And don't imagine matters were easier in Hobart. It was common knowledge how Mr Gordon once rode on his horse for three days through the bush in order to dance at a ball—at the Bellevue, I believe—where he was much disappointed to discover that the settlers and officers all had to waltz with each other. You must realise that even in Hobart there were thirty men to every woman. Who knows what desperation would have done to Mr Gordon and the ten other fellas down here if it hadn't been for the Castle Morton Jerry.

'Well, like I tell you, things being so desperate on the island at that time, the Governor got in touch with Mrs Elizabeth Fry in London and a committee was formed to send a transport ship to Hobart filled with "desirable, free and single women". This was the *Castle Morton*, built in Nova Scotia,

472 tons of copper-sheathed white oak and black birch. On board were two hundred young women, some of them the most beautiful and elegant ever to come to Van Diemen's Land. Plus a Chaplain, a naval Surgeon and a Matron to keep those women clean and orderly on the four-month voyage to "Hobart Town on the Derwent"—where they were to enjoy free board and a roof over their head and a lot else beside. Only trouble is, after four months at sea, the *Castle Morton* got disoriented in a southerly coming up the channel. Instead of sailing into the Derwent, where she was first sighted, she sailed without realising it into the mouth of the Huon nearby. You listening now?'

'Yeah, I'm listening.'

'You'll be listening real good, I reckon, when you hear what my granddad told me about that altogether memorable day. Ralph watched it all happen. He was settled on the sandspit here when mid-afternoon came through the cold front from hell. A storm blew up and he observed a ship in distress. He didn't know there were two hundred eligible women on board, including some convicts from the London Female Penitentiary. All he saw was this sailing vessel off Bruny Island dragging her anchors and in danger of being wrecked. The southerly carried the ship past the entrance. Ralph could see she was in great danger. The rapidity of the tide made him fear that she might be forced on the west side of the sandspit and he hoisted a bed-sheet on a pole, but couldn't keep it up in the violent wind. So he ran to Mr Gordon's farm and requested two of his men to go with him and make a fire on Bluff Point and another on Norman Cove to guide the ship in.

'The smoke of one fire was seen on board. A stay sail was hoisted and the ship bore westward, clearing the sandspit with the help of the steering fires.

'Ralph alerted the crew to the dangers of another sandbar and directed them to sheltered water. He shouted "Starboard!" and they hove round. "Port!" and they did so. He told them: "Let go your anchor!" They did so. And then the gale died down as suddenly as it blew up.

'It was coming on dark when Ralph launched his whaleboat and rowed out with the help of Mr Gordon's two men.

'The Master who pulled Ralph on board was Mr Henniker. He was sufficiently wary to keep his passengers down below and out of sight until he had ascertained where he had anchored, plus the identity of his young saviour. Beside Mr Henniker stood the Chaplain who had fallen down a hatchway in the gale and dislocated his shoulder. Beside the Chaplain stood the Surgeon and Matron. All four officials stood in a row and stared by the light of Mr Henniker's lantern at Ralph and the two disreputable-looking figures who had clambered with him on deck, systematic thieves and liars both of them, and both with faces blackened from the smoke of the bonfires they had lit and dressed in trousers and jackets stitched from the skankiest-smelling kangaroo skin.

'Ralph overcame his natural shyness to take control. He told the Master that if he kept on the east shore on the mud flat he would be sheltered from any further gale.

'The Master thanked him. Then he said: "I have 198 women on board bound for Hobart who have suffered much seasickness." And explained that he was most anxious to disembark them after so many months at sea and constant drenching by storms and heat. He looked again uneasily at Ralph's two companions and then at Ralph. "This is Hobart, right?"

'"Yes, yes," said Ralph, a quick-witted fella. "This is Hobart all right."

'"I was expecting," the Master said, "I was expecting something bigger." He had seen through his telescope two clearings and a bark hut. None of his crew had been before to Van Diemen's Land. He had imagined a bend on the river surrounded by cleared banks covered in buildings.

'"No, you have arrived in Hobart," said Ralph, "most certainly. This is what we like to call the...the outskirts."

'"The outskirts," the Matron said glumly.

'"We were expecting a Landing Committee," threw in the Chaplain, wincing.

'"I will go this moment and fetch them," promised Ralph, and said that he would be back with the Landing Committee at first light.

'Well, as soon as Ralph rowed ashore he ran helter skelter all the way to Mr Gordon's house. As it happened, Mr Gordon knew about this Girl Boat and its cargo of Reformers. It was because of the *Castle Morton* that Ralph found Mr Gordon saddling up, preparing for another long ride through the scrub to Hobart. Even so, his spirits were considerably reduced at the idea of having to compete with 3,000 single men at the wharf. And not only 3,000 men. Also waiting in Hobart were the Ladies' Committee composed of all the respectable matrons of the colony and excited to inform the passengers of the *Castle*

Morton that their Committee had enabled each and every one of the 198 to be engaged in service and provided for respectfully. There were in addition at the dockside a small squad of police waiting to march the women under guard up Macquarie Street to the government hotel, "The Bellevue", which had been appointed to house the newcomers. I tell you, lad, the arrival of this ship was a large and significant event, and it caused quite a stir. Once word got out that the *Castle Morton* had been spotted at the mouth of the Derwent more crowds turned out than for the execution of Matthew Brady. Mr Gordon didn't stand a chance. Nor did Mr Hacking, nor did young Ralph, nor any of the other eight assigned men in the valley. And that's when the jerry comes down the river to assist.

'In the night the southerly eased off into a light offshore wind. Early next morning a current of cold air tracked down from the mountains through the gullies and marshes and fed into the river. It hit the warmer water in a tube of dense rolling mist, a big cloud of it that spilled out into the channel and locked the ship in a chill moist fog.

'On the *Castle Morton* they woke up to a virtual whiteout. Couldn't see a thing. They knew it was a beautiful day, bright and sunny outside. But inside the jerry, the Master couldn't see the Matron shivering across the quarter-deck, leave aside the sourness of her expression. He certainly couldn't see that they weren't in Hobart on the Derwent.

'At eight o'clock that morning Ralph rowed out Mr Gordon and Mr Hacking, both dressed in their neat Sunday best, to the ship. Noise travels over still water. They could hear the coughs below deck as the women put on the new set of clothes that the Matron had issued, the demure uniform to include, of all things, a veil.

'Mr Gordon introduced himself to the Master. He had been at Harrow public school before he became a forger and spoke well, at least well enough to put the Master at his ease.

'"I regret that this mist has kept away the Ladies' Committee. They have sent me as their representative. You may tell me with complete confidence anything you would have told them."

'"Then I will tell you, Mr Gordon, that never have women been more commodiously accommodated as on this passage. You may be assured that much attention was paid to guard them against evil. From the moment they boarded in Woolwich, I urged upon them the most decorous and orderly conduct and a strict obedience to the regulations which the Chaplain and Matron thought needful to adopt. And this morning I impressed on them, I dare say for the thousandth time, how the Governor will take a truly paternal care of them on their arrival in Hobart Town."

'"As you say, they will now be in excellent hands," said Mr Gordon in his Harrow voice.

'The other officials were keen to follow the Master's lead and trumpet their own contributions. The Surgeon-superintendent was a long-nosed martinet called Guthrie. He said: "I was asked by Lord Goderich to land them as uncontaminated as they were sent on board. This I have done. No spirituous liquors were allowed, no visitors."

'The Matron, who had mustered the women every morning to check their personal health and cleanliness, said: "I think they all have high hopes of marriage to wealthy settlers. Most have already been assigned as general servants. One or two are very bad, but a considerable portion of them are respectable and deserving characters."

'Then it was the turn of the Chaplain: "I have told them the measure they have adopted in leaving their native land to go into a foreign country is a matter of vital consequence and under the Divine Blessing it may prove of the greatest benefit, but otherwise the very reverse. By their good conduct or the contrary they will form their own characters."

'"Well, let's get on with it," said Mr Gordon, enthusiastic to speed along the process of disembarkation. He urged the Master in the strongest and most persuasive terms to remain with his crew on board, and promised to make it his topmost priority to arrange with the port authorities to have the *Castle Morton* fully provisioned with fresh water, mutton and oysters as soon as the mist dissolved.

'Relieved to be shot of his charges, the Master ordered the women to be led up on deck and watched them step into Ralph's whale-boat in groups of ten at a time. They sat with their faces obscured in their veils, their hands resting on their bags, and Mr Gordon and Mr Hacking were most careful to say nothing as Ralph ferried the first party ashore, where a cart and three men waited to escort the women to Hobart, that is to say "Nettlepot", as Mr Gordon, who came from Cumbria, had baptised his three-roomed establishment.

'Once on shore, Mr Gordon and Mr Hacking were replaced in the whale-boat by two willing rowers who laboured under the strictest instructions to remain in a state of cemetery silence until they had landed safely every single female. Only on the last journey did it prove impossible for the rowers to contain themselves. Ralph told me how the jerry had barely swallowed the *Castle Morton* behind them when his two crewmen began touching up the women and trafficking to obtain their services at the lowest penny. If the women couldn't see them, they knew where their hands were!

'The jerry lasted until late morning before the sun broke it down and it disappeared, and Master Henniker looked around and saw through his telescope that he was anchored in the middle of nowhere.

'I won't go into the disgraceful scenes that were enacted under Mr Gordon's roof. Let us simply say that the women who came ashore that morning swiftly became acquainted with our habits. But they turned out well, some of them particularly so. They'd have been wasted on respectable landowners, your great-grandmother most of all.

'Her name was Harriet Fay. She was the daughter of a Baptist minister from Richmond, a respectable servant and useful, delicate woman whose mistress regretted parting with her and who had been engaged by a gentleman as a governess to his brother's children in Hobart.

'As I say, I don't know what happened over the next days and weeks at "Nettlepot" or at Miles Cottage, which was Mr Hacking's place, or here at Two Mile Creek where Ralph had taken Mary Malvern, a pert and artful young pencil-maker with a round face who'd been transported on suspicion of stealing fur and fourteen yards of bombazine. I do know that surprisingly many women chose to remain in the valley after the mistake was discovered, and these included Harriet Fay and Mary Malvern. Harriet's conduct especially was said to disappoint all expectation formed of her in London. When it was known that she was living with some men in the country in an improper way, a delegation was sent by boat, a sort of rescue mission to sail her back to Hobart, but she declined the advice of the Committee, saying: "I'd rather be hanged than leave here." And after living myself in this same cove for eighty-two years I reckon I know how she felt.

'So don't go knocking the jerry, lad. Without it, you'd be piss in the wind. And now help me up. And when you've done that you can look behind you. All the time I've been talking, it's been turning into a fine day.'

Adrienne Eberhard · 2001

Orange Bathers

It was 1973. Lycra hadn't been invented then, or if it had, had not yet made its way to southern Tasmanian beaches. Myra's bathing suit was orange, the sort that dried quite slowly, and it was laced at the chest with a white thread. If Myra had been older—a teenager, say—this would have looked quite sexy, but at eleven the bathing suit was entirely demure.

They had come to Roaring Beach for a picnic, her mother, her two brothers, Mrs Carruthers, Jean and Jean's two sisters. It was a work day—the summer holidays—and both fathers were absent. She'd never been to this beach before. It stretched on and on in a beautiful white arc, and there was a river which they'd crossed by a rickety, wooden bridge before turning into the beach. They'd had to come through Dover but there was a coast road for going home.

All morning Myra had been excited—a chance to wear her new birthday bathers, a whole day to prance in them pretending to be a bathing belle or one of those underwater swimmers in the old black-and-white movies, pointing her toes and swirling about. White sand, too, in which she could make Robinson Crusoe tracks. Her brothers didn't seem so excited. They were older than Myra. She thought they probably wanted to be going somewhere by themselves, not with their mother, Mrs Carruthers and Myra and her friend. Still, Jean's older sister would be there. They ought to like that.

Myra's family drove down in a separate car to the Carruthers'. They stopped for ice creams in Dover and then sped out along the dirt road by the sea. Myra pressed her nose against the back window, ignoring her mother's pleas not to put sticky fingers everywhere. She felt inordinately happy and knew a lot of it had to do with her new bathers. She'd also been given some flippers for her birthday and was looking forward to wading, ducklike, with her flapping feet. She wondered if Jean had a pair of flippers, whether they could be a pair of wading birds.

'Myra, stop breathing on the window. You'll fog it up and make it all greasy.'

'Myra's daydreaming again.'

'Stop it, Myra. Why don't you kids play I-spy or something?'

Peter nudging her in the ribs with his sharp elbow. Tom passing judgment. Her mother joining in.

Myra was oblivious to most of it. She could see the sea and the long stretch of beach and she was imagining adventures for herself. As soon as the cars stopped Myra was out and running on to the beach. She heard Mrs Carruthers' voice booming out at Jean and her sisters, and probably at her as well. She didn't care. In a house that voice would pull her up short, but not here, not when there was so much open space and blue sea. She ran to the sea's edge and dabbled her toes. It was quite cold. There were flecks of foam and white caps on the waves. Still, the sun was shining, the air was warm. Myra ran back to the others, who were carrying picnic baskets and blankets and cordial flasks.

She helped Jean carry the folding chairs for their mothers. She was secretly pleased to find out that Jean didn't have any flippers, just her plain, blue bathing suit without the novelty of being laced at the chest. They dumped the chairs, helped their mothers arrange everything and then stripped off to the freedom of their bathers. Myra's mother smiled at her in her new suit and said, 'You look lovely'. Mrs Carruthers didn't say anything, but Myra could sense her disapproval of the white thread lacing. She had known Mrs Carruthers wouldn't like her bathers. Myra grabbed Jean's hand, grasping her flippers in the other, and they were off. They raced across the white sand, eyes squinting, hair flapping and then sank in an exhausted heap near the river, or lagoon as Myra thought of it.

They sat sprawled in the sand, digging at it with sticks and hands and heels and toes.

'I like your bathers,' said Jean.

'Thanks.' And after a pause, 'I like yours too.'

'Mine are really plain and ordinary. Not like yours or Nancy's.'

'Nancy has a bikini on! I bet Tom and Peter can't keep their eyes off her!'

Bikinis seemed highly risqué to Myra. More so than the white lacing at her chest.

'Mum says you and I and Jenny shouldn't even wear bathers.'

'Why not?' asked Myra, greatly surprised.

'She thinks we're still too little. That they're unnecessary.'

'But, but what about our bosoms?' Myra said, astonished, using a word she had heard her mother use.

'Well, we haven't really got any, have we?' said Jean.

'I have. They're growing.'

'No they're not! You're flat as a tack.'

'I'm not. I have so got a bosom.'

Jean just clucked her tongue and raised her eyebrows, rolling her eyes in that annoying way she had.

'But what about, you know, everything else?'

'I don't know,' said Jean, starting to tire of the conversation.

Myra felt mortified for the sake of her own body, and her new bathers. They were so orange. They had such lovely white piping on the shoulders. And they had the white lacing at the chest. They made her feel very special. Like Liza Minnelli in the bits of *Cabaret* she'd glimpsed through the crack in the lounge-room door when she was supposed to be in bed. She couldn't bear to think what it would be like to have to give them up.

'I'm hungry,' said Jean. 'I think I'll go and get a sandwich.'

'Okay.'

Myra watched as her friend idled back up the beach to the dark group that was her mother, Mrs Carruthers, and Nancy and Jenny, Jean's two sisters. Her brothers, she could see, were miles away up the other end of the beach. The allure of Nancy's bikini couldn't have been that great.

Still feeling slightly astonished by the conversation, Myra sat up on her knees, her legs folding back under her. She pulled the straps of her bathers down and wriggled her wrists out of them, letting them hang from her waist. She stared down at her 'bosom'. Saw the pale pink nipples like little flowers. She touched them with her fingers, felt the flesh shrink and her nipples tighten. She cupped them in the palm of each hand and imagined what it would be like to have a proper bosom, one that protruded and spilled into her hands. She stuck her shoulders back and her chest out, pretending that she was Marilyn Monroe or Liza Minnelli. When she did this it seemed as though her breasts grew, as though there were large, creamy swellings beneath the pink nipples. She placed her hands behind her in the sand, sticking her chest up as high as it would go. She moistened her lips, let her hair swing against her shoulders, imagined she was being photographed. It was funny how doing this made you feel older, naughty. She wondered if Nancy ever did things like this in her bikini. She wished there was a mirror she could see herself in. See these new breasts, this swelling body. Feeling suddenly self-conscious, she hastily pulled her bathers up again, noticing how the laced white thread seemed to be stretched over her chest, tighter, in a way she was sure it hadn't before.

Myra stood up and wandered closer to the lagoon. She waggled her hips, tried to pout her lips, thrust out her chest. She ran her hands over her breasts, believing she could feel them grow in the warmth of the sun, under the caress of her fingers and through sheer determination. Tiring of this after a while, she put her flippers on, thinking she would be a wading bird. But after a few desultory steps she stopped, feeling that for someone growing a bosom this was very childish. She stooped, took the flippers off, then lay down in the shallow water. She decided she would loll in the water, roll around and let it lap against her skin. It felt warm and silky, like little fingers touching her all over. She 'swam' a little, kicking her legs and walking her elbows along the bottom, then tried to do the splits. It was difficult under water, but she liked the feel of the water, the way it seemed to caress her body. She could see Mrs Carruthers walking in her direction. For a moment of panic she thought she was coming to take her bathers. She turned over in the water again, facing away from Jean's mother.

Suddenly, she felt the most excruciating pain between her legs. Underneath the fabric of her bathers, like she'd been stung or bitten. She stood up shrieking. Mrs Carruthers heard the cry, saw Myra and came running.

'What is it Myra, what's wrong?'

Myra was crying now, trying to rub the pain away.

'It hurts. It hurts,' she sobbed.

'What does? What is it? What's wrong?'

'It hurts,' cried Myra, 'down there,' she whispered. 'I think I've been bitten by something.'

'Well come here then and let's take your bathers off. Quickly!'

Myra howled again and shook her head. Mrs Carruthers had her by the shoulders and was trying to wrench her bathers down. Myra was saying 'No, no, don't.' She felt wildly upset. She didn't want to take her bathers off, didn't want

Mrs Carruthers to see her bosom or any other part of her, didn't want to lose her precious bathers.

So they tussled, with Mrs Carruthers getting angrier and angrier, forcing Myra to sit down and finally pulling the orange bathers off in one, long movement. She tossed them aside where they lay bright and discarded in the sand. Myra looked at them mournfully. Mrs Carruthers bent to examine her but Myra was up and running. She wasn't going to have anyone looking at her, least of all Mrs Carruthers. She ran and ran, hearing only Mrs Carruthers' voice ringing with sarcasm and stabbing at her like poisonous darts: 'Such modesty! And at eleven! It's not as though you've got anything to hide, Myra!'

Rohan Wilson • 2011

The Needle in the Shoe

The two men had met many times. The writer had said what he wanted to say. Confessed and, in confessing, half made amends for the many faults of his life. All of it recorded in the biographer's tight script. They sat together now in the minimalist beach house the writer had built himself, warmed by the sun blasting through the huge glass walls, below it the Tasman Sea and the orange coastal stone. Talk turned to old loves, heartbreaks, mistakes.

She was a friend of my sister's from university, the writer said. Technical college it was back then. Girl by the name of Miranda Miller. Blonde. Never out of a skirt. The Whipsnake we called her.

Sounds like a real terror.

Let me give you the character sketch. There was one fellow, Pill was his name. He'd gone really head over heels for the Whipsnake. She played up to it. Kissing him and whatnot. But never more than that. Never anything you might call affection. It drove this Pill mad. One night he gets well and truly pissed, and he pulls the bar towel off the bar. Spills all the beers. Spills my beer. Then he throws the towel at her.

Jesus.

Yeah. Well, I saw a lot of that. Blokes she'd played up to. Left bruised and sour. And I was wary of her.

The biographer took this down in the leather-backed journal balanced upon his knee, the pen now and then making a scraping sound on the page. So she was interested in you?

Oh yes. She told me that a lot. She'd give me these kisses on the neck. On the ear. Tiny soft things. But I didn't want to be another corpse in her flower-starred meadow, you see. I wanted to stop my ears with wax.

The biographer nodded as he wrote. Sounds like Miranda might have been sort of a model for Watto in *Dark Black Days*, he said. Watto and Johnny share a similar history. At least that's my impression.

The writer stood from his recliner and walked away to the windows. This was his habit, gazing out across the bay to the headland, chin cupped in thought. In the bay stood a single dome of rock fouled white with bird leavings. Waves rose and shattered.

He put his hands in his pockets. You're right about that, he said. He turned to his biographer. Am I that bloody transparent?

Whether it was meant as a question the biographer wasn't sure. He waited, pen a finger width off the page.

The writer continued. It's been years but I still feel the needle.

The biographer scratched this down. Needle. He put a question mark beside it, underlined it. He hoped he would remember the context.

As the writer stared at the mountainous coast curving off into a haze of oyster-grey sea he continued to speak. Wisdom begins at the end, he said. But I was too long in getting there.

In what way?

Her father had left early on. Out of the blue. She remembered it vividly. The way her mother had burned his clothes in a kero tin after he'd gone. Burned his craypots and his ring nets. We'd drink and she'd tell me about it. More than anything she wanted to be a success. To prove the mongrel wrong, she'd say. To show what a mistake it was to leave.

The writer stepped back from the windows and crossed the dark hardwood floor to the dining table. It sat twelve though the writer was childless and unmarried and who all these guests might be was a mystery. He pulled back a leather chair and sat.

That must have affected her, the biographer said.

Yeah. It was like I'd found her subclause. I could see in a moment how it had altered her life. See it everywhere. The carry-on around fellas. The hard yards she put in at school. Chasing a job. Saving money. It all fell into place.

He took an apple from the bowl on the table. Each one polished and stacked precisely. He did not bite but turned it in his fingers, assessing the colour. He replaced it with the rest, squared it. That story of hers drilled into me, he said.

What do you mean? You stopped resisting?

Yeah, I did.

Because of what she told you?

Because she was not what I had imagined.

The biographer flicked to a fresh page and wrote on. And this was nineteen-seventy-one, he said. Two years before you published *Dark Black Days*.

Seventy-one. Yeah.

The writer rocked back in his chair and folded his arms, the language of a younger man. His eyes inside the crease lines were bright and searching when he spoke again. She stayed one night at my house. Just one. It was the only night we spent together. This was her idea. She wouldn't have sex. Not under my parents' roof. She wanted to treat me differently, she said. I was different to the rest. Better. Important. But we talked and kissed. I had by now begun to feel strongly for her.

The biographer was writing steadily. He looked up. So what happened?

Well, she found a bloody job. As far from Launceston as you could get. She was leaving a couple of days after our last exams. That was always her plan. She hated Tasmania. We all did, of course. Young 'uns do, don't they? But she was steadfast about getting out. Absolutely bloody steadfast.

There passed a few moments of quiet as the biographer took this down. On the page was a pencil sketch he'd done of the writer at work, hunched over his old Olivetti, feeding in a new sheet from a paper stack. He wrote around the picture and under it. With the final word caught he straightened up, cleared his throat. And she just left? he said.

The writer leaned forward. I sat with her on the night before she flew out. The Mowbray Hotel it was. There were some others there too. I forget. It was loud. A band was playing. We drank cider, I know that. She kissed me a lot. Later I reached across the table and took her hand, and I looked at her and I asked her to marry me. She smiled and glanced around the room. I waited. It was very noisy. I wondered if she hadn't heard. So I said it again. She was looking around and smiling. She didn't say a word.

What did you do?

I got up and walked out.

You walked out?

My oath I did. She was so silent. So cold. I didn't want to see her again.

Maybe she didn't hear you.

The writer laughed and it was unpleasant. His face settled into a hard grin. And that there is the needle in my shoe, he said.

The biographer was nodding his head as his pen tracked across the page. The fact you walked out?

The fact I will never know. It drove me to drink for a long while after. Just the thought of it. Had she heard me? The music was loud. She wasn't that cruel person I imagined her to be. She never was. If I had just stayed, if I had just talked to her, it would have been otherwise. But I had left. I was no better to her than her useless bloody father. By the time I understood her, she was gone. And so I wrote out of grief. Eventually all that became *Dark Black Days*. Other parts went into *Under a Weight* later on.

Pretty fruitful, said the biographer.

What's that?

I mean that grief. It was useful. You wrote *Dark Black Days* and then *Under a Weight* out of it. They're your best works.

Wasn't much of a trade, if you ask me. For a couple of second-rate books. Not much at all.

Your whole career might have its genesis in that one moment at the Mowbray. Incredible.

Yes. But who would want it? A pain that leaves you drunk for weeks. Leaves you laid out like a boxer.

I reckon anyone would take it.

Then anyone can have it. I can think of a hundred better ways to live.

He found her in South Fremantle. Miranda Swan, née Miller. It was an expense he had not budgeted for, flying out to interview this woman. He extended the limit on his credit card. If she had no story to tell it was a dead loss. He was worried, but he went.

She was waiting in her front garden beneath a spread of green shade trees. An elegant woman, even in summer shorts, blonde hair salted with grey but her eyes lively and blue. He walked through the ground cover of leafy tropical shrubs. There was no fence, no path. She waved and showed him inside.

The day was hot and dry. He took a big glass of iced water from her and drank it all without thinking. Then he pulled out his journal and started making notes of what he saw. It was a grand place. Wide wandoo floorboards the colour of tea. High ceilings and pressed-tin dadoes. He wrote and sketched as she pegged out her washing.

They sat at the kitchen counter to talk, the marble cool on his arms. He put to her the questions he'd mapped on the flight so that one led naturally into another, the intent behind each concealed. How long had she been here. Why Fremantle. Her husband. Job. Tasmania. Her father.

He was a goodhearted old boy, my father, she said. He's been dead ten years but I still miss him every day.

The biographer hesitated, then wrote it down. So you got on well with him?

Yeah. I knew what my mum was like. He left for a reason. I left too, in the end.

She smiled as she spoke, crossed her legs and uncrossed them. When he moved on to the writer, her manner grew more restrained. She remembered the writer, remembered him fondly. But she seemed bemused by the biographer's questions.

He called me the Whipsnake, she said, 'cause I only looked harmless.

Yes, he told me that.

Why are you interested in him? she said after a moment.

The biographer closed his journal. It was a question the writer had never bothered to ask. Was it self-evident that people would be interested? Or did the writer suspect his biographer's motives but chose not to pry?

I had a girl in high school, the biographer said. Natalie. She broke my heart. His books just came along at the right time for me. It helped me understand things when I was a teenager. Things you can't learn.

She raised her eyebrows. Like what?

You know. Women. Love. The bullshit that follows.

What does he know about women?

The biographer shrugged. A lot of people think he's Australia's greatest writer.

I wouldn't know, she said. I don't read books much.

What did you make of him back then?

He liked to have fun, she said. He danced. He drank a lot, which was great 'cause I did too. I don't know. He was a nice sort of bloke. But he wasn't good with women.

How do you mean?

Are you married? she said.

No.

Then there's no use telling you. You're no good either.

The biographer glanced around the kitchen. On the walls were portraits of children and grandchildren, the sort done at Kmart. There were wedding photos too. In them she was young, and he saw now why the writer might have longed for her. She had a quality.

The night you left Launceston, he said. Can you tell me about it?

She laughed. Oh come on, that was years ago. How could I remember?

You went to the Mowbray. There was a band playing. You drank cider with him.

Did I? You are a little mole, aren't you? Digging all this up. What else does he say about me?

Ah, well. You'll have to buy the book to find out.

Oh, very canny, she said, and she laughed and it was charming.

The biographer smiled. Miranda, this Miranda, the Fremantle grandmum, touched him on the hand then the way a girl might. It gave him a thrill. Those eyes of hers like cut glass inside a tanned and freckled face.

She put her elbows on the counter and covered her face briefly, then steepled her hands before her mouth. Yeah, we did drink cider, she said. We did. And we had some fish and chips. Yeah. He paid. He was a nice bloke. He always paid.

Did he say anything to you?

She looked at him warily. Like what?

I don't know. Anything.

He asked me to marry him. Asked me twice, actually. But he never said goodbye.

The biographer frowned, and nodded.

Is that so hard to believe? she said, studying him. I heard that a lot when I was young, you know. I love you. Marry me. All of it.

So you said no?

I didn't say anything. He wasn't serious. I thought he knew me better. But I was wrong about him.

Did you ever think about it later?

No. Not until you called. Tell you what, I wish I had though. He must be loaded by now.

Back in his hotel room he opens the journal and goes through it again, gets things straight in his mind. He pulls out his phone, brings up the number and hits it. He will tell the writer. She heard him.

As it is ringing, he thumbs through his notes. Needle in my shoe. Pain that leaves you drunk. And beside it another absentminded sketch of Natalie.

He lowers the phone. It is ringing still, an insistent sound like a child wailing in the distance. He hangs up.

Danielle Wood • 2011

None of the Above

In her house on the mountainside, Gretel is almost in the sky. This morning she has been up long enough to watch it turn from black to ochre to shredded pink-grey to its present mottled blue, gradually washing out of itself the bright mark of a three-quarter moon.

She has sung nursery rhymes. She has read the same book over and over again, turning its thick cardboard pages and reciting its refrain—'that's not my monster.' She has looked down at her baby girl's sucking mouth and lightly furred head with its patch of cradle cap, and silently declared 'that's not my child.' She has put the dozing child into her cot, and though tired beyond measure, Gretel has not the heart to go back to bed herself. She has learned that there are times when no sleep at all hurts less than the little that is never enough. Instead she looks in the bathroom mirror at her dirt-coloured eyes and lifeless skin, and thinks 'that's not my face.' She folds gro-suits and blends pumpkin, and thinks 'that's not my life.'

Above her kitchen sink is a window with a view down over the city. It's a small city at any time and from any angle, but from this window it appears small enough for her to cup in her hands. She watches Matchbox cars inching in squares around the city's heart and imagines flinging up the sash window and reaching out to scoop up all the houses and offices and warehouses and apartments, and then crumbling them like stock cubes into the water of the river.

'Boredom,' her mother would diagnose, if Gretel were to tell her mother about making city soup in the basin of the Derwent. 'You've always tended to wild thinking when you're bored.'

The nurse at the child health clinic might have had another diagnosis, except that Gretel had cheated on the test. Or was that true? *Had* she cheated, exactly? Or was it just that she'd been able to beat the questions at their own game?

The child health clinic was a small fibro cube in a quiet and out-of-the-way street and the nurse was an extravagantly freckled woman of capable dimensions. She sat with her chair lowered and her Birkenstocks securely earthed on the carpet tiles.

'And how are *you*, mother?' the nurse asked, after the baby had been stripped and weighed and measured, her tiny hip joints inspected, and her clothes reapplied.

Gretel knew that the nurse's aura of calm was probably supposed to transmit to her, as it clearly did to her baby, who was sagging contentedly into the nurse's broad lap. But instead it kindled a panicky desire to grab the nurse by her arms and implore her to look around her. To see. All you had to do was flake open a newspaper, or flick on the news, to know that calm was not justified. All you had to do was look up at the sky and you'd see the cracks forming. But of course, Gretel did not grab the nurse. Compliantly, she sat in the clinic's armchair and gripped the cup of very hot tea that the nurse had topped up with a stingy amount of low-fat milk.

'In the last seven days,' the nurse read out from the sheet on her clipboard, 'I have looked forward with enjoyment to things, a) as much as I ever did, b) rather less than I used to, c) definitely less than I used to, d) hardly at all.'

'Actually,' Gretel said with a little laugh. 'It's none of the above. I've looked forward to some things more than ever.'

She was thinking of her morning showers. At about seven-thirty am, she would go into the bathroom and shut the door behind her. She had come to love the door, which was panelled, and painted white, and she had also come to love the blessed metallic clink sounded by the sliding bolt when she shot it home. With the door locked, the room became a box—a white cube disconnected from the rest of the house.

Gretel would shuck her clothes and turn on the water and stand beneath it, gradually turning up the heat until her back and shoulders were scarlet. In the windowless room, she could imagine that outside it was not seven-thirty am, but 10.30pm, and that when she emerged, she would put on clean pyjamas and slide into the cotton sheets of a turned-back bed, in which she would sleep through the night. In the whiteness of the bathroom, she could even rewind herself out of the nightmare of motherhood. She could push the baby back inside of herself: dematerialise her from flesh and blood to the sweet and ghostly status of being expected. In the shower, Gretel could still believe that her life was something that she was sketching in pencil, and that she had not, in fact, blotted her copy paper by making a mark as indelible as a child.

Beyond the searing sheath of water, beyond the shower curtain, beyond the bathroom cube, Matt would be looking after the baby. He had not yet complained about the length of the showers, but sometimes when Gretel emerged from the bathroom, he would be already in his coat and standing by the front door, doing nothing more than waiting to hand over the child. In these moments, if in almost no others, Gretel did not feel guilt. That was the wonderful thing about showers—they were such everyday, reasonable things to want. When her shower came to an end, she would stand on the bath mat—the hot water cylinder exhausted—knowing that the best part of her day was now over.

'Well, that's wonderful,' said the nurse, looking pleased and proud.

It is almost seven am and the sky beyond the kitchen window has turned properly blue with the rising of the sun. Down in the city, the buildings and cars have switched off their lights and a ferry is wearing a groove into the surface of the river with its comings and goings.

Gretel empties the sink of its soapy water and long, floating islands of pumpkin puree and wonders why she has lately been remembering strange things. Didn't they say nature abhorred a vacuum? Well, perhaps this was how her mind proposed to deal with hers, by sucking old and unregarded memories out of their chambers and blowing them up to fill the void, magnifying even the smallest details. Perhaps this was how minds survived hibernation: by laying down stores of image, thought and sensation for later use. Perhaps this was what memories were for: to provide nourishment for those times when the mind has nothing left to eat but itself.

It is thirteen years since her final year of school and Gretel has never before in all that time had cause to remember her mid-year practice exam in geography. Now, though, she recalls that it was held in the assembly hall, in order to give a feel for the Real Thing. Her school was historic enough to have some classic old buildings, and wealthy enough to have quite a lot of new and sleekly architectural ones, but the assembly hall was an ugly sister whose construction dated somewhere in between. Its walls were made of flat grey bricks with the occasional textured one sticking out like an invitation to climb up to the row of windows that ran along under the ceiling, letting in a stripe of heatless sunshine.

On the day of the exam, the hall was set out with rows of square, grey Laminex desks, each with a fresh exam paper laid face-down on its surface, but as soon as the doors opened, students spilled all over it, girls tipping fluorescent highlighters and barley sugars out of their pencil cases, boys skewing the desks as they bundled their oversized knees and shoes underneath them. Gretel chose a desk about eight rows from the front and Jesse sat down next to her and reached out one leg so she could twine her ankle around his but Mr Andrews—who usually just rolled his eyes—sternly gestured them apart.

Mr Andrews was standing at the front of the room under a big clock that wasn't usually there and which was also part of getting a feel for the Real Thing.

Gretel was good at exams, but her mother had warned her not to be too cocky because it might turn out that she, like her father, was good at nothing except exams.

'And you can see for yourself how far that got him in the Real World,' her mother had said.

To seventeen-year-old Gretel, the Real World was invisible, but solid, like everything you can't see on the dark side of a window at night.

Mr Andrews said: 'Your time begins…now.'

Q1. The length of the Tasmanian coastline is:

a) 4882 kilometres
b) 5400 kilometres
c) 3300 kilometres

Gretel hovered her pencil above the page and looked up at the assembly hall windows that held nothing but sky. A sky that she knew. Even if she had been in a coma for a really long time and woke up not knowing her name or what year it was, she would still know from that particular shade of pale blue that it was winter outside. She looked at the sky until she noticed, in the top corner of the furthest window, the smudged thumbprint of a daytime moon.

How far was it to the moon? she wondered. And if you unravelled the coastline of Tasmania, could it be made to stretch the whole distance? Well, that would depend. On where you drew the line. On whether you measured at high tide. Or low. It would depend on how far you went upstream into the rivers and whether or not you took your measurements all the way to the places where rivers became creeks, and split apart into many creeks that wended their ways up into the mountains. And on whether or not you measured offshore islands, and whether or not you included all of them, even the ones whose outlines disappeared with the tides. It would depend, too, on how precisely you measured. Gretel pictured herself rolling out a ball of string on a pebbled beach, curving meticulous spans around every last pebble at the water's edge. She smiled at the thought. Then, beneath c), she wrote d). And in the white space beside it, gave her answer.

When the exam was over, she and Jesse got into her tinny little Corolla and joined the Friday afternoon traffic heading for the coast. At a service station on the edge of town they ate hot chips and changed out of their school uniforms, and a little after that they took down Gretel's P-plates in readiness to cruise into the drive-through of a country pub where they bought cheap wine. Finally, they turned off the highway and took the long, winding dirt road that led to a campsite where they set up their tent by torchlight and got stoned.

Little penguins were crooning in the dunes as Gretel and Jesse stumbled along a narrow path that led through the scrub and onto the beach. There they started to kiss, and then to strip off their clothes. They didn't care that the sand was cold because sex was still new enough and mid-year exams were over and they were reckless inside a swirl of dope and winter wind and blurring stars.

Like Gretel, Jesse had parents on the permissive side of things. In Gretel's case, it was because her parents almost never spoke to each other that it was easy to slip into the grey area between them. But Jesse's parents were slack in a far more considered way. They'd moved to Tasmania with a view to surviving the Cold War by growing backyard vegetables and building an underground bunker in the grounds of their hobby farm, and they believed that seventeen-year-olds—who might at any moment have to pull an adult's weight in a post-apocalyptic world—should start practising independence and responsibility. Gretel didn't know it then, but at the end of the year, his parents would take the family back to Sydney since the nuclear holocaust had turned out not to be so imminent after all.

Gretel lay on the sand with Jesse still on top of her, his head resting on her collarbone, her fingertips blending into the soft, curling stubble of his dark hair. Above, the clear night sky was immensely black against the white spill of the Milky Way, and Gretel worked out that if she crossed her eyes just a little, she could prise the moon and stars from their firmament and make them look as if they were coming loose and just about to shower down all over the two of them.

Jesse propped himself up on one elbow.

'What'd you pick for Question 1?' he asked.

'Such a romantic question,' she said.

'No, really. What'd you pick?'

'What'd *you* pick?' she asked.

'I went for a). Split the difference. Four thousand and something kilometres'd be about right, wouldn't it?'

'Maybe,' she said. 'But I chose d).'

'There was no d),' he said.

'There was on my paper,' she said.

'You didn't.'

Jesse looked at her, incredulously.

'You can't do this shit forever, you know,' he said.

'It was only a practice exam,' she said, laughing, but his face was so serious that it was like getting a glimpse through that darkened window of what he would look like all grown up in the Real World.

'So what *did* you write?' he asked. 'For d)?'

A moment ago, she might have told him. Now, she didn't feel like it.

'Nothing special,' she said. 'Just shit.'

Behind Jesse's shoulder, Gretel stretched one hand up towards the sky and the small amount of light that there was on that night seemed to cling to it, making a luminous outline for her fingers and thumb. Though joined, still, to Jesse, she felt her separateness. She knew precisely where she began and ended. She could feel the very edges of herself. Of her hands, fingers, feet, toes. She had very long hair then—fine and pale—and she felt the full measure of every strand, and that of every eyelash, and eyebrow hair, and of all the hairs on her arms and her legs. She could feel the overhang of her fingernails, the rippling ins and outs of every pore of her skin.

She felt her outline as a crystalline filament, glowing. And as she concentrated upon it, she sensed its unravelling. She became a single strand drifting upwards, threading stars onto herself as if they were tiny beads. She scribbled herself in finest silver all over the black of the sky. *Virtually infinite*, she wrote, in huge cursive letters. And even when she was finished, there was still easily enough of her left to lasso the moon.

The baby cries. But Matt is up, and Gretel can hear him burbling to his daughter as he gets her out of her cot. He comes into the kitchen and kisses Gretel good morning and the baby reaches out for her mother, so Matt bundles her into Gretel's arms. Gretel's body takes up the weight as if it is something to be expected. And though it causes her to sink back down into all the heaviness of her days, at the same time she feels the force of her love for her child, dragging like a ploughshare over the surface of her heart, opening it up, rolling it over, exposing all its tenderness.

'Good morning, sweetpea,' she coos.

'How long've you been up?' Matt asks as he goes about the business of getting the coffee percolator going.

'Since about three.'

'What have you been thinking about?'

Perhaps she is only imagining it, but she senses something faintly diagnostic about the question. She knows that he has been worried, and perhaps it is because she doesn't want to worry him any further that she thinks it best to say nothing of unravelling coasts or unhinged stars or the lost infinity of her youth.

'Nothing much,' she says. *Just shit*.

The kitchen smells of coffee now and he is standing close beside her as he puts out a finger and touches her high in the centre of her forehead. Drawing his finger down, he traces her profile, through the middle of her eyebrows, down the length of her nose, along its underside, over her lips and chin. The finger travels down her throat to her breast and across to the baby's belly and up over her little chest and the fatty curve of her cheek. It keeps going, tracking over the baby's soft skin all the way to the place where the sunlight coming in through the window is coating each and every flyaway strand of her impossibly fine hair.

Tahune Linah • 1896

In the River

It was a heavy, all-night downpour—heavy even for the ever-moist West Coast, where rain is never prayed for. The three piners—Jones, Sullivan and Oliver—listened to its patterings on their tent and rejoiced. They had a cargo of logs all ready for transport to the sea-board, but an unusually dry spell had kept the river low. A flood is the Tasmanian pine-cutter's waggon, railway, or lighter—the means by which he gets his goods to market.

Daylight saw it raining as consistently as ever. The river roared along with a full pressure of dirt-discolored water—sweeping away logs, trees, and the varied flotsam and jetsam contributed by the forests through which it took its course. The men hurried an early breakfast, for there was work ahead. They were soon at it—clearing and starting laggard logs; pushing others clear of the eddies into the run; and averting threatened 'jambs'. Wet, cold work—yet exciting for the spice of danger in it. There is a fascinating wildness in the disorderly procession of flood-borne logs. Their passage is fraught with many uncertainties. Now arrested by low extending arms of the river scrub; now carried forward by the smooth, swift fresh of the deep reaches; on, ever onward, to the mad swirl of the rapids, over which they shoot erratically, now hurled right out of the water, and again diving into the depths; the noise of their contact with the boulders resounding above the din of waters. An ever-varying picture of man's utilisation of the forces of Nature to serve his ends.

About mid-day the party decided to embark in their punts and follow their timber. Rain was still falling, and the river increasing in volume. Securing their effects, away they went, scarcely any pulling being necessary other than to assist the steersman, whose post is no sinecure when so much debris is awash.

All went well with them for about half of their journey—the worst half—till they came to a rapid at the foot of which a small island divided the stream. Just as the boat was fairly in the swift 'run', at the top of the fall, she grated heavily on an unnoticed submerged snag—a sharp and deadly obstacle which tore the thin planking of the boat's bottom as if it had been brown-paper. In an instant she filled and rolled over, throwing out her crew, who were swirled forward by the furious rush of icy water—bruised against the rocks, and half smothered. Oliver went down stream for some distance, till at last he managed to grasp some bushes and pull himself ashore. The others effected a landing on the island, which was but a few inches above water. The wrecked boat was swept clear away.

Oliver lay till he regained his breath. Then he looked round for his companions, whom he had not seen since the capsize; he knew that neither of them could swim. His coo-ees brought no response—nor could they have been heard far above the din of the river. He mounted a small promontory, from which he could see up and down stream for half a mile or so. On the little rocky islet, surrounded by the raging torrent, he saw his two mates. Sullivan was busy about a small log which some former flood had stranded, Jones lay apparently inert and helpless—though not dead, as Oliver first thought. Their position was precarious, as the river was steadily rising. Sullivan, working with all his energy to get the log clear of the bushes, was too occupied to notice his mate's signals. It was evident that Sullivan meant to use the log as a means of escape. He carried his hapless, injured comrade to it and secured him on the log with strips of shirting and their leather belts. Oliver waited till the island was nearly covered, then hurried down stream and took up a position on a point where the river made a bend, and stood ready to render assistance— praying the while that the log would swerve inshore.

Presently he saw them coming—Jones stretched out but firmly lashed on; Sullivan, stripped to the waist, sat astride, swaying from side to side in his efforts to keep the rolling thing balanced, and maintaining his place by holding on to something which girdled it. Fairly in mid-stream, the log held its course. Oliver could do nothing—what could be done? If it had only run into the eddy there was a chance, but things were not ordered so. Sullivan saw him as they swept past. With a smile on his face, he waved his hand in farewell, shouting 'Good-bye, old chap. We're bound—' The remainder was lost. There was another rapid ahead, and Oliver watched them to their doom. He saw the log roll over, as, with a sudden shoot, the resistless waters tossed it onward. He saw it a second or two later with but one figure on it—him who was tied.

At the river's mouth the workers securing the logs as they arrived were horrified to find one bearing a ghastly, battered burden. Sullivan's plan had miscarried, and his last resource was transformed into a hearse for Jones. Sullivan was denied the poor privilege of 'decent burial', as he was seen no more.

The river kept its secret.

A. J. O. • 1905

The Salted Claim

When silver and other minerals in abundance were being discovered on the West Coast, and all Tasmania went mining mad, Sullivan, amongst others, found his way there. Labor was in great demand, wages were high, and he easily found work.

But work—ordinary honest work—was too tame and unremunerative for him, and beneath a man of his abilities, in his opinion. So, although he took a job here and a job there just to keep himself going, he spent most of his time visiting one claim after another and acquiring as much knowledge of mining (industrial and financial) as he could, and looking out for an opportunity to make one of his brilliant strokes.

After a while he thought he saw his way, but to carry out his scheme he required assistance, so he looked out for a suitable accomplice. Just then he chanced to meet Homer, the very man he would have chosen; and Homer, on learning his scheme, at once joined him. But he wanted a third, and his thoughts naturally turned to Potts. Potts, too, he learned from Homer, was also on the Coast, but a good many miles away. Sullivan at once sent Homer to fetch him, and Potts promptly came.

Sullivan took them to a certain claim he knew of that had been worked for a short time and then abandoned. It had yielded a rich percentage of gold for a few weeks, but the reef was only eight inches wide and had narrowed as it went down, and the gold had been a mere patch, the shoot running out at both ends, so the claim had been thrown up.

But on this same claim Sullivan had found another reef, about two yards wide, and cropping out across the whole ten-acre section, but barren. It was not the right kind of quartz to carry gold; at least gold is very rarely found in such quartz. This claim Sullivan applied for in Homer's name.

Going over this barren reef, which only cropped out faintly here and there and had to be searched for in the intervals, Sullivan skilfully salted certain parts which had become more or less friable from exposure to the weather. He had got a small supply of gold for the purpose. He then, with his mates, carefully covered up their work and set them to open up afresh the abandoned shaft, while he went down to Strahan seeking whom he might devour.

Now, there were at that time, when all Tasmania was mining mad, many capitalist speculators—some experienced, hard-headed men, some inexperienced and gullible—all on the look-out to have a throw for one of the rich prizes that abounded but could only be located by experiment. It was quite on the cards that you might get £100 for every £1 you laid out, but the chances were far more than a hundred to one against you.

It was an inexperienced investor that Sullivan was in search of. But how to get hold of one of them?

Before long he heard of one who was staying at the hotel at Strahan, and was intending to go up towards Mount Lyell.

Sullivan went to the hotel, managed at dinner to sit next to this individual, whose name was Simpson, got into conversation with him, and exerted all his charms. He spoke so courteously, displayed so much intelligence, and told such racy anecdotes, that he soon made the favorable impression he desired. They talked, of course, like everyone else, chiefly mining, and Sullivan learned that Simpson intended starting for Lyell the next day but one, and had hired a horse, which was to arrive next day. Sullivan appeared as much pleased with Simpson as Simpson was with him, and said he hoped to have the pleasure of meeting him again soon, as he himself, as it happened, was going up Mount Lyell way about that time. But never a word did he say about the claim.

That afternoon he sent particular instructions up to his two mates.

It was necessary that Simpson should somehow be got to stop at the claim (which was near the Mount Lyell track) on his way up. But how to get him to do so? Sullivan could not suggest it. Neither Potts nor Homer could be expected to draw him there, as they were both much too suspicious looking customers to attract anyone into the bush with specious stories of gold reefs, and no one else would be likely to recommend Simpson to an abandoned claim.

On the morning the unsuspecting Simpson was to commence his journey, Sullivan watched him sit down to breakfast, and, stepping into the stable, he tied a fine strong thread round the horse's fetlock, well in under the hair, so that nothing could be seen, or even felt, when the horse went lame, as he certainly would do after an hour or two, from stoppage of the circulation. Then he stepped out on the Mount Lyell track. Simpson started later, travelling slowly, as the way was rough. He had not gone many miles when his horse started to go lame, and got steadily worse as he went on.

Presently he met Potts coming along. Potts saluted him cheerily, and then stopped suddenly and eyed the horse. Then he said, 'That horse of yours will never carry you to Mount Lyell.'

'I'm afraid not,' replied Simpson; 'I can't think what's the matter with him. He was all right when I started.'

Potts bent down and carefully felt the horse's leg up and down. 'I think I know what's wrong,' said he. 'I've seen that kind of case before. An hour's rest and a good bathing with hot water will set it right. If you like to come to our camp, which is close by, I'll soon put your horse on his legs again. I was going a mile or so down the road, but it's no great consequence, I can do that another time.'

Simpson thanked him, and accompanied him to the claim.

Here Homer received him with the best manners he could muster, and, producing the customary billy of tea, poured him out a pannikinful piping hot.

While Simpson was sipping it Potts put a fresh billy of

water on to heat for the bathing process, and soon proceeded to bathe the horse's leg.

While Homer engaged Simpson's attention Potts slipped his knife in under the hair, soon found the thread, and cut it. Rather a difficult job it was, as the flesh had swelled up round it. The leg really did want bathing.

Meanwhile Homer began talking about their claim; how rich it was, and how anxious they were to keep it and work it, but found it difficult for want of means, and wanted a partner with a little money, hinting that they would sell it for a reasonable figure if they could not get anyone to join. He admitted that the claim had been worked and abandoned, and that the reef had narrowed downwards, for Sullivan had strictly enjoined them to speak nothing but the exact truth, and though it was contrary to their nature to adhere strictly to it, still they kept reasonably near it.

Potts bathed his horse and then joined them. He urged the exceeding richness of the reef, and said he could show gold in it visible to the naked eye, and, taking Simpson to the shaft, he did show a few specks, and said, what was quite true, that a reef that narrowed in ten feet down was quite likely to widen again in the next ten feet, and that gold shoots often ran out and then re-appeared richer than ever. Simpson, however, was not charmed, and after a while got ready to go, thanking the two men for their help and hospitality. The last thing Potts said was: 'Well, we are going to start for Strahan presently for fresh supplies. If you want to communicate with us you will find us or hear of us at the hotel there for the next three days.'

'All right,' said Simpson, and he rode off.

About a mile up the track he met Sullivan, and stopped for a few minutes' chat, and presently mentioned the reef he had been shown, adding that he did not think much of it.

'No, neither do I,' answered Sullivan, 'I know it well. It has been tried before and abandoned. But if you are looking out for an opening of that sort I know of one not very far from here that is really promising.'

'Then why don't you take it up? asked Simpson.

'Me!' replied Sullivan, smiling, 'I'm a poor man; how can I take up a claim. Even if I could scrape up enough to pay the survey fee and the Government rent, I'd be no further on. To work a mine requires money.'

'Then it's no use to you?'

'No; the mine, as a mine, is no use to me, but the knowledge of the reef is. I wouldn't sell my knowledge for money, but I'd sell half a share of the mine to anyone with money, who could work it or float a company to work it, and leave me the other half—or even a third.'

'It must be a rich reef to be worth buying on such terms.'

'Well, I believe it is rich. I believe it's a fortune. But I ask no man to buy blindfold. All I ask is, that if, after seeing and testing the reef, he concludes to take the claim up, he will give me a share in the mine. If he doesn't think the reef a good one he can let it alone; if he does think it good, he can and ought to pay me—not in money, I don't want that, but in shares only—for the opportunity which I find him. It's hard lines if the poor man who never can take up a good thing when he finds it is to be left out in the cold altogether—never to have even a share in a good thing when he finds it.'

'That's reasonable enough. I wouldn't mind having a look at your mine. That, at any rate, can't hurt either of us.'

'Just so; but you'll excuse me, sir, in showing you the mine I'm parting with my knowledge. If you'll give me a written acknowledgment—well, I'm a poor man, as I said before, and here's a chance for me I may not get again for some time. If you'll give me a right for a quarter—hang it, for one-fifth—in the event of your taking up the claim. I'll show it you straight away, it's no distance off. Remember, you run no risk. I'm not asking for money, only for a share in the venture—a paid-up share, mind.'

'Very well; I'll give that if I find it worth taking up.'

'Then just come a few hundred yards further on to the Madam Percy claim, where we can get paper and ink.'

So they went on to the Madam Percy, got paper and ink, and the agreement was duly made out, signed, and witnessed.

'Now retrace your steps,' said Sullivan, and he took his companion back to the claim he had just left finding it deserted for the time, Homer and Potts having left, as they had said they intended. Sullivan picked up a pan, a pick, and a shovel, and took Simpson up the hill and into the scrub.

'The reef I mean is on this very claim,' he said, 'but these two duffers know nothing about it. I don't exactly blame them either, because they are neither experienced prospectors nor bushmen, and anyone might walk over the reef a dozen times without noticing it. That often happens when the scrub is thick and the reef only peeps out here and there and looks to the inexperienced eye just like ordinary rock. I only found it out myself by accident. See here,' said he, stooping down, drawing the bushes aside, and disclosing a piece of rock just showing above the soil. 'Here's some paper. I'll tear it into ten or a dozen pieces, and we'll take specimens from as many different places and test them, each separately, afterwards. You take the pick yourself, if you like, and break off a little.'

Simpson did so. The top, having been long exposed to the weather, was friable, and broke up easily. Sullivan put some into one of the pieces of paper. He then took Simpson further on, and looking about, presently found, or rather managed to let Simpson find, another outcrop, and then another, and then another and another, repeating the process of taking some of the surface stone from each.

'Now,' said Sullivan, stepping the distance from one outcrop to another across the hill, 'you see there's a width of six feet actually showing; and as it's wildly unlikely that the whole width shows, the reef is pretty certain to be a good many feet wider, but we'll say it's only one foot wider. Then we have a reef seven feet wide. Now for the length.' He then took Simpson along the hill for a good distance, finding bits of outcrop here and there, and taking specimens from each. He then turned back, counting his paces, and tested the ground in the opposite direction. 'There,' said he presently, 'There's four chains of a reef seven feet wide, that's clear, anyhow. Now we've got to test the quality.'

Returning to the camp he hunted about in the tent

till he found a pestle and mortar. 'Now try some of your specimens,' he said. Simpson pounded them up roughly—several of them—and trying them in the pan separately, saw gold distinctly in almost all of them, several quite large grains in some.

Simpson got rather excited. 'It certainly looks promising,' he said.

'All right,' said Sullivan. 'Now you take those specimens back to Strahan, and have them tested carefully before you decide.' Then he added, 'And you may as well get some expert's opinion upon them.'

Sullivan, of course, would much rather he did nothing of the sort, but he reflected Simpson would be almost certain to do so in any case, so it would look better if he suggested it, and the mere fact of him proposing it would make Simpson perhaps less insistent on doing so, or, at any rate, satisfied with less of it.

'But what's the use of all this?' asked Simpson. 'Those two men hold the claim, and they believe in their little reef, so they'll hold on.'

'That's nothing,' replied Sullivan. 'I know they believe in it, and therefore will ask a good price for it. But they can't work it. They know that. They haven't the money, and they'll take two or three hundred pounds for it, you'll see. And my share of the purchase money can be deducted from my receipts, with interest, when my receipts come in.'

'Well, we'll see about it,' said Simpson, and rode off.

Next evening Sullivan reached Strahan. He noticed Homer and Potts sitting in the hotel, but made no sign, and sought Simpson upstairs. He found him in a state of suppressed excitement. He had had the specimens tested separately. Only two of them had shown no trace of gold; the others had yielded from a few pennyweights to over five ounces to the ton, an average of two ounces fairly distributed along the whole line of reef. He had shown the specimens to an expert, who had said the result seemed all right and very satisfactory, but remarked that that kind of quartz rarely contained gold, though he admitted it did sometimes. He asked Simpson whether it was all right, and warned him to be careful, asking whether anyone was wanting to sell him a section. Simpson had replied, 'No; not for money, only for a share in the mine.'

'That looked well, at any rate,' the expert had replied, but still had warned him to be careful and get further tests.

Simpson, however, was satisfied, and not only satisfied, but eager. A reef seven feet wide, four chains long at least, and yielding over two ounces average along the greater part of the reef, was too dazzling a bait to be resisted.

The sellers did not know what they were selling, and the man who did know would not sell at all, but insisted on staying in and taking his reward out of the results. There was a risk, of course—a risk that the reef might pinch out, or the gold shoot run out; but that was the regular and inevitable risk in all mining. If he was not going to run any risk he had no business to speculate. Moreover, his intention had been from the beginning not to buy into a proved mine, the cost of entering which would be proportionately high and yield only a good interest on the outlay; but to buy cheap into an unproved mine that promised well, in the hope of making a fortune; and here was exactly the chance he was looking for.

He did not say all this to Sullivan, but Sullivan understood his thoughts as well as if he had spoken them, and maintained a discreet silence.

'Well, what do you think it worth?' Simpson asked at last.

'That is for you to decide,' replied Sullivan cautiously.

'Would a couple of hundred buy it, do you think?' asked Simpson.

'Scarcely, I fear,' replied Sullivan. 'You see the fellows thoroughly believe in that shaft of theirs, and feel it a real grievance to be obliged to sell out. I expect they'll stand out for more. Besides, after all, the shaft *may* also turn up trumps. Reefs that pinch often widen out again, and lost gold shoots re-appear. The odds are equal both ways, and the mine certainly yielded a big percentage one time. If it was me I'd willingly go another hundred, or more if necessary.'

'Well, we'll see what they say.' So saying, Simpson stepped out and called Homer and Potts.

We need not follow the bargaining. Homer and Potts first pretended to want to join rather than buy them out, then asked first £500, then came down to £400, and finally accepted £300, plus the rent they had paid (£10) and £10 apiece more to cover their expenses. The cheque was made out, the transfer signed, and the parties separated.

Next day the three confederates sailed by the steamer, renewed their acquaintance as soon as they were out of sight of the wharf, and finally arriving in Hobart, cashed their cheque and proceeded to enjoy themselves.

If anyone thinks Simpson was taken in too easily he can never have witnessed a mining mania. Thousands on thousands of pounds were invested on far less grounds than were presented to Simpson. I know a case in which no gold had been seen, nor even a reef established. A mere cap of quartz was struck at the bottom of a shaft, and the finders carefully abstained from testing it, but floated a company. The shares were taken up quickly.

James Leakey · 1871

The Tasmanian Devil

The obscure hunter who first, in the heat of his admiration, gave the name of devil to the Ursian sarcophilus, probably dreamt little that the title would not only remain to the species, but that a learned naturalist would one day endow the kind with the generic Diabolus, adapted unmistakably from Garth's energetic sobriquet.

The original term was indeed more homely still—in fact, too low and trivial to have survived in serious print; and Garth owes it, no doubt, to his immediate and prudent substitution of the more parliamentary term of devil, that he remains the founder of the family name.

Garth was an illiterate farm domestic, employed chiefly as a ranger by his master, Lazarus Hart. His history begins and ends with the one solitary incident connecting his name with the sarcophilus, and he is entirely indebted to the subsequent fame of that distinguished quadruped for being remembered at all in the annals of Tasmania.

Lazarus Hart, on the contrary, was one of the few independent settlers surviving at the granting of the charter. His reputation is founded on a lifelong struggle with adversity, ending in a triumph achieved too late to be enjoyed by himself, but infinitely profitable to his children and successors. It is not the place in these pages to sketch his history as a model colonist, but he has every claim to be noticed as a naturalist of merit, and especially in connection with the life and habits of the devil.

I had never the satisfaction of seeing old Hart himself. He had been for some years dead when, accidentally in London, I made the acquaintance of his son Elias. His son's first words were addressed to me in the form of a rebuke, too well deserved to be not acutely felt, but I had ample solace in the friendship that ensued. We were a large party assembled as guests of a common friend, and all sportsmen of more or less pretensions. We were recounting in turn our adventures, and as I had acquired less fame in a recent campaign than I thought myself entitled to, I am afraid I betrayed ill-humour in my appreciation of the doings of others. I remember I inveighed especially against the modern fashion of extolling the Australian brotherhood, whose exploits I regarded as mild recreations when contrasted with ours in the East. I had no curiosity, I said, to essay my arms beyond the ancient continent. I had encountered in Europe the bear and the wild boar, the jaguar in America, and in Asia and on the coast of Africa the leopard and the buffalo. I was aware I had still hard labour to perform to earn a name, and from the accounts that reached me Algeria seemed the field of all others for a huntsman resolved at least to deserve renown, although perhaps not destined to secure it. 'What business,' I added pompously, 'had a sportsman who is in earnest, to waste his prime in trapping wombats or in coursing boomers over the easy plains of New South Wales, whilst the lioness leaps, with her cub in her mouth, over the garden gates of Blidah? Why, gentlemen, there isn't an animal in all Australia that, in open ground, would face my old hound Hero!'

'That's all you know about it, master,' said Elias Hart, with a smile of assurance that left me no hope of his being wrong. 'I can tell you of a creature,— it is true no longer found in Australia properly so called, but still common enough in the remoter backwoods of Van Diemen's Land,—that would not only face your Hero in the open country, but would refuse to move an inch out of his path to let a drove of bullocks pass. Did you never hear of the Tasmanian devil?'

No; I had never heard of the Tasmanian devil. I had imagined, on the contrary, that the zebra-wolf, and the dingo, or native wild dog, were the only carnivorous quadrupeds not positively insignificant on the whole continent and in all the islands of the new world. It was nearly two years later that the first authentic notice appeared in print of the Ursian sarcophilus, or Texus Diabolus of Gray. I therefore listened with greedy ears to Hart's highly interesting, though somewhat inelegant, narration.

'The devil,' he continued, 'is a beast of about the size of a large bulldog, in appearance something between a polecat and a bear, but in kind a poucher, like the opossum or the kangaroo. There are devils in nature of many kinds and characters.

The wild cat is a devil, the rat is a devil, and so are the fox, the Indian buffalo, the stone marten, and the zebra. But the devil of devils is the devil proper, or, as they called him formerly in the blue report books, the Ursian sarcophilus. And it is not only we English that call him devil, his name in French is *diable*, and in German *teufel*, and I am told the Royal Society has given the Latin name of devil to the whole race.

'His natural propensities are those of the gluttonous or sluggish kind, and he will be quiet enough when gorged with flesh and left to undisturbed repose, but the slightest provocation, the merest and most unintentional observation will turn him at once into a veritable fiend. He then becomes instantly the very type of senseless fury, attacking all before him, dead or living, and flying with equal fierceness at a mastiff or a barn-door. Nor is there, whilst life is left to him, either truce or quarter; as long as a shred of flesh remains to tear, or a last bone to shatter, he fights on regardless of the numbers that surround him, or of his own subsiding strength, until at length his jaws snap faintly, and his life goes gradually out with an infernal snarl.

'Though taken young, and brought up in captivity, his nature undergoes not the slightest modification. He lives to the last the same surly life, and usually dies in some mad struggle with the bars of his cage. After years of experience he repeats the same acts of profitless and exhausting frenzy. Without apparent motive he rushes at the wall, beating the air like a rabid lunatic, uttering long growls that seem to choke him, till they break out suddenly into a piercing bark. He shows not the smallest attachment to his guardians or feeders, whom he menaces and swears at from the moment they approach him till they pass completely out of sight. When tired out or overfed he becomes stupid and sleepy, rolls himself up into a corner, and falls into a leaden slumber from which it is not always easy to rouse him. Nothing can be cheaper than to feed him. He will be satisfied for days together with huge bones, which he cracks up like biscuit, and usually swallows entirely.

'The full-grown devil is an animal of strange appearance. His coat is rough, and looks like a blanket brushed the wrong way; the head and stomach are of a brownish black; the tail is black also, but with a large patch of white just above the insertion. An apron of white covers the chest, and there are spots of white on the muzzle and the front paws. In the wild state his habits are nocturnal, and he appears as sensitive as an owl to the action of the solar rays. Whilst the sun remains on high, he keeps within the clefts of the rocks, or under the roots of trees, where he sleeps so soundly that the noisiest pack may pass in quest of him without awaking him; but no sooner do the shades begin to fall, than he issues forth in search of prey, and then, woe to the living thing that passes windward within scent. Beast or bird, large or little, all fall before him in instantaneous helplessness. Once fairly griped, the victim, whatever his kind, is doomed inevitably. A feeble squeak, an unconscious struggle, and all is hushed except the muffled crepitation of bones smashed up and swallowed with the flesh that covers them, the impartial monster making no distinction of morsels.

'His gait is something similar to that of the brown bear. In walking he plants on the ground the entire sole, which imparts to his movements a kind of solemnity in keeping with his heavy structure. He is, nevertheless, more active than he seems, and hunts with an agility scarcely surpassed by his enemy and neighbour, the Tasmanian wolf. In pursuit of his prey he gives tongue like the jackal, and his peculiar voice, resembling a grunt and a bark emitted simultaneously from the same mouth, betrays him at times to the impatient huntsman who has quitted his fatiguing ambush for the chance of a casual encounter.

'Contrary to what might be expected, the flesh of the sarcophilus is succulent and good. It is said to be in taste like veal. It is certain that the esteem it was held in by the original settlers was not the least of the many causes of his total extinction in almost all the inhabited districts of Tasmania.

'The female bears from three to five cubs, which she carries about with her in her pouch until they grow too big to get into it. She loves them tenderly and licks them conscientiously, and no doubt, to save or shield them, she would attack an army, or plunge into a blazing fire. This is a redeeming quality, and the devil is entitled to his due.

'His voracity renders him an easy prey to the trappers. The clumsiest snare suffices, provided it be strong enough to hold him. Any bait attracts him that can be seen or scented—a dead bird, a piece of flesh, a fish, a knot of mussels, or even a lump of lard. He rushes blindly upon all that tempts his appetite, and has been found transfixed upon a greasy spike used in a tanner's yard for stretching skins.

'It is more difficult to secure him by means of dogs. No single dog will attack him twice, and he will fight any number, till he falls completely exhausted. His great strength, his rage and intrepidity, and, above all, his fearful teeth, sometimes against incalculable odds, determine in his favour a mortal strife, in which at first no chance of life seemed possible. The huntsman arriving, finds the quarry gone, and the humbled hounds dispersed or disconcerted.

'The early colonists had much to suffer from the ravages of these animals, which glided stoat-like into their unprotected yards, and destroyed in single nights entire stocks of pigs and poultry. They were consequently forthwith marked for vengeance and extermination. Snares were laid for them in all directions, hunts were organised, and trackers engaged and paid by contribution. It followed that the devils diminished with sensible rapidity, whilst those that remained took gradually refuge in the thickest woods and rockiest caverns, till at length they disappeared completely from their ancient haunts, and were only to be seen or heard of in distant or inaccessible retreats.

'The settlers were at first quite ignorant of the sort of animal they had to deal with, and a story is told of a young Dutch colonist of the name of Breeboorst, who lay in wait one night to take revenge on what he supposed to be an opossum or a dasyure. Armed with a stick, he waited long for the coming of his imagined enemy, and was just about to dismiss the boy that kept him company, when he heard a rustling amongst some dry leaves which he had strewn expressly at the entrance of the hen-roost. He thereupon, with a plank, closed quickly the hole through which he supposed the yard to have been entered, and ran forward to confound the robber face to face. At first he could perceive nothing, but presently descried two small eyes intent upon his movements from an adjoining shed. Nothing doubting, he ran forward, and aimed at the marauder's head what he deemed to be a decisive blow. The next moment he found himself on the ground moaning with pain, and remembered no more till he discovered himself in bed, with his father on one side, and on the other a veterinary surgeon, who was the only doctor in the colony. It appeared the blow had been no sooner struck than the devil had rushed on his aggressor, and seizing him fiercely by the lower part of the leg, had thrown him with violence to the ground. At this moment the boy, with great presence of mind, had let loose the dog, which in turn had flown at the devil and diverted his attention from the prostrate youth. The dog was killed in the encounter, and the devil would have returned to his former victim had not the youth's father arrived in time, and paralysed the desperate animal with a gunshot close from the muzzle. The bone of the leg was splintered, and young Breeboorst was long in recovering. He afterwards vowed vengeance on the whole race of devils, and became in time the most determined and foremost of their persecutors. He is still alive, and takes pleasure in relating how the vexation retarded his recovery when he learnt that the infernal brute which had well-nigh bitten his leg off had been allowed to escape with its life. The father had supposed it dead, but the tenacious villain had revived during the flurry of the adventure, and had profited by it to depart unseen.'

Hart here resumed the thread of his personal experience, which he had quitted to discourse a moment on the natural history of the singular quadruped he had brought before us. He told us how for years his father and kindred had grappled with famine and fever in lands which he aptly described as refractory to human intrusion, and how at last they had surmounted all obstruction and installed a thriving farm amidst the astonished marshes of Fort Morcomb. Hart's choicest hunting feats were those achieved in pursuit of animals for daily food, but none were to me so attractive as those where the game was the Tasmanian devil. Of these he recounted several, and amongst them was the incident already noticed, where we made the acquaintance of the ranger Garth, whose happy coarseness had extemporised a name, which experience had found appropriate, and science at length adopted. The Ursian sarcophilus had before that time been called at hazard the Tasmanian boar-wolf, the piebald bear, the grizzly badger, and sometimes even the Australian badger, a name since given to the phascolome or wombat, the happiest and least offensive of the whole marsupial family.

Hart's business in England was to fetch from Cornwall, and take back with him to Australia, two orphan nieces, the last of his father's family remaining in Europe. On the eve of his departure, some weeks afterwards, I bade him adieu with something of a longing heart. I had, nevertheless, no notion at that moment of going in the same direction. It was not till long afterwards, when his words had worn me with their incessant echo, that I began to think seriously of passing into Austral latitudes. Elias was no more a carpet Nimrod than his father. He had been a real and rugged adventurer, and like those of all genuine sportsmen, his accounts were unexaggerated and his good faith sure. I felt, therefore, founded in believing I should find the devil not only a grim and desperate antagonist, but one to which an ambitious huntsman might worthily attach his name, as Paul to the Indian tiger, and Adrian MacCulloch to the shark.

Whilst absorbed one day in these reflections old Hero came into my bedroom. He had been my companion over two-thirds of the globe, and it was fair he should be now consulted on what concerned him, if possible, more intimately than it did myself. 'Hero shall decide!' I exclaimed unconsciously aloud, and taking him caressingly by the two ears, I asked him if he felt game to go with me to Australia, and there have a shake with the devil. The dog smiled, and wagged his tail; and I then and there decided at once to go.

I could have started immediately, had I chosen to go in a convict ship, and four months later I could have secured a privileged cabin in a Government packet. I adopted a middle, and as it turned out, a more commodious course, by engaging a berth in an emigrant vessel bound for Sydney, and advertised to sail from Gravesend in the course of the ensuing month. I had written to Hart, and was anxious to be his disciple for a few weeks, in order to save golden time, and in order, if possible, to do the right thing first. He resided in a house built entirely by his children and himself, at an almost unknown place, called Settler's Increment, and situate halfway between Sydney and Inlet Corner. From Inlet Corner I was informed there were merchant ships sailing often for Van Diemen's Land; the destination of Sydney was, therefore, the best that could have offered.

I arrived at Sydney the day before Christmas Day, after the sulkiest voyage I ever remember. The passengers, though three parts paupers, avowed or in reality, were perpetually mysterious and false, telling untrue stories about their past, and giving themselves airs to maintain fictitious actualities. They were, moreover, dirty in their persons, and idle and trifling in their ways, or only serious when gambling. I wished the colony joy of such an ungainly cargo. Hero excepted, and a dog belonging to no one, the captain, and some few of the crew, were the only amiable beings in the ship; but these latter were occupied incessantly, the winds being adverse continually, and the weather occasionally tempestuous. My pleasantest souvenir of the *Julia Boult* is the captain's astonishment on partaking of a gannet, which I had shot on board, and which I insisted on cooking before him. He declared at first he would never touch it; but the fumes of the roast seduced him, and, after sending in his plate for a second help, he candidly admitted that gannet was as good as duck. The sole secret is to skin the bird as soon as shot, and then quickly to remove the fat and oil-glands, before the flesh has time to catch the rancid taste of the secretions.

I had business at Sydney, and an introduction to a banker. My business was soon over. It lay with a doubtful debtor, to whom I had years ago lent thirty pounds, and as I had kept the statute running, and had claimed interest under the Act of George, I hoped in part to defray my excursion, and, what was of far more value, to excuse myself to Hart for having gone out of my way by a circuit of two hundred miles. My chance of being paid was the more promising that my friend was said to be amassing money. My first care was, therefore, to look him up, and I was too well served by fortune in my researches to trace him home. My first and only informant was by mere chance an inspector of police, who was able to inform me that my debtor had been in Sydney gaol for the last six months for embezzling wool, and had a year and a half to stay there to complete his time.

My visit to the banker was scarcely more engaging. At first he received me civilly enough, though somewhat condescendingly; but on my happening to use the word 'colonial', in reference to his house, he informed me haughtily that well-bred people reserved that word for gum and sugar, and were at the pains to find some less contemptuous term for the establishments of the gentry of the town; and I have since read in a book on Australia that the use of the word 'colonial' is expected to be confined by strangers exclusively to the produce of the country, and that visitors from home give great offence by applying it to the inhabitants of the towns.

The few other folks I met with seemed equally determined to keep me in my place. Mortifying hints were whispered at my side at dinner about the rise and fall of empires. Historical comparisons were drawn and commented on, with applications intended evidently for my especial humiliation. In connection with home I could hear of nothing but old-world fallacy, stagnation, selfishness, protection, aristocracy, prejudice, atrophy, and extinction, whilst all out here was freshness, progress, freedom, life, and renovation. One young lady told me that the British oak was doomed to wither, in order to make room for the Australian gum-tree, whose roots were destined to monopolise the soil. Of course this made me feel very small indeed, and I was quite concerned about the British oak; but what could I do to prevent its withering, if the gum-tree wanted so much room? At last I apologised for belonging to the mother-country, and was allowed to depart with a severe admonition.

Refreshing indeed after all this was my reception at the home of Elias Hart. On arriving at Settler's Increment I put up at an inn which stood invitingly at the entrance to the village. For this Hart reproached me in a tone that touched me to the quick, and he then immediately despatched a man with a mule and cart to fetch my luggage, and at the same time to take a sheep to the innkeeper as a compensation for the loss of his guest.

Hart's interior was a model of unostentatious comfort, and his hospitality of that unboring kind which allows the guest to exist unconsciously; a contrast to the afflictive zeal of certain hosts, of which the defenceless victim lives in hourly and nervous dread. His family consisted of himself, his wife and sister, nine children, and four labouring domestics. Nearly everything consumed or worn by the family was manufactured on the farm, the corn ground, the wool bleached and spun, and the horseshoes forged and fitted. Hart bade me observe that he had reached the point where specie was the least required, and further that he economised the profits of the miller, the baker, the butcher, and most other intermediates. He admitted, however, that such an Arcadian state would be impossible in denser civilisation, or where land was costly, or required to be tilled expensively.

He was at this time suffering from the effects of an accident, and I joined his family in dissuading him from accompanying me to Van Diemen's Land. I had written him from London, and though I had informed him I should start before I could receive an answer, he had replied on the chance of my delaying, and in his letter he had engaged himself to go with me. It was now, however, arranged otherwise, and he gave me instead a letter to Augustus Hamilton, of Woolnorth, whom he told me I should find a sportsman of the right sort, although bred in London, and a Cockney both in speech and physiognomy. Notwithstanding this assurance, the name of Augustus Hamilton inspired me with involuntary awe, and I shuddered at the recollection of the swells of Sydney; but I quieted my fear with a mental promise to be vigilant, and especially circumspect in employing the term colonial.

Six weeks later I had passed the straits, and was jolting fast but heavily towards Woolnorth in the postman's car. I found Augustus Hamilton in bed, in a very dirty kitchen, with live fowls on his table pecking at the remains of his supper. He sprang to the ground on seeing me, wiped a chair for me with a stocking, and was soon shaved and ready to receive me becomingly. I gave him Hart's letter, and also a packet of which I had taken charge for him, and which appeared to me, with other things, to contain money. We were very soon sworn friends, and I perceived with satisfaction that Hart's estimate of his friend was correct. I was nevertheless besieged in his presence with a vague, but ever-recurring souvenir. I had certainly seen that face before, but I was quite unable to seize the recollection. At last, in a moment of animation, his features took an expression which distinctly recalled to me his identity, and I asked him without hesitation whether he had not seen me before. The question seemed to make him uneasy, and he replied in the negative. I then said, 'You cannot have forgotten me in Cursitor Street. Is not your real name Nathan Cocksedge?'

Poor fellow! he assented in a tone of chagrin, which made me regret bitterly that I had been so clever. He seemed, however, to be relieved in the end that there were no more secrets between us, and as I tendered him my hand, I assured him that Augustus Hamilton should be to me thenceforth inviolable, and that Nathan Cocksedge was consigned to oblivion. My acquaintance with Hamilton, as he must now be called, arose out of things by no means grateful to my memory. My friends had fondly destined me to become an attorney, and I had gone so far in the profession as to complete my articles with the bygone firm of Brooking and Surr, of Lombard Street. Those were the good old times of the red-tails, the rare old days of the declaration-books and the special originals, when, in a twinkling, for a debt of forty shillings, you could put a struggling tradesman to a cost of as many pounds. Those were the days of arrest on mesne process, of bail in chambers, of bum-bailiffs, nabsters, and men of straw. The calling of a town attorney was then indeed a scald upon the face of London, and richly justified the mordant sarcasms of Pope and Johnson. The country attorney shared in the profits, but was not always privy to the oppressive working.

During my apprenticeship Hamilton was known to me by reputation both as a nabster and a man of straw. A nabster was a sheriff's bull-dog, or sub-aid to an under-sheriff's officer's man. His business was to fly provisionally at the throat of a refractory defendant, and pin him till the arrival of a legal reinforcement. Of course he was responsible for all sorts of consequences, but it was seldom advisable to attack him. A man of straw was a mysterious and taciturn individual, who paced round Clifford's Inn with a single straw sticking accidentally into the side of his shoe. To this individual resorted the unscrupulous suitor who was hard pressed for a witness, a deponent, or a surety, and it was old Brooking himself who convicted Hamilton of some such delinquency, and procured him a year's imprisonment in the city gaol.

On the whole I think I detected in my breast a Pharisaical satisfaction at finding myself the patron and secret-holder of a grateful sinner. In any case I felt no kind of repugnance at accepting his useful and devoted friendship. I felt, moreover, that the change of name and scene, the distance from temptation, the contact with wild beasts and virgin clods, the unsparing sacrifice of his person, and the long privations of the bush, had thoroughly condoned his wickedness, and restored his being to its rightful and natural condition. I was perplexed to know how it came that, with such an unrustic youth, he had become so hardened and adventurous a ranger. He replied that I had only known him in his ostensible profession. He had subsisted chiefly by poaching in the night at Kingsbury, and that his arm having been there broken in a fight with the keepers, he had been driven to the unholy trade which had ended so unhappily in London. We then moralised awhile on the cutting circles of our small existence, and agreed that our present meeting, so singular in appearance, was, in reality, as natural as the least surprising of our daily occurrences, and we then dismissed the subject, to devote ourselves exclusively to the engrossing business which had brought us together.

A week's preparation enabled us to start for Nobbler's End, where Hamilton informed me we should procure fit men and dogs for the dangerous game we were in quest of. We took with us, in the way of food and cooking utensils, what seemed to me an embarrassing provision; but it turned out to be none too ample for our need. We should, indeed, have been thankful for an extra supply of brandy, of which I imagined we were taking a most suggestive and compromising quantity. At Nobbler's End we had to wait five days for the return of a party of rangers, who were gone for wood to the forest of Little Hampshire. I, for one, however, declared myself well paid for the delay. The men brought back with them, emptied and in good preservation, a brace of bandicoots and a good supply of parrots, poplocks, bister pigeons, and several other kinds of birds. All these I was curious to taste, and found them to be, without exception, excellent. I am convinced there is little, if any, flesh or fish in creation not fit for human food, if scientifically cured and cooked with skill.

At length, through alternate tracts of sand and brushwood, we reached the limit of the Little Hampshire flats, and proceeded up the Spalding Hills, in serious pursuit of the Ursian sarcophilus. Our party consisted of six men, including Hamilton and myself, and seven dogs, including Hero. I felt at times a little nervous about poor old Hero, notwithstanding his spiked collar and his prodigious strength. I knew his courage, and dreaded to see him smart for it undeservedly, from his entire ignorance of his opponent's mode of warfare. I was told the devil, once roused, entirely neglects his own defence, and thinks only of wounding his aggressor. When attacked by a dog, his plan is to seize it by the fore leg, and if he gets fair hold, the bone snaps at once, and the dog limps off disabled. Hero had earned applause in many a sanguinary fight, and I felt truly pained at the thought of witnessing his defeat in his old age, and possibly his death, from the grip of the hideous beast we were expecting to encounter; and I felt the more touchy on the subject, that Hero had become the admiration of the hired rangers, who were provokingly impatient to see him, as they expressed it, 'tackle a devil fasting.' Fasting applies to the animal when roused from his sleep in the daytime, a proceeding which redoubles his natural irritability, and which he resents with his utmost ferocity.

I was startled from this unpleasing reverie by the report of a gun some yards ahead of me, and presently Hamilton presented me with a charming little grey quadruped with yellow feet, of about the size of a guinea-pig. It is known classically as the Antechinus flavipes, but goes popularly by the name of the yellow-footed pouch mouse. It was a female specimen, and had the pouch sufficiently developed. I skinned it on the spot, and have still the spoils at home. The remains we cooked for supper, and had only to regret that they afforded us so scanty a repast.

The next chance of a shot was mine. I was attracted by a rustling behind me, and, turning quickly, was in time to take aim at an animal of about the size of a rabbit, just as it was about to disappear in the hole of an immense tree. I fired, and the animal fell amongst the lower branches, where it hung lifeless and unreachable. Hamilton climbed the tree like a cat, and threw me my shot, which I was highly impatient to examine. It turned out to be the long-eared pig-foot, so called from the length of its ears, and an extremely faint resemblance of its feet to those of the hog. It was first named the tailless cherop by its discoverer, Michael Edwards, who caught it alive in the hole of a tree, and found it to be without a tail. Other specimens were, however, taken afterwards with tails nearly a foot long, and it became clear that the first individual had merely lost his tail by accident. The name continued nevertheless through the vice of habit, until Gray inscribed the animal with authority under the name of Castanotos, from the chestnut colour of its fur. This animal also is a marsupial, as indeed are nine-tenths of the quadrupeds of Australasia. Owen tried to explain the phenomenon as a provision of nature against the effects of drought. 'What,' he writes, 'would become of the helpless young ones whilst the mother was gone, perhaps a two days' journey, in search of water? It is necessary she should take them with her, and for this purpose the pouch is indispensable.' But Owen's theory broke down before the instance of the dingo, which is not a marsupial, and which exists and thrives under the very conditions which Owen regards as fatal.

Meanwhile we had been able to discover no trace of the sarcophilus, and Hamilton gave orders for returning to our encampment at Nobbler's End, and there packing up for a longer journey westward. A two days' march from the camp brought us to the edge of an immense plain bestrewed with loose stones, over which we had a fatiguing pull of nearly three hours. On the other side, passing westward, we came to an acclivity covered with tall herbage, and interspersed with rocks. Towards evening we reached a sort of rocky platform, from which Hamilton pointed out a spot in the distance where he had assisted in killing a sarcophilus, and afterwards in roasting and eating it. It was there, he said, we should find the devil if anywhere. The place, he believed, had been undisturbed for years, and he knew there were devils in the neighbourhood.

The whole of that day and the next was spent in beating fruitlessly the covers. We then moved higher, as Hamilton began to suspect the game had been molested recently, and had found by experience that the rocks were safer than the bushes. At nightfall we held a council, and determined to keep watch till moonlight, on the chance of surprising a sarcophilus hunting on scent, at which time, as has been said, the animal betrays its passage by its voice. The dogs were then chained up and the fire extinguished. Towards midnight I fancied I heard the grunt of a pig, and suddenly remembering that the voice of the sarcophilus was said to be something similar, I called softly to Hamilton, and bade him listen. But Hamilton had no need of my warning; he had caught the grunt himself, though farther off, and I heard him fall immediately at full length on the ground. I did the same without knowing why, but I learnt afterwards that Hamilton had taught himself to interrogate the ground like a native bushman. Presently I heard the grunt again, but less distinctly. Hamilton lay still, and so did I, though I began to get tired of a posture which seemed to me a waste of caution, as, whether up or down, it was too dark to be seen by any known organisation of optics. I had since heard, or fancied I heard, the grunt a third time, but still there was no movement. At last I got up, with as little noise as possible, and was about to creep on to Hamilton, when, all at once, guided I suppose by some indication which had escaped my less fine senses, I heard him give a long, low, thin whistle, which quite made my hair stir with excitement. This was a notice well understood by the rangers, for I immediately afterwards heard the chains chink faintly, which apprised me that the dogs were being held in readiness. Hero was close by my side; in fact, he never left me, but he lay as composedly as usual, and appeared not at all to understand my eagerness. We were only three guns, including myself, two of the rangers having merely spears, and the fourth a horse-pistol. The moon rose shortly after, and we were able to converse by signs; but morning dawned and found us still expectant. The game had wisely followed its inspirations, and left us shivering from stillness. The amount of brandy I absorbed that night was positively indecent, but it left no trace of either dryness or nausea, and I believe it saved me from the ague, especially the liberal portion I poured into my boots.

Next day was a total blank, and I began to fear the devils were resolved to balk us. Towards evening, however, my hope revived, and before night I had the envied quarry at my feet. I had strayed a little from my post to follow a strange-looking bird that greatly excited my curiosity, and I owe it to that wilful distraction that I lost the opening and most interesting scene of the encounter. It was not a long, low whistle that recalled me this time to my obedience, but a series of boisterous halloos, that told me clearly there was an end to ambush, and that the battle was declared in open and unmasked hostility. Shout followed shout in quick succession, and then there came a howl, so long and dismal that old Hero pricked his ears and sprang forward in the direction of the sound. I called him back, determined to have him under my own immediate control, and we hurried on together to the scene of action. As I tore through the brushwood, the horrid stubs gored my feet and sadly impeded my advance. I had scarcely noticed them whilst picking my way leisurely, but now in my haste I found them a most cruel obstruction. I nevertheless got rapidly through, and I shall not forget the scene which broke on my view as I emerged into the open ground. With his back to a large overhanging stone, there stood, half crouched before the dogs, the most horrible-looking beast imaginable. Not that his contour was villainous: in form he resembled a badger, but his physiognomy was literally diabolical, and quite explained and justified his apparently exaggerated name. What struck me first was the look of sarcasm expressed by the drawing down of the corners of the lips,—an expression taken also by the ass, when over-tormented, and unable to intimidate or escape from his tormentors. His jaws were just wide enough apart to reveal his large white teeth without parading them, and from between these issued a continuous growl, that seemed to unwind from a bobbin in his throat. But what most arrested me was the animal's infernal eyes. The eyes of the wild cat are said to be the most savage-looking in nature, but there is about them an expression of uncompromising ferocity, which is frank and unmistakable. Such might have been the eyes of Marius, which disarmed the affrighted slave commissioned to execute him in his prison. The eyes of the sarcophilus are small, black, leering beads, fraught with design, but close and impenetrable. Such must have been the eyes of Burke, whilst hiding the plaster in his hat, and watching the friendless Italian boy from the dark arches of Great Queen Street.

When I first arrived on the ground, the wounded dog was still howling piteously, with his tail curved under him, and holding up his right fore foot. The five others were close to the devil, dodging within distance, but not venturing to close with him. One, the smallest of the five, appeared the most resolute, fixing him steadily, and apparently watching his opportunity. A shot had been fired, and evidently with some effect, as the devil was bleeding from the ear. One gun was on the ground, bitten short off at the slope of the stock, and the closeness of the dogs prevented the use of the other. On seeing Hero, the men at once hounded him on the devil; and, not hearing my half-muttered counter-orders, looked petrified at his apparent want of courage. At last the small dog closed, and the others took heart immediately. A fearful strife ensued, in the midst of which I let loose Hero with a shout, meant to explain his previous passiveness, and which he now redeemed abundantly. With one bound he reached the devil, and fastened fiercely and heavily on his throat. This turned the scale at once, for the poor devil was already at bay with the whole pack, and Hero's weight and galling collar completely mastered him. On seeing him thus pinned, a spearsman stepped forward and ended the fight abruptly with a mortal thrust. The devil then turned on his side, still eyeing the dogs defiantly, till his life went out with a snarl that seemed to go right down and expire underground.

The first dog was maimed irreparably, and his master shot him on the spot. Two others were wounded badly, but not incurably, and one had got blinded by some accident not explainable. Hero had not a scratch, and I felt it my duty to make it well understood, for his reputation, that it was I and not he that had fought shy at the beginning.

We flayed the devil then and there, and half salted his carcase. We afterwards lived on it for two days, and were sorry when it came to an end. I cannot say it tastes like veal; it is more like leveret, but lighter in colour, and less close in fibre. The dogs took their share, but without any show of eagerness, and they all of them preferred soaked biscuit. I preserved the jaw-bones and teeth, and still regard them as the most eloquent souvenir I possess.

A few weeks afterwards I was again with Hamilton at Woolnorth, and preparing to take leave of his hospitable kitchen, which he had had well cleaned for my accommodation. He implored me to return after a visit I purposed making to Hobart Town, and he promised me a rare kangaroo hunt in the savannahs of Port Richardson. But my time was now running short, and I was anxious to return to the mainland, to explore the southern districts before winter with Hart and his two sons, as had been agreed, if health permitted. My acquaintance with Hamilton had obliterated Cocksedge, and I felt able to conciliate the two individuals by the simplest application of a rule of charity. His devotedness to me—and he had shown me much during a five days' illness from marsh fever—had been utterly disinterested, for he had in reality nothing to fear from any indiscretion of mine. He consented to my defraying the expenses of our excursion, but refused a ten-pound note which I pressed on his acceptance. I allowed him, at his urgent request, to accompany me to the coast, and he remained my guest at Willan's Bay until the vessel sailed for Inlet Corner. I fancied, as I bade him adieu from the side of the ship, that I discerned in his face a more complicated emotion than usually arises from the mere severance of a temporary tie. Whether that were so or not, I cannot say with certainty; but I am certain of this, that my feeling for him, as his form disappeared in the distance, was wholly purged of its former Pharisaical admixture.

Roy Bridges · 1930

The Magistrate

She saw them ride across the paddock at sun-down—Laird, and the young Ensign Wall and his men of the 63rd. She was elate that she had triumphed over, avenged herself on, Laird; through her they came too late; Larry was well away in the ranges.

Mellis, in drink, had boasted at the inn that Larry was to be laid by the heels that night; no longer were the Heydons to work their will and their way through the district, now that Mr Laird was Police Magistrate. Colonel Arthur had picked his man well. Larry had been seen sneaking about Mellis' house on the very night the sheep were stolen. Mr Laird would have the young rogue under lock and key by dark, and held for trial, and it would not be long before old Dick Heydon and his boys, one and all, were called to full account. Mr Laird had sworn this to Mellis as gentleman to gentleman.

Harris, the landlord, had told her this. Fortunately she had pulled up at the inn, thinking to find her brothers there, and to order them home! At Harris' warning she had come galloping home, in wild anxiety for her brother, and in hot hate of Laird. She had sent Larry scurrying off for the ranges; Rod and Will had followed for safety, for Laird must have a wide choice of counts against them. Still, to her thinking, her brother had not stolen Mellis' sheep. Larry was courting Mellis' girl, and had met her on the night of the loss.

Laird! She had beaten Laird. She had no part in—she hated and feared—the Heydon law-breaking. But Laird!... Supercilious, pompous fool! Puppy!...Passing her by on the road without a bow in response to her nod and smile; pretending not to know her, not to remember the night of the 63rd's ball in Hobart Town; and he, the little wisp of a man, presented to her, and claiming dance after dance, and presuming to make love to her, so that he had filled her mind for all the weeks thence to that meeting on the road. He had passed her by then without a word, being newly-appointed Police Magistrate for the district, and puffed up with arrogance and insolence; considering her, as old Heydon's girl, not safe or fit for him to know!

She watched Laird and his men approach the house; they scattered to surround it; Laird dismounted at the gate and walked swiftly up through the neglected garden—a lean little man, white-faced, neat and precise in dress—in black coat, white breeches, high black boots and high black hat. He carried a switch in his gloved hand; he seemed unarmed. She heard him rap upon the door, and, no one answering, rap more loudly. She heard her father roaring her name; he was now deep in drink; the men and the women servants were in their huts. She must go down and meet Laird.

She glanced at herself in the mirror. Swiftly she smoothed her dark, disordered hair, and set in her ears the rings with coral pendants which had been her mother's; the corals matched the redness of her lips. She had a regretful thought of her new muslin gown in preference to her dusty, tattered habit. She moved slowly down the stairs, heedless of her father's snarling demand why, in the devil's name, hadn't she answered the knocking at the door? She moved as slowly through the hall, loosed the chain, and unlocked the door.

Laird stood against the redness of the sunset, white-faced and impassive. He bared his head at her sharp question: 'Well, what is it? What do you want here?'

'You are Miss Heydon, I think,' he said quietly. 'I want to see your father. The matter's urgent. My name is Laird.'

She motioned to him to enter the hall; she went to the door to the right of her, and thrust it open. Old Richard Heydon lolled in his chair, at table. His face was flushed, his hair unkempt, his dress disordered, and his cravat loosened from the soiled and crumpling linen at his throat. A candle guttered from a silver stick; the tallow was spilled on stained mahogany; the curtains had been drawn heavily against sunglare. The room reeked of Jamaica rum, and was clouded with Brazilian tobacco-smoke.

Laird had followed her, and stood in the doorway—the mean, little, stilted figure. She noted with satirical amusement the contrast between the two men. Heydon lurched from his chair, striving with fuddled brain to assume the air of dignity and breeding which had belonged to him before the years of dissipation and destruction of all the standards of race and youth.

'Mr Laird, I believe,' he mumbled. 'Why, sir, you honour me...Kate, my dear, a chair and a glass for Mr Laird.'

'No, thank you,' Laird said stiffly. 'I'm not here as a guest. I have to tell you that I'm looking for your son Laurence. Where is he? If he's at home, call him here...The house is surrounded by my men...'

Heydon, with instant change from sneer to snarling rage, roared out: 'You dare to stand there and tell me—'

'Mr Heydon, we'll waive the question,' Laird interrupted with a flash of his steel-blue eyes. 'The charge is laid by your neighbour, Mellis. Sheep-stealing! Where is your son?'

'Not in the house!' old Heydon cried, with tipsy triumph. 'And not where you'll lay hands on him!'

'I must direct search of the house.'

'Oh, search! Search!'—reaching out his hand for the bottle. 'But you'll not find Larry. Hey, Kate—he'll not find our Larry, will he? The lad's well away from here?'

She said, not looking at Laird: 'Mellis is a drunkard and a liar. He has lied to you. My brother had no part in the affair. He is not in the house, as my father's told you...Search the house, if you insist; but you'll only waste our time and your own.'

She was aware that Laird held his eyes averted from her, and that his lips were compressed; he appeared to listen with intentness. She faced him, and cried out with sudden passion: 'Oh, call in your men, then! Search the house!'

He made no answer to her. Pointing his switch at the sodden, sagging figure at the table, he demanded: 'Why has your son left the house, if he's not guilty? Why hasn't he stayed to face the charge? He's clearly had a warning.'

'Why's he away?' Heydon mumbled with tipsy triumph. 'That's *his* affair and mine, not yours! I know Mellis for a rascally perjurer, as I know you for one of Arthur's pimps, Mister—Robert—Laird!'

Laird was impassive still; he swung round without a word; he went to the house door and cried sharply: 'Wall!'—and young Wall appearing—'Tell two of your men to search the house. Heydon says that his son's away. He's received warning, and he's ridden off to the hills. But we'll be sure!'—and, lowering his voice, he muttered to the lad apart.

Heydon sat sucking his pipe, and sinking, with a fresh draught of rum, into a half-stupor. With disgust Catherine Heydon stepped from the room, drawing aside contemptuously as two of Wall's men entered the house. Laird had left the hall, but when she approached the doorway she saw him standing by the porch, and he would have drawn back into the hall. He turned instantly; she was conscious of his pallor, and of the glitter of his eyes.

'I beg for a word with you, Miss Heydon.'

She stood gazing at him in silence—her hate of him expressed in burning eyes and in sneering lips.

He averted his eyes from her. He said, and his voice was hard and rasping: 'A word and a warning, if you will! I'm here in this district with definite instructions from His Excellency.'

'You are one of Arthur's creatures!' she sneered.

'Name me as you wish. I am the Governor's servant! His Excellency's orders vitally affect your brothers—I exceed my duty in speaking to you and giving you this warning. The charge of the man Mellis is one of many for investigation.

Your brothers are under grave suspicion. I say this—that whatever the result of my investigation, whether of this charge or of the succession of complaints made against your brothers, I'll carry out my duties. Rigorously! Without care or concern except for duty.'

'Why do you tell me this?' she asked, her look intent upon him.

'You have influence, I don't doubt, over all your brothers. They are young men, and their lives may yet be of high value to the Colony, not merely thrown away.'

'I ask you,' she persisted, 'why do you tell me this?'

His eyes met hers; she saw the flame of his eyes and the twisting of his lips.

'Pray answer the question for yourself, Miss Heydon!'

The summer heat had endured beyond sundown. The breathless air was thick with the smoke of bush fires. The windows were open to the stifling night, yet the candles burned before the mirror with a steady flame.

Catherine saw the dim reflection of herself in the blurred dressing glass—black ringlets, pallor; the long coral pendants like drops of blood, the misty whiteness of her muslin gown. Her eyes were sombre, her mouth colorless and lined about. She was, she realised, the pale ghost of herself, through the strain of these months of terror, months of conflict.

The Mellis affair had brought new disaster on the Heydon family. Laird, with Ensign Wall and his men, had sought his quarry in the ranges; he had pressed hard upon the brothers; magistrate and military had fallen into an ambuscade.

Young Wall, shot through the body, and lying in the town, was reported to be dying; Laird himself had been slightly wounded in the shoulder; two of the men had been killed. Laird had directed thence constant pursuit; new troops had been brought from Headquarters. The boys were driven from range to range, from hiding-place to hiding-place; their horsemanship and their knowledge of the country as yet outwitted Laird and the troops.

Catherine had not set eyes on her brothers all this time. Her father had met them from time to time at this or that point in the ranges, having roused himself from his drunkenness to succour his sons, carrying them stores and ammunition. He was persistent to his daughter that the boys had had no part in the attack on Laird and his soldiers; the three denied it; they were not alone on the ranges. The remnants of Brady's gang were yet abroad; Wall and his fellows had been ambushed by these men.

All the Heydons' misfortunes were due to Laird! Old Richard threatened a bitter reckoning.

Laird! Catherine had met Laird riding by the road to the town on several occasions. Always he had halted to greet her, his strange eyes burning as from cavernous depths, his face white and tormented, his speech harsh and broken. He had uttered no word of her brothers and his direction of the pursuit of them, pretending only concern for herself and sympathy with her in her anxiety; his speech confused, faltering, he would fall suddenly to silence and ride away.

She told herself that she hated him. She called him a madman; yet, in her secret thoughts, she felt no wonder at him, estimating and understanding. Realising the irony of it—this man, Police Magistrate for the district, compelled by duty to activity against the Heydon sons, and mad for Heydon's girl! Fearing to be diverted by her from the path of duty. That was why he had ridden past without a sign of recognition on that first day. Remembering the night of dance, of sentiment and laughter in Hobart Town!

Irony! Her father's degradation, drunkenness, had involved all of them—the boys, herself. Heydon—with this great house of his and all his acres—had been broken in spirit by her mother's death, and had sought oblivion from the bottle. His name had become a byword in the Colony, the boys had grown up undisciplined, and lawless for sheer joy of a mad game, wild rides through the night, horsemanship, and cunning matched against the Governor's men.

She was alone this night in the great house. The cottages were empty of the assigned servants: all had been withdrawn by the Governor's order—a new count against Laird! But how should the drunken father of outlaws, and their sister, be allowed the charge of assigned servants?

Alone in the house! Heydon had been absorbed, mysterious, and busied in writing during the morning. He had ridden off at noon without explanation to her, and he had not returned.

She was roused from gloomy thoughts by the sudden moaning of the wind about the house, the banging of a shutter, and the fluttering of the candle flames. She rose from her chair, and went to the window, but looked on an impenetrable blackness absorbing bush and cleared land. The sky was wholly overcast; the puff of breeze had ceased, so that the night seemed breathless and soundless save for a distant stirring of the bush as the wind passed inland, and the low drumming of the seas to the east. She leaned from the window, listening intently, and feeling a drear foreboding, arisen, doubtless, from her realisation of her loneliness, as from the weeks of mental strain and terror for her brothers. If they were taken they would surely hang; and Laird was pledged to take them.

So, with relief, she heard at last afar the sounds of hoof-beats; a rider was coming swiftly. She assumed instantly that her father was returning; she took the candlestick, and hurried down the stair into the living-room. The old man would be worn out and famished; she must spread a supper for him.

She set the candles on the table. The windows were open, and the tattered curtains were flapping with new gusts, preluding the rush of the merciful sea breeze. To stay the wild flicker of the candle flame she hastened to draw the shutters and half-close the windows, despite the heat. She took a cloth from the sideboard, spread it, and set bottle and glass and dishes. With the candlestick in her hand she hurried out to the kitchen. She carried in bread and meat and a jug of water.

The candles cast white flickers through the room—on the stained, lime-washed walls hung with sporting prints, the heavy furniture of mahogany, and the faded cushions and curtains. She had a bitter thought of the decay and disorder about her: the house was symbolic of her father's life.

He had come to Van Diemen's Land in possession of considerable means and energy, early in Lieutenant-Governor Sorell's time. He had prospered till his wife's death, and had seemed likely to build up a great estate even in the young, disordered Colony. Now he was a drunkard; the sons of the fair, delicate wife were outlaws through him; the ruin of his life involved their lives in ruin.

She heard the hoof-beats sound up to the gate. She wondered not to hear Heydon cry out her name and ride about the house to the stable-yard, but to hear the gate swung open slowly, footsteps on the porch, and a rapping on the door. She snatched up a candle and hurried to the door, but, ere opening it, she cried out sharply: 'Who's there?'

She trembled to hear the answer—'Laird!'—and hurriedly opened the door. He stood bare-headed; she saw in the flicker of the candle the whiteness of his face and the eagerness of his eyes. She whispered: 'Come in, please!'—and she drew aside till he entered the hall. She closed the door then, and locked it. Silently she went before him into the living-room.

He threw down hat, gloves and riding-whip upon a chair. She saw no pistol at his belt. A black cloak swung open from his shoulders.

Facing him, she whispered, trembling: 'Why do you come here, Mr Laird? Do you bring me...ill news? What is it, please?'

Seeming startled, colouring, and staring at her, he said sharply: 'Did you not send for me?'

'Send for you! What do you mean, sir?'—standing aghast before him, and having a sense still, despite her concentration on him and his answer, of the coming of the winds, like riders sweeping wildly to the house. 'Why should I send for you?'

'But your letter!'

'I wrote no letter.'

'Is this a joke, Miss Heydon?' he asked. 'A letter was handed to me this evening. It was signed with your name. It implored me to come hither to-night, for you needed help from me.'

Shuddering, she said: 'And you...accepted this as coming from me!'

'Miss Heydon,' he answered, his eyes averted from her, 'I hoped—that is, I believed—the letter to be from your hand. Who should have written the letter and signed it with your name?'

She did not speak; she stood staring at him still, wide-eyed and striving for control.

'Who should have written a letter except you?' he said harshly, and with white blazing wrath. 'Is this a trick—a trap for me? Answer me!'

'A trick!' she whispered. 'A trap! Yes, yes, I think—'

His lips were sneering; his eyes now bent on her were pitiless and accusing. 'A trap baited by you—is that is? I should come alone to the house—alone, your letter said! Your brothers are here—is that it? Waiting for me! Where are they?'

She cried out: 'I set no trap! I have no part in this! How dare you?'

Leaning towards her, he said swiftly: 'When I was first appointed to this district—first was called on to administer justice in it, I feared you—for your influence on me, and your appeal to me. I feared you lest you should turn me from my sense of duty—justice; I feared knowing that to carry out the Governor's orders and bring security to honest folk I must first move against your father and your brothers. I thought to do this—strove to put you out of my mind; all this while, striving, striving. I have known no peace, no rest of mind and heart, for you are more to me than duty, honour...And I have come hither this night—unattended this night—because you summoned me. Loving you!'

'I wrote no letter. I would have written no such letter.'

'Who wrote it, then?'

'I do not know! One of my folk—one of them, beyond doubt. So as to have you here and retaliate on you. Go, please! Go now! Before they come!'

'Yet, ere I go—'

'Oh, in Heaven's name, sir, don't stay, don't palter here! Go!'—and her voice rising to a shriek—'Too late! Too late!'

The wind came crying all about the house; the candles leaped and flickered ghost-white on his pale face, on her pale face, and showed the gleaming of her tears. About and all about the house the sea-wind rolled; about and all about the house this beating, crying, wind; but hoof-beats sounded through the clamorous wind, and voices hoarse, triumphant!

He stood calm, resolute; his lips curved in a smile. She gasped with terror: 'Come! The stairs! Hide in my room, while I hold them here; declare you are not here!'

'But my horse! They saw my horse at the gate when they cried out!'

'I'll vow that, hearing them come, you slipped through the house and away. And while I keep them here, climb from the window; the gale will hide the sound...Too late! Ah, Heaven, too late!'—hearing the kitchen door crashing open, the mutter of voices, the tramp of feet in the hall. Grasping his hand and whispering: 'You love me? Love me?'

'Before Heaven!'

'I'll save you from them. Help me!'—and leaned against him. Instantly his arms were about her; so they stood, facing the grim figures crowding in the doorway—old Richard Heydon and his three sons. Heydon's pistol covered Laird.

'Hands up, Laird! Out of the way, Kate! Out of the way, I say!'

She cried out: 'What does this mean? Father, what would you do?'

'Settle our score with Laird. It's a heavy one. I tell you to stand aside, Kate. You in his arms! You making love with him!'

'You'll not lay hands on him. You'll not! Father, boys—for Heaven's sake—Oh, for Heaven's sake, listen! Listen! Larry, make them listen—make them! Can't you see—can't you understand—all of you?...Mr Laird thought the letter—your letter, father—was from me—and that I cared for him, as I *do* care. And as he cares for me. He's asked me to marry him...Marry him! Do you hear me? Father, boys—you're not going to hurt me—not going to break my heart?'

'Is this true, Laird?' Heydon muttered, lowering the pistol.

Laird, stepping forward, said coolly: 'It is true. Your daughter has done me the honour to accept me. And more: I have information for you—affecting you all...Will you listen to me? There is no need for further strife among us—for any hostile action on your part against me, or on my part against you...Mellis' daughter waited on me today. She gave me the reason for the lad Laurence's presence at her father's farm on the night of the loss...The miscreants who attacked us in the ranges and shot Wall and his men were taken last night, and brought down into the town this morning. Sheep-skins at their camp showed the Mellis brand...There is no definite charge, then, against any of you lads. There is no outlawry! Let me add this: I have erred grievously—I have been grievously misled—at the very start of my magistracy—in my injustice to you. I shall not err, I feel, in future interpretation of His Excellency's instructions to me. The Governor plans only the restoration of order to the Colony, not the transformation of headstrong lads into outlaws...'

Smiling then—'And I feel, naturally, that your activities—energies, knowledge of the bush—possibly widened these past weeks—will be of value in the service of the Crown, not ranged against it. I have wiped out—dismissed from mind—less definite charges. The past is the past; the future is your own...Is there an end, then, to strife among us?...There is! There will be a stronger tie!'

And, while the father and the brothers stood staring at him in silence, he turned smiling to Catherine. He grasped her hand; his eyes alight, touches of colour on the pallor of his cheeks.

He said: 'I hold you to your promise—your pledge to me!...I'll not release you, sweetheart, all my life...'

Geoffrey Dean • 1971

The Meat Merchant

My mother gave birth to me at home with the aid of a midwife called Sister Bean. 'In the humiliation of a woman's travail, a woman wants a woman. Not some gerrymandering, clumsy fingered, prying quack with the sensitivity of a breakdown truck.'

My dad said it.

Unfortunately for everyone, my dad had 118 rabbit traps set that day. He wouldn't leave a trap set for more than two hours without doing a check. 'Selling 'em in pairs with their skins stripped off is insult enough—no need to torture 'em as well.'

We owned forty-six scruffy acres at the back of town, packed tight and thumping full of cultivated bunnies. Fenced conscientiously with chicken wire in a grand pretence of rabbit-proofing, it was a festering sore to the authorities.

'What can they do about us?' my dad asked. 'Nobody controls 'em like I do.'

All day long I apparently had resisted the world, and during that time Dad kept up an incessant travelling from the scrubby creeks and hillside warrens to my mother's labour room.

Checking and resetting ten traps at a time out there, he would then race back down the stony banks, over the post-and-rail fence—three steps through the fowl-yard, spraying squawking fowls into the bare-limbed trees before him. Three bangs on the door.

'How's it going Sister? Good, good, I'll be back in eight minutes.' And off again before the indignant chooks had recovered from the recent upheaval, not knowing that in exactly eight minutes' time they would have had to repeat the whole damned affair. My mother said I was born to a world that a little stranger could only interpret as being anti-fowl.

A boy! I lobbed amongst the towels and sheets seven trips in. My dad's eight minutes had stretched to fourteen as his flight through the hills became less vigorous. His puffing sprints had become something of an interminable, soul-destroying, all day marathon.

'He'll be able to carry the traps. How long before he could carry a dozen traps?'

Sister Bean shot him into the kitchen, where she mixed him an egg flip from what might well be the last production of our terrorised fowl-house.

My mother expected me to at least be a marine biologist. (A career she had envisaged for herself at the age of eleven—before, of course, she met *Him*, who didn't allow her time to breathe, let alone study plankton.)

In due course, four more little strangers had—if you'll forgive the assumption—blessed my parents. Mostly raised on rabbit meat, fowl-manured vegetables and cow's milk.

Although my mother was willing to go along with the rabbits and the traps and the forty-six acres she was determined *Her* children weren't going to take after their father. She was English and consequently allowances had to be made. On top of that she was middle-class, mixed-up, phoney-valued but instinctively honest. She was a mess. Looking back I realised she was a contradiction. Though she hated individuality and considered it a lingering curse of pioneering Australia she, the ultra conformist, was fascinated by it. Perhaps, because it was diametrically opposed to her own prissy upbringing, she married my father, who was as individual as Ned Kelly—he strode through life in metaphorical blinkers. My father allowed no padding in his life; no shadows; no subtleties. 'Complication was the invention of fools.' He said it often. Curiously enough, I found him more complex than my mother.

Thus the battle for our education started. As a result of my mother's false values, I was enrolled at Clydesdale College for young gentlemen—or gentlemen's sons. I don't remember which.

It was my father who took me to the railway station. 'It will be easier for you to find out yourself,' he said, as a way of farewell. 'Easier, that is, than opposing your mother's middle-class snobbery. You'll know what to do, when the time comes.'

The time came the next morning. In respect to some heinous tradition, each boy, grey-suited, slicked and scrubbed and quailing was requested to answer the first roll call: name, age, sex—in a school for boys?—and father's occupation.

'Peterson, Charles William...12...male...Business Man.'
'Grover, Peter Harold...13...male...Architect.'
'Millar, Douglas George...13...male...Grazier.'

The monotonous interviewing rippled and flowed along the rows of boys—till it was my turn.

'Quinn, Henry Hamford...13...male...Rabbit Trapper.'

The last two words dropped like stones in the pool of disbelieving silence. Class Master Raspin, save his old school soul, only made an almost indiscernible pause in the flight of his pen across the paper...

'You're a fool,' my mother said. 'You take after your father.' Her hand to her mouth. 'Heavens, how can I? I told them... you at least could have said Meat Merchant. You're irresponsible—just like your father!'

She retired, fiery-cheeked, to the sewing-room-cum-verandah-cum-spare bedroom. During the next three hours she made two summer dresses for my sisters and a pair of purple corduroy shorts for an obscure six-year-old cousin I'd never heard of.

Meanwhile, infamous and vanquished, I limped off to join my father in the hills. He was striding in front of me, cleaving into the sunset to lay his traps before dark. When I caught up with him he was hammering in the last anchor spike. His face was expressionless, he just passed me the trap hammer and we walked home in the dust without a word.

That night at tea he said to me, 'Seeing you're back so unexpectedly from school and not yet enrolled in our local one, you can give me a hand to get rid of the rabbits tomorrow.'

He was scowling, for my mother's sake.

In a way, she was right. He *was* a meat merchant. A seller of meat. In a horse and cart, moving through the early morning streets, he had a bell which he rang every minute and, like a town crier proclaiming kingly laws, he called them from their beds.

'Rab-be-oh-oh, all-oh-fresh-oh.'

The simple words he put to a tune that was both cajoling and inspiring. Like rabbits themselves, popping out of their suburban burrows, the housewives came to meet him. Be-curled, be-slippered, heads in scarves and their dressing gowns pulled tight at their throats to keep out the cold, they clamoured at the sides of his cart for the youngest, the biggest, the cheapest pair.

My dad coaxed, chastised, pleaded and wooed them. 'C'mon, ladies, you'll all get the best—don' fight now. Two pairs Mrs B—crikey your old man'll be hoppin' to work tomorrow. Don' forget to spit out the bones ladies. C'mon now; don't shove.'

Everybody fought and joked and their laughter vaporised in the morning frost. I sat on the seat in front of the built-in meat safe, warm in my jacket and scarf, happy and unblinking; mostly forgotten.

Had I not wanted to escape that day from Clydesdale, I could have said anything. For my mother's sake. Especially in view of the fact that later my two sisters also disappointed her when they were expelled from the Wilton Park School for Young Ladies after only five months, for the crime of organising a protest march in the school grounds against the Rabbit Eradication and Myxomatosis Bill.

For my mother's sake I could have said Grower, Wholesaler, Retailer. He ran his business from pregnant doe to dressed pair. He was his own advertising manager. His bell-ringing and repertoire of wise-cracks put him in the category of a showman, a side-show spruiker. His dexterity with the dollar made him cashier and accountant, and for an added laugh he could roll the coins through his fingers like a juggler or a magician.

I didn't have to say it for myself, or my brothers and sisters. Not for my father, who didn't need to know, only for my mother, bless her, who was English and probably never would understand.

Margaret Scott • 2000

Preserves

'Waste not want not' was one of Mrs Zena Bromyard's favourite precepts. She said it very often to her daughter-in-law and the girls who came to help out in the kitchen. She reminded them that in the old days when the steamer brought supplies only once in three months everyone had to learn to make do with whatever lay to hand. She had grown up in a house built by her father from split timber straight from the bush with chaff bags lining the inside under the wallpaper. Other bags were dyed to make mats for the floor. Mrs Bromyard's mother sewed rabbit and possum skins into bed covers and coats and used grated sassafras bark in place of nutmeg. Every box and button, every tin and scrap of thread was hoarded and reused in one way or another, and every bit of wool was knitted up, unpicked and used again.

Not that all this thriftiness had made Zena Bromyard niggardly. She was one of the best cooks in the district, famous for serving three vegetables every day for three hundred and sixty-five days of the year. Her picnics were legendary and her fruitcakes and sponges sure-fire winners at every show. Her jellies and jams, her chutneys and sauces, her bottled fruit and vegetables had carried off trophies all over the state. Towards the end of the Second World War she had even featured on the front page of a leading newspaper under the headline IF YOU'RE TIRED DON'T READ THIS STORY OF A HOME-INDUSTRIALIST. Below this were photographs of Mrs Bromyard making cheese (Cheddar, cottage, buttermilk or cream); picking out cabbage seedlings in her seed house; holding up a conger eel she'd caught from her powered dinghy; stalking game with her rifle ('quail and other edible birds to be prepared as a table delicacy'); packing home-made crystallised fruit for her son and his mates in the RAAF; and inspecting a flitch of bacon from her smokehouse. There was also a picture of a vast pyramid of Kilner jars containing twenty-five different types of vegetable and thirty different types of fruit, part of a special one-woman show that she was preparing for the Country Women's Association's annual exhibition in September.

Each of these jars carried a label cut from one of the used envelopes that Mrs Bromyard collected for this purpose, and on each label, under 'Raspberries' or 'French Beans', she had written in her finest copperplate a date and the name of the property that was her home: *Shendlestone*.

This name had been part of her life for as long as she could remember. It has been printed across the bottom of a picture that had hung over the fireplace in her old home. On winter evenings after tea when the whole family was gathered round the fire—all busy, of course, with useful tasks, knitting, sewing, making dolly-pegs or fish hooks or some such—little Zena had peeped up from time to time at the picture, repeating to herself the beautiful name that flowed through her mind like a clear wavelet whispering among pebbles on the beach. In the foreground of the picture there was a man in a broad-brimmed hat with a long stick in one hand. Zena though he might be a shepherd although there were no sheep to be seen, just a sweep of a green pasture and, at the top of the rise an enormous house, *Shendlestone Manor*, at which the man with the stick was gazing very intently. The house—a great oblong stone place—was far larger than any building that Zena had ever seen, larger even than the Town Hall in Hobart. It had row upon row of windows and, at the front, a huge porch supported by pillars with steps on three sides. This, her father said, was where her grandfather, Jabez Lamprey, had lived until, after a terrible quarrel with his elder brother, he had set out almost penniless to seek his fortune in Australia. Apparently he had failed to find it and died at an early age, leaving a wife and three sons with nothing but a few small heirlooms, scattered sparks from the blazing glory of his former home: the picture, a mourning ring with a sprig of asphodel picked out in diamonds on a jet shield; the works of Alexander Pope printed in six calf-bound volumes in MDCCLXVI; and a gold brooch in the shape of an ivy leaf with a pearl nestling like a softly glowing berry in the crease above the stem. Somehow Grandma Lamprey had managed to survive and bring up her family of boys without selling any of these treasures.

'She'd rather've cut off her right arm,' said Zena's father. 'Though she always made sure none of us went short. Always had good food on the table. Always had us all properly dressed. Just like your mother.'

In fact Zena's mother, though she worked all the hours God gave, was an altogether softer, tamer person than Grandma Lamprey. It was Zena who turned out to have inherited her grandmother's fabulous energies and driving purpose. By the time she was fifteen she could hoist a case of apples on to her shoulder and run with it like a man, milk fifteen cows, turn out a hundred pounds of best butter every week, speed through a heap of starched pinafores with a gophering iron and bake a better loaf than her mother.

'Hard work,' she said—and went on saying—'never killed anyone.' But she saw very clearly that hard work hadn't done much to help Grandma Lamprey or her parents get ahead. It turned out that her great uncle, master of *Shendlestone Manor*, had been a real no-hoper. He had frittered away all the Lamprey money through fast living so that Jabez's family had never seen a penny of it, and the great house had fallen into the hands of strangers. With no capital behind them and large families to feed and clothe, Grandma Lamprey and her sons had spent all their lives battling to keep their noses above water. They'd managed to hang on to their little hoard of *Shendlestone* relics but, like the man in the picture, had remained stuck in the same spot, unable to move towards the palace on the hill or claim any more of the splendours hidden away inside. Zena, on the other hand, meant to be mistress of a place she could be proud of. Not a palace, but the best house in the district with big rooms lined with something better than chaff bags, a modern range, a proper bathroom and a lovely garden with lawns and an ornamental fish-pond as well as flowers, vegetables and all kinds of fruit trees.

Her chance came when Herbie Bromyard began looking at her sideways in church and turned up one Sunday evening at the Lampreys' back door with a bag of Democrat apples from the new orchard he had put in at Mercer's Bay. He was a mild-mannered, hard-working young man, rather like Zena's father, but his arrival threw Mrs Lamprey into a fearful state. The Bromyards were well-to-do and well-respected. Everyone looked up to them. And Mrs Lamprey on getting home from church had taken off her Sunday best to help Zena's young brothers cart water to fill the copper for wash-day in the morning. So she had to send one of the boys up to the house for her corsets and good clothes and change behind the dunny before she could come flustering in to greet Herbie.

By this time, warmed by Zena's interest, Herbie was sitting in the parlour describing the two hundred acres on which his father had set him up several years back. He owned the two points enclosing Mercer's Bay as well as a great swathe of land facing the sea. Working with axes, crosscut saws, a stump-jump and a bullock team he and his men had already cleared at least half the property and he was putting in apple and pear trees as fast as he could go. The first trees he'd planted were already bearing well. To prove this point he offered Zena a Democrat which she ate with appreciation while Mrs Lamprey hovered in the doorway and Herbie went on explaining how eventually his orchards would cover eighty acres and how he was starting to cut timber for apple cases in the sawmill that he'd built.

A few weeks later he took Zena on a tour of inspection, pointing out the new packing shed, the sites he'd chosen for barns and workshops, the paddocks where he'd chipped in grass seed for horses and cattle, and the slab hut in which he was making do until the homestead could be erected. He asked Zena her opinion on the best spot for his permanent home, although there was really only one choice—a flattish area at the top of the rise sloping up from the sea, right in the middle of the spreading acres of fruit trees. As they walked up and down the site Herbie did his best to keep pace with Zena's ideas on bathrooms and fish-ponds but his attention kept straying to other parts of his property: a new dam; two men felling a tree up in the bush; the four Jersey cows he'd added to his herd.

It was much the same when, a year or so later, he brought Zena home as a bride to the hut at the top of the track. Every night after tea they'd light the candles and sit down opposite one another—Herbie with his elbows on his knees, patiently cutting scions for grafting in the orchard, Zena leafing through catalogues of pressed steel wall and ceiling panels from the House of Wunderlich or making sketches for the builders who came every day to work on the homestead—sketches of every detail from the pantry shelves to the semicircular fanlight that was to go over the front door with the twelve letters of *Shendlestone* arching round the rim.

Once the girls had gone off with the scones and sandwiches for morning tea, the kitchen seemed very quiet. Zena relished these moments, alone in the room at the heart of the whole farm, when she could hear from far away voices, engines, the stutter of hammers, the faint jingle of harness. It seemed as though she could feel her vigilance spreading out to every corner of the property and receive back from the farthest ranks of trees, the cattle dozing in the deep grass of the paddocks, her son's new house on the hill, messages that told her all was well.

From the window of her kitchen she could oversee, still more satisfactorily, the packing shed and the sawmill lying at the foot of the track beyond her flower garden. She watched her girls setting out plates of food on the bench under the big wattle; Herbie and his men filing out of the mill; the workers who'd been cleaning up the packing shed ready for the picking season gathering round the big billies of tea she'd sent down. Then Syd Hemp came up the track from the road, leading two horses back to their paddock, all of them slouching along with their heads down, kicking up puffs of dust, while scrawny little Norm Hemp, who followed his father everywhere, scrambled up on the fence and began teetering along the top like a tightrope-walker.

The sight of the Hemps made Zena bristle with exemplary energy. She turned back to the two dozen jars of apricots she'd bottled after breakfast and sat down quickly to write the labels. There was nothing special about this batch—nothing fancy, like the exhibits she'd taken to preparing for the bigger shows. For those she now chose fruit or vegetables exactly matching or carefully graded in size, carved sometimes into scallops, cubes or even flower shapes, and arranged with the aid of long-nosed tweezers in elaborate towers, swirls and spirals that rose like jewelled sculptures in their glowing syrups.

Even when her bottling was of a more modest kind, Zena usually enjoyed putting the finishing touches. She took pride in the look of her elegant black lettering on the white labels, and, as she placed the jars in line on her pantry shelves, she relished the sense of having made provision for the future, preserved a bountiful harvest, added another course to the wall she'd raised against the onslaughts of chaos and decay. But, today, her glimpse of Syd Hemp dragging his feet in the dust and his child acting the fool had tainted her pleasure. There was no excuse for such people—feckless, work-shy, never taking the least bit of care over how they looked or anything they did. When she was young she and her sister, Bella, had got up every morning at five to give a hand with the horses or the milking or whatever they'd had to do. Then they'd got all the little ones dressed and helped cook breakfast before walking four miles to school. One year she'd won a prize for the pupil walking the most miles to attend classes. She never missed a day. And then at home after school it was work, work, work all over again. They had to cart all their own water in those days and struggle with a brick oven, scraping out all the ashes before they could bake their bread. But you never saw any of them slopping around looking like the Hemps—far and away the most down-at-heel of all the itinerant families who came to *Shendlestone* at picking time.

Always the Hemps arrived first, wanting to move into one of the pickers' huts before Zena had made sure the whole lot had been properly cleaned up for the new season. And always they hung around after the picking was finished, hinting that they'd like to stay on through the winter. Time and again she'd told Herbie they'd be better off without the Hemps but on this one issue, mildly, peaceably, he took his own line. He had a soft spot for Syd and said he was a marvel with the horses.

'Well, his wife's no marvel,' Zena would snap. 'And the children are a disgrace.'

Then Herbie would mutter something about 'poor old Syd'.

'Poor old Syd! Poor old Syd! If the chap's such a marvel why doesn't he make something of himself? Get a home together, get his family something decent to wear?'

Sometimes she wondered if draggle-tailed Ida Hemp was all there, wandering round with her ropey hair hanging down her back and her skirts trailing in the dirt. She had no idea at all how to bring up children. It wasn't just the ragged filthy clothes. Norm and his brothers and sisters were skinny as rakes, they had scabs on their knees and elbows, and every year Zena had to get the district nurse to come and check their hair for nits and make sure they weren't coming down with anything catching. She couldn't, after all, risk Tom's babies picking up something nasty.

The thought of her two grandchildren lightened Zena's mood. Tom's wife, Pat, though she couldn't always see eye to eye with her, was a good mother. Baby Ronny was a dear little fellow and his sister Jenny was the pride of Zena's life—the prettiest little thing you ever saw with bright blue eyes, beautiful blond hair, and skin with the warm summer bloom of a ripe apricot. Born less than a year after Tom had come home from the war, she was two and a half now, trotting everywhere, into everything, clever as a boxful of monkeys. Zena tried not to show her preference or her pride but sometimes at night when she and Herbie were on their own she'd burst out with some story of what Jenny had said or done: 'D'you know what she said to me today? Well, I was just filleting a bit of flathead and she picked up this scale. Just a scale off the fish on the end of her little finger. And she said, "What's this, Granny?" And I said, "It's a scale, Jenny, off the fish." And d'you know what she said? She said "No, Granny, scales is for weighing sugar." Really. That's what she said and she's not three till September.'

Jenny was always interested in everything her grandmother did, everything that happened in the kitchen. She was particularly fond of the pantry—just the sight of the big shining jars on the upper shelves, the different colours of bottled beans, pears, raspberries, carrots, and lower down the massed jams, jellies and chutneys with their taut cellophane caps, the fish curled in brine, the smoked mussels packed in oil. She would stare and stare with her head tilted back as though filled with wonder at the sheer height of Zena's ramparts against want, disorder and the pace at which the seasons ran by.

Later in the day, thought Zena, Jenny would want to see the bottled apricots. But it would have to be some time towards evening because after dinner Zena was going into

Pyana to present prizes at the school. It seemed queer to be doing this in February, just when the school year was beginning, instead of back at the end of last term. But in December there'd been a big scare over diphtheria and the prize giving had been cancelled. So today was the great day with somebody coming down from the Education Department in Hobart and afternoon tea for the pupils, parents and visitors after the ceremony.

In summer Zena kept her bedroom curtains closed, so when she went into the room to change it was cool and dim after the hot dinner-time bustle, and the scents of camphor, eau-de-cologne and beeswax seemed, in the half light, more pungent than usual. She pulled open a drawer, put on her corsets and silk stockings, twisting round to make sure the seams were straight. She put on cool, slippery lingerie and the frock pattered with black, cream and heliotrope flowers she'd bought to wear at her father's funeral under her black, edge-to-edge grosgrain coat. Leaning forward to peer into her dressing-table mirror she combed back her hair and then turned her head this way and that. She had a good look at her teeth, wiped a powder puff over her nose and cheeks and stood back to size herself up. She thought she didn't look too bad for her age—tall, upright with her flowered dress settled smoothly over her hips. After she'd put on her edge-to-edge coat, her best hat with the spotted half-veil, and her court shoes, she came back to the dressing table, took the *Shendlestone* ivy leaf out of her jewel box and pinned it carefully on to her coat just above her left breast.

When she stalked into the kitchen carrying her glacé kid bag and gloves, the girls, Ruby and Joan, stopped in the middle of washing up to stare at her. They said she looked lovely and went out with her to the car, carrying the tins of shortbread and lamingtons she was taking as a contribution to the school tea. Then they stood together, waving, as she drove off in the Humber down the track to the packing shed and on towards the road above the bay.

It was a still, hot afternoon. The Supervisor from Hobart had to pause in the middle of his speech to mop his face with a handkerchief. While tea was being served several of the guests went outside to get a breath of air and stood around in groups looking anxiously at the southern sky. There was thunder about. Most of the parents from fruit-growing families were on tenterhooks, worried that a gale of hailstorm might sweep down on their orchards and wreck their harvest just as a whole year's work was coming to fruition. Zena remained quite calm. It was no use, she told them, meeting trouble half way. Yet, at *Shendlestone* she and Herbie had done just that, carefully placing their orchards so that the bush-covered hills to the south protected them from the worst of the stormy weather. There'd been a few years when the crop hadn't quite come up to expectations but the Bromyards had never suffered a really severe loss like some of their less provident neighbours.

Driving home again Zena reflected that it had all gone off very well. She'd handed out copies of *David Copperfield* or *The Water Babies* to the prize winners and presented certificates for proficiency in first aid. Afterwards she'd given a short speech on how to succeed in life. She'd made some notes on a card but found she didn't need to refer to them. 'Make up your mind what it is you want,' she'd told the children, 'whether it's having your own farm or a nice house or whatever it is, and work hard. That's my advice. There's no reason why you shouldn't succeed if you use commonsense and are prepared to work.'

During the vote of thanks Mr Dunn, the head teacher, had referred to Zena's own success as a 'home industrialist' while the Supervisor from Hobart had congratulated her on both her speech and her lamingtons.

When she turned off the road Zena had to get out of the car to open the big gate with *Shendlestone* painted on a plaque on the top bar. There was not a breath of wind. The bay was as still as a millpond with the low cliffs of the far bluff reflected in the water. As she was pulling the gate back she was struck by how quiet it was, much quieter than it had been in the kitchen earlier on when she'd stood and listened to the far off reassuring sounds of a working day. Now, for some reason, although it was long past the time for afternoon tea, there was no sound of sawing from the mill, no beat of hammers. Only once, as she got back into the Humber after closing the gate, she thought she heard someone shouting, then the sound was cut off as though a lid had been dropped.

She drove up the winding track between the oak trees Herbie had planted for her over thirty years ago. Then, as she swung round the last bend and came in sight of the packing shed, she was startled to see a crowd of people standing round the bench by the wattle tree. Her first thought was that Ruby and Joan had got behind with their work and brought down the things for afternoon tea over an hour after the proper time. She was really angry, thinking she couldn't turn her back for a minute without everything going to the pack, but as the car slowed she saw Herbie push out of the crowd and come running towards her, no hat on his head and his face all creased with worry.

'What?' she asked, getting quickly out of the Humber.

'My Lord, I'm glad you're here, Zene. It's Syd's boy. He came off the fence.'

Zena clicked her tongue in exasperation. What did they expect?

'Now, I s'pose he's broken something,' she said angrily. 'Has someone phoned the doctor?'

'Ruby's gone up. And Joan's getting a bit of warm water…'

He took her arm, hurrying her along towards the wattle tree, saying it was barely five minutes since it happened—Syd had only just put Norm on the bench—and how lucky it was she'd turned up when she did.

Everyone knew Zena was the President of the Pyana branch of the Red Cross and had handled dozens of accidents—fractures, gashes, burns, a leg crushed by a falling tree, somebody gored by a bull. They all looked relieved to see her and fell back to let her through. She jolted the straps of her bag up her arm and stripped off her gloves, still possessed by indignation at not being able to go off for five minutes without something going wrong, the Hemps' failure to take proper care of their kids, and the bother of having to cope with what seemed to be a bad accident just at the busiest time of the year. Probably she was going to have to find some way of getting Norm up to hospital in Hobart. 'I ask you!' she thought. 'As if I hadn't got enough to think about!'

As she came up to the bench, the first thing she saw was Syd Hemp on the far side, leaning forward for all the world like a shopman behind a counter. She looked down at the boy—his little ragged jacket, his shirt half pulled out of his shorts, the thin legs sticking out, the dusty broken boots. Someone had put a folded coat under his head and she saw it was soaked in blood. The child's hair was all black and spiky and more blood had run down over the bench on to the ground where a viscous crimson pool gleamed in the dust. Syd, who must have been trying to stop the flow, was holding a blood-stained cloth in one hand.

'Dived off the fence,' whispered Johnny Spratt—a good worker—making a quick dipping motion with his hand. 'Right on this rock.'

'Wasn't too far to fall though,' said someone else, more loudly. 'Couldn't 'a done himself a lot of harm.'

Zena lifted one of Norm's arms, looking sideways at his face, part turned towards her with half-shut eyes. She stared at the snub nose; the front teeth, that looked too big for the face, resting on the lower lip; freckles scattered over the white skin; smears of blood and dirt, and as she was trying to find a pulse she noticed that the child's wrist was so small that she could have put her thumb and forefinger round it with room to spare. She looked down at the grubby little hand with its black-rimmed nails, then thumped her bag on to the bench and scrabbled in it, searching for her powder compact—her best one with a shell embossed on the gold lid. When she found it she held the mirror in front of Norm's mouth and nose, waited, peered at the glass and saw to her astonishment that she was still wearing her hat with the smart spotted veil. Then she dropped the compact back into her bag, reached out and quickly drew her hand down over Norm's eyes.

By this time Syd had come round the bench and was standing beside Zena. When he saw the mirror with not a trace of mist on its surface, not even the faintest dimming of its brightness, he clapped one of his great red hands over his eyes as though he was trying to keep his face from falling apart. Then, to Zena's horror, the hand slipped to his mouth and, standing there in his battered clothes, covered in sawdust from helping in the mill, he began to weep and, lurching forward, fell against her, blubbering into the shoulder of her grosgrain coat.

The whole crowd knew in a moment what had happened. Five or six men came round Syd, patted his shoulders, took hold of him, muttered 'Come on, mate, come on. Let's get you out of here. Come on, Syd.'

'You do your best,' he sobbed, lifting his face. 'You try to do what you can for 'em. But what's the point? Eh? What's the point?'

Herbie was there and Tom.

'Where's the mother?' asked Zena. She was shaking like a leaf.

'It's alright. They're looking after her...'

Always at times like this everyone relied on Zena to take charge.

'I'd better have a word,' she said, looking round. She caught sight of Ida sitting by the fence clutching her baby with her hair hanging round her face. There were four or five people crouching round her. Johnny Spratt was putting a blanket over Norm.

'Are you right, Mum?'

Tom was holding her arm, peering anxiously at her face.

'You don't look too good, Zene. D'you want to go up to the house?'

Zena broke away and began to run. She pulled off her hat and lolloped up the track in her fine get-up with the gold brooch gleaming in the evening sun and her best shoes plunging through the dust. There was sawdust all over her black coat but it seemed cruel to brush it off so she left it and didn't even make a move to brush herself down when she was back in the quiet of her kitchen. She sat at the table and, when Herbie came hurrying after her, told him to give her a minute to herself. After a bit she got up to put on the kettle, thinking someone would be bound to want a drink. The pantry door had been left half open. She saw a last brilliant ray of sunshine strike across her exhibition jars so that the glass sparkled and the sculpted fruits shone golden, scarlet, emerald and pearl in their translucent columns of rich juice. They seemed queer and alien like pagan idols from a distant country.

'I'd better go to Ida,' she thought. It was her duty, it was what she was expected to do. But what would she say? All she could think of was Norm's blood on the ground, his limp hand and the father blubbering 'What's the point?' The question rang and rang in her ears like the trumpets that brought down the walls of Jericho.

It was a wild night. The storm that had threatened in the afternoon broke as dark was coming on. Dr Moore arrived just after tea and when he'd looked at Norm, laid out in one of the barns, and done what he could for the Hemps he had a word with Herbie and Tom who were worried stiff about Zena.

'Never seen her like this,' Tom kept saying.

'Been overdoing it, I expect,' said the doctor comfortably. He left her some sleeping tablets and promised a nerve tonic for later.

In the morning Zena was fit for nothing. She tried to get up but when Herbie urged her to stay in bed, and Tom and Pat came down, and Ruby and Joan insisted they could manage, she gave up and lay back on her pillows. There'd been deaths at *Shendlestone* before—one of the pickers, old Garnett, had dropped dead from a heart attack just before the war and not so long ago a nephew of Herbie's, a silly stuck-up young chap who knew it all, had rolled a tractor up on the hills and broken his neck. Zena knew what to do. There were the police and coroner to be dealt with, the grave site to organise, funeral arrangements to be made. She ought to be up seeing to these things, taking all those burdens off the Hemps. As it was she felt as weak as a kitten and scared that if she opened her mouth she'd burst out crying.

At about ten, Pat turned up again, this time leading Jenny by the hand. The little girl looked puzzled by the strange sight of her grandmother lying in bed. They both kissed Zena on the cheek and tried to get her to drink a cup of tea they'd brought her. After a few minutes Jenny sidled over to the dressing-table and started trying out a hair brush from the set with the tortoise-shell back, and poking about in the jewel-box. Pat sat down on a cane chair by the wardrobe, for once at a loss for words because she and Tom had talked the whole thing over and agreed to avoid mentioning the Hemps or anything that Zena might find upsetting. Eventually she said, 'That's a lovely lot of apricots you did yesterday, Mum. What's next? Greengages is it?'

'I don't know that I'll be doing any more. What's the point?'

Pat was flabbergasted.

'Well,' she said after a bit, 'we all enjoy 'em and they're good for us. Look at Jenny. She loves your fruit. She gets hours of pleasure just looking at it, leave alone eating it.'

'But what if she wasn't here?'

'What d'you mean? She is here. She's here now. Aren't you, sweetie?'

Zena lay in bed till nearly dinnertime, breathing the familiar scents of the room, listening to the far off sounds of the farm which were all going on again today as though nothing out of the ordinary had happened. At about twelve she got up, put on one of her house dresses and tidied the dressing table. Jenny had left half the contents of the jewel box scattered among the brushes and combs. There was the

Shendlestone mourning ring with the jet shield lying on a pin-cushion. Zena picked it up and turned it over in her hand. As she stared at the ring she made up her mind to give it to Ida Hemp, along with a box of stuff from the pantry. And she'd tell Herbie to let the Hemps know they could stay on through the winter—if they still wanted that when the time came and the Bromyards were still growing fruit at *Shendlestone*.

Rachael Treasure • 2011

The Mysterious Handbag

Dr Posthlewaite had been dead exactly a week. While his wife thought of this, she picked up her needle, bent her head and began to stitch buttons onto silk. A tingle of delight ran up her bony spine while she imagined sewing the eyes of his corpse shut tight. Prick of cool needle, thread running, tugging, through cold skin.

He had been the 'good doctor'—a much admired surgeon. A pillar of the community. And, for the past forty years, she had been the doctor's wife.

Life with the doctor made her feel like an empty handbag. It was a strange way to feel, but Mrs Posthlewaite would often sip her chamomile tea at her sewing table in a patch of afternoon sunlight and consider her handbag theory carefully. From the exterior she looked like a neat, functional and socially acceptable handbag. She knew she was a touch on the old-fashioned side. But she was certain she had more style than the other bum-bag-wearing, gym-going grannies like Mrs Smithers, who lived in the flat next door.

The very personal and private space inside 'Mrs Posthlewaite-the-handbag' had been emptied over years of living with the puffed-up, self-important doctor. Now, at the sewing table, she felt the anger simmer inside her empty space again as the doctor's little white dog clawed runs in her stockings and whimpered to be fed.

With cool, polite distance Dr Posthlewaite had come home to her each evening. She, the neat wife in the neat home with no children...just an annoying little dog. Mrs Posthlewaite would hear the doctor's pompous booming laughter coming from the stairwell as he flirted relentlessly with Mrs Smithers. The smile on his red round face evaporated when he crossed the threshold into the plush flat and placed his wooden box of personally engraved surgical instruments on the bedroom chair. The little dog, so delighted to see him, danced in circles at his feet and piddled with excitement. Steaming dinners were placed before him while he sighed and frowned.

Mrs Posthlewaite's garments, meticulously stitched, hung in the dark space in the sewing-room cupboard. She no longer proudly showed her husband her sewing. He used to glance at the neat navy pleated skirt or the finely embroidered blouse with his eyebrows raised. Then his eyes lifted to her face and he mocked her with silence. His surgical stitches saved lives. His needles pierced living flesh. His skills and status attracted gushing buxom nurses, who fussed and danced in circles around him.

Sometimes, when the doctor attended conferences interstate, Mrs Posthlewaite dragged the heavy surgical books from the shelf to stare at the diagrams long into the night. The human form was put together like a complex garment. Diagrams of flesh transposed themselves into sewing patterns in Mrs Posthlewaite's mind. As she gently fell into the pages, she dozed off, mouth open, bedside light shadowing her wrinkled skin. She dreamt of her childhood, when she had helped her father skin rabbits, possums and wallabies. Young girl's fingers wrapped around the smooth wood of a well-worked hammer. Girl's hands tapping tacks into skin. Stretching moist pink hides on boards to dry. The dream would shift to her tidy kitchen where she pounded meat with the hammer. Dinner for the doctor.

Occasionally, they ate out at social occasions. Chest puffed out, the doctor took her on his arm. She was introduced as 'the doctor's wife'. Her empty space was momentarily filled with this important fact. Other women patted her husband's arms and squeezed his important hands with delight. They cast amused glances at Mrs Posthlewaite's neat grey bun, ankle-length tweed skirts and stick-like limbs. In the crook of her arm hung a very safe navy handbag, which matched her shoes. Handing her a twenty-dollar note, the doctor would send her home early in a taxi.

After one such occasion, Mrs Posthlewaite discovered a handbag under the Volvo's passenger seat. The bag was of a curious pale-blue silk in which purple roamed when she moved it in the light. Light also danced through little opaque cornflower-blue beads, which were sewn over the silk giving it a curious texture. Irresistible to stroke. Her fingertips, seduced, couldn't help but travel over cool silk then bump up and over smooth pert beads. Although the bag was small it was stuffed full. There were dazzling red, racy lipsticks, glittering nail polishes and golden tubes of jet-black mascara. Light danced in diamantes as Mrs Posthlewaite pulled from the bag a silver comb. Entwined between the grinning teeth were wisps of blonde hair. Black silk lined the private space inside the bag. Her fingertips slid to the silky corners of the bag's dark little universe and met with smooth glass. Golden French perfume was held in a bottle shaped like the torso of a curvaceous woman. Mrs Posthlewaite clasped the torso around its waist. She reached for the gold star gift tag that swung from its neck. Looped handwriting read, *From the good doctor*.

She drove the Volvo and the silken handbag to the supermarket and there she emptied her soul some more as she filled up her shopping trolley. The day after she calmly passed the handbag back to the gaping doctor, he came home with a squirming, whimpering ball of white fluff in his clean pink surgeon's hands.

'For you, dear,' he said, handing it to her awkwardly. 'It's a Maltese terrier...with a pedigree, of course. Name it what you like.' Then he took his place in his leather upright chair to watch the TV news. The puppy, she supposed, was meant to keep her there. To show her that he cared. As she mopped up its puddles on the plush coffee-coloured carpet and pulled on pink rubber gloves to pick up its little brown cigar-shaped messes, she cursed it, but like her husband, she endured it. She named the dog Gigi, after the French perfume she had found in the bag. Every day, when the dog demanded food, or brushing, or playing or walking, Mrs Posthlewaite obeyed, but quietly seethed inside her empty space. Since the doctor had died the dog had taken to sleeping on the bed where Dr Posthlewaite once had lain snoring. When Mrs Posthlewaite tried to move her, Gigi would curl up her lip and growl. In the mornings, when Mrs Posthlewaite stepped from the door to take Gigi for a walk, the dreadful Mrs Smithers was there cooing and clucking over the dog. The dog snuffled, wuffled and piddled in excitement—often on Mrs Posthlewaite's neat navy shoes.

One day, instead of walking the dog to the city park, Mrs Posthlewaite marched to the nearest haberdashery store. She tied Gigi to a pole outside the shop, left her there yapping and went in. She bought elegant pearl buttons, exclusive white silk, strong white cotton and a length of lace. Returning home she placed the goods by the sewing machine and turned her attention to Gigi. She ran a tepid bath for the dog and lay the dog's brushes out on a towel.

'Good dog, Gigi! Bath time,' she called.

That night, while Gigi slept in her basket, Mrs Posthlewaite went to her husband's cupboard and pulled out a solid wooden box. Laying it on the kitchen bench she undid its brass clasp and took from it the cold steel surgical instruments that had once been held in the doctor's smooth hands. She spread the perfect, gleaming scalpels and scissors onto the bench. From the kitchen cupboard she took a large bag of salt.

'Gigi! Come here,' she called.

For several weeks Mrs Posthlewaite barely left the flat. But tonight she knew it was time. In her sewing room, stooped over, her bony foot pressed down on the pedal, her sewing machine whirred into the night. She wore a faint smile as scissors glided through silk and the needle pierced the willing hole of pearl buttons. She hoped Mrs Smithers wouldn't hear the grinding sound of the sewing machine in the dead of night, but she knew the Valium would not allow the cloud in Mrs Smithers' head to lift.

After a grey morning shower of rain the sun burst through the kitchen window.

'Time to go shopping!' announced Mrs Posthlewaite airily. 'Some new clothes, some less sensible shoes…even, perhaps, some French perfume.' She made sure she timed her departure with Mrs Smithers' morning journey to the mailbox, solely for the purpose of showing off her brand-new home-crafted handbag. She grabbed her keys and enjoyed trying the new clasp on the bag. Rather than toss the keys in she let her fingertips slide in and out so she could feel the lining of cool white silk. Instead of placing the handbag on the crook of her arm she hung the long, lace-trimmed straps from her shoulder. Her hand ran down the straps to touch the bag's most striking feature, the exterior. It was white and fluffy and her fingertips delighted in the feel of it. Her strokes paused when her fingers met with perfect pearl beads, stitched on with precision.

As she caressed the furry handbag Mrs Posthlewaite smiled and said, 'Come on, Gigi—we may even call into the pet shop and buy a kitten. After all, I've always liked cats.'

Joan Wise • 1950

The Conquest of Emmie

Six dead rabbits strung on a piece of fencing-wire were fastened around Emmie's waist. Deftly she skinned two kangaroos, tossed their carcasses into the scrub and carefully put their skins in the sugar-bag along with little Johnnie.

All her life Emmie had lived in the Lake District, helping first her father with his few sheep and his trapping, and now helping Sam.

Sam was all right, but he had promised to build her a house. Four rooms she wanted—no more, no less. She herself had helped split the timber, and they had lived in a tent while Sam built the first room. Then Johnnie was born, the cow got sick, the horse got lost in the marshes, and Sam got tired. Emmie made a bag sling for Johnnie, fastened him on to her back and resolutely went on with her trapping. There was nothing slack about Emmie!

Sam sat on a cushion of dried bracken, his back against a chock and log fence. The sun, the scent of the ti-tree and even the tangent smell of the marshes was good. He had first met Emmie, six scrubs back, on the slopes of Table Mountain. She had been helping her dad with kangaroo snares.

'Too much for a slip of a girl carrying them heavy carcasses home for the dogs,' Sam had thought, and each morning neglecting his own bit of trapping he had made it his business to appear in time to carry her catch for her.

Conversation came slowly, but this simple gesture formed an unspoken bond between them.

Sam altered his position, for even bracken after a time can become tedious. Funny how soft he had been, promising Emmie a house. It was that damn' Moss with his quick-and-ready tongue and two empty rooms in his old man's own house. Emmie was all right when Moss was away. Why couldn't he stay at his fishing!

Moss Jones had two professions. In the summer he and some mates worked a trawler, filling big contracts with mainland fish markets, and in the winter he came home to live with the 'old man' and went trapping. A precarious income, but, with no responsibilities, what matter? The old man was happy enough. He had his pension.

Moss was small, energetic and quick-witted. He got drunk every Friday night and thought about Emmie.

The rabbits bobbed against Emmie's knees as she trudged wearily around the edge of the marshes. Johnnie beat his fists incessantly on her back and her neck ached.

Then she met Moss. She didn't altogether like being caught by Moss doing Sam's job and, what's more, wearing his old coat and hat. But Moss was waiting, sitting on his hunkers watching her pick her way between the sags and fallen timber.

'Y' back again?' she inquired resentfully.

Moss nodded and unfastened the rabbits from around her waist.

'I'll carry these across to y'r new 'ouse.'

'It's not finished yet,' she shuffled her feet uncomfortably. Mockingly Moss raised his bushy eyebrows.

'The timber's split,' she went on hastily. 'Sam's waitin' for it to season.'

'It was seasoned last winter, afore I went fishin',' Moss laughed.

Emmie smiled indulgently, 'I knew as soon as I seen you you'd be makin' trouble agin.'

'I'll always make trouble until—'

'Y' still got y'r brushwood on, Moss,' she broke in coyly.

Moss put his hand up to his tangle of beard.

'It's comin' off tonight.'

Johnnie began to whimper and thumped her neck even harder.

"E's hungry. Come in and find Sam, Moss?'

'I seen 'im last night, when I got off the bus, didn't 'e tell you I was 'ome?'

"E must 'a' forgot,' said Emmie slowly. 'It won't 'urt to remind 'im.'

Sam was the mail-carrier. On Mondays and Thursdays he would collect the mailbag from the postmistress, walk two miles with it, and fasten it to a post on the edge of the Lyall

Highway. The Hobart-bound bus would gather it up, and then on Tuesdays and Fridays Sam would walk out and collect the bag of incoming mail. He always felt he had been talked into this job by Emmie, who was so set on 'steady money' as she called it.

Not that he minded much, for he gathered up all the news as he went along. Much more than Emmie read in the papers. But he always felt uneasy about leaving Emmie alone. Especially when Moss was in the district.

Now the beggar was home again. Well, there was nothing for it but to finish the damn' house. It would be a bit hard now that he had no horse.

'These wimmen!'

Sam rose awkwardly from his bracken seat and rubbed gingerly those parts affected with pins and needles. Perhaps Moss's old man would lend him his old crock of a horse; it would be better than nothing.

He gathered an armful of sticks and busied himself with a fire. Moss and Emmie were approaching. It wouldn't do to be caught napping by Moss! Out of the corner of his eye he saw Moss help Emmie over a log. Carrying her rabbits, too! A cunning look spread over Sam's face. Perhaps Moss would even give him a day or two's work on the house. After all, he would be with Emmie!

Sam was a man of his word. Four rooms, no more, no less. Unlined and thatched with bark and leaking with the first thaw.

Moss helped odd days all through the winter, and then went back to his fishing.

Emmie managed to hammer the last nail into place before she was obliged to take the bus into Hamilton, where Maggie was born that night.

Sam reluctantly took over Emmie's rabbit-run. It meant getting up early and going to bed late. What a pity Emmie had such fancy ideas for making a bit of extra money!

The house was horribly gloomy without her banging about; and he found himself dropping in more and more often on Moss's old man. Dull-eyed and living in the past the old man shuffled about making pots of tea and muttering endlessly. He was lonely, too.

'I won't be 'ere much longer,' droned the old man for the fiftieth time. 'What's gonna 'appen when I'm gorn? Who's gonna milk the cow, feed the pig and look to me boy?'

A trickle of tea ran down his chin and dropped on to his already stained waistcoat.

Sam swigged his tea, rolled himself a cigarette with some of the old man's fine-cut and thought uneasily about Emmie. Women were the devil with their naggin'!

'Who'll look to Moss?' the old man inquired fretfully.

'I dunno,' said Sam. 'Guess 'e'll manage f'r 'iself; 'e seems t' have a way with 'im.'

'Yes, always knows what 'e wants and goes arter it—gets it, too,' the old man nodded.

The next day Sam borrowed the old man's best suit and went down to Hamilton to collect Emmie, Johnnie and Maggie.

'Why, Sam!' said Emmie, somewhat surprised. 'I didn't know you was comin' down for us. Is anything the matter?'

Sam removed the old man's hat and mopped his head. Rolling his eyes, he turned away from Emmie. Then like a shot burst from him.

'It's the old man...thinks 'e'll peg out soon...Moss'll take over. Won't be able t' go fishin' then...'E might be wantin' a missus...What about it?'

The flush on Emmie's cheek shot down her neck. With amazed wonder she eyed Sam. Never had she heard him say so much before. And all because of her.

Nonchalantly she gathered Maggie and her few belongings up.

'Well, what about it?' Sam said sharply. 'Can't y' speak up, woman? Pity t' waste me trip down t' Hamilton. Parson says he'll marry us right away!'

''Ere, take me string-bag; I'm glad y' didn't let Moss beat y' to it,' said Emmie proudly.

Biographical Details

A. J. O. (Arthur James Ogilvy, 1834–1914) was born in Calcutta, and educated there and in England. In 1851, following the death of his parents, he migrated to Tasmania to join his uncle who had a large property near Richmond. An active member of the Richmond community, he became absorbed in social and economic issues, and in 1894 chaired the conference that saw the birth of the Democratic League, the forerunner of the Tasmanian Labor Party. He later became interested in evolution, publishing *Elements of Darwinism* in 1901. Around this time he also wrote a small amount of fiction and poetry. 'The Salted Claim' was published in *Sullivan and Co.* (1905), a cycle of connected yarns presented at the time as a novel.

Carmel Bird (1940–) was born in Launceston, Tasmania. After graduating from university she lived in Europe and the USA, before settling in Melbourne. She has worked as a secondary-school teacher, and has taught creative writing in various tertiary institutions. Her published works include nine novels (three of them shortlisted for the Miles Franklin Award), five collections of short stories and three manuals on writing. She now lives in Castlemaine, Victoria. 'The Woodpecker Toy Fact' was first published in Bird's short-story collection *The Woodpecker Toy Fact and Other Stories* (1987).

Roy Bridges (1885–1952), the younger brother of the writer Hilda Bridges, was born in Hobart. After graduating from the University of Tasmania he pursued a career in journalism with various newspapers, including the *Tasmanian News*, the *Mercury* and the Melbourne *Age*. In 1930 he returned to Tasmania with his sister to live on Wood's Farm near Sorell, the home of his mother's family. With thirty-six novels and numerous short stories to his credit, Bridges is Tasmania's most prolific author. 'The Magistrate' was published in the *Australian Journal*, June 1930.

Marcus Clarke (1846–1881) was born in London and migrated to Australia in 1863, after his family's financial problems had dashed his hopes of a career in the Foreign Office. A successful journalist and a prolific writer of plays, novels and short stories, he is famous as the author of *For the Term of His Natural Life* (1874), a vivid indictment of the convict experience in Van Diemen's Land. 'The Seizure of the *Cyprus*' was first published in the *Australasian*, 9 April 1870.

Geoffrey Dean (1928–2011) was born in Hobart, Tasmania, and though he travelled the world as a young man, working at a variety of jobs, he was always drawn back to his home state. A productive short-story writer, he published more than fifty tales over six decades, winning numerous literary awards along the way. His work has been published in the UK, the USA, Norway and China, as well as in Australia. His short story 'The Town that Died' was adapted for TV by the ABC in 1986. 'The Meat Merchant' first appeared in the Australian Labor Party magazine, *New Horizons*, in 1971.

Adrienne Eberhard (1964–) was born in Dover, Tasmania. She has published several collections of poetry, including *Agamemnon's Poppies*, *This Woman* and *Jane, Lady Franklin*. Her poems and short stories have appeared in a range of Australian journals, among them *Southerly*, *Island*, *Westerly*, *Voices*, *Meanjin*, *Siglo* and the *Australian*. She lives in Tinderbox, and divides her time between writing and teaching. 'Orange Bathers' was first published in *Island* in 2001.

Henry J. Goldsmith (Henry James Goldsmith Armstrong, 1846–1916) was born in the Huon Valley, Tasmania. He is the author of two novels and one short story. 'The Hermit of the Huon' appeared in the *Australian Journal*, January 1875.

James Leakey (1824–1871) was born in Exeter, England, one of eleven children of the painter James Leakey, Snr, and brother of Caroline Woolmer Leakey, author of the early convict novel *The Broad Arrow* (1859). It is believed that Leakey, a solicitor, spent only a short time in Tasmania, after travelling there in order to accompany his sick sister on her voyage home to England in 1853. 'The Tasmanian Devil' appeared in *St Paul's Magazine*, London, in 1871.

Tahune Linah was the writing name of J. E. (John Ernest) Philp (1869–1937). Born in Franklin, Tasmania, he was a bushman, sailor and pioneer, as well as a writer. As Tahune Linah (borrowed from the Tasmanian Aboriginal language name for the Huon River) he contributed a small number of poems and short stories to the *Bulletin* and the *Tasmanian Mail*, as well as a series of articles on his bush adventures for Hobart newspapers. His most important work is the maritime history *The Whaling Ways of Hobart Town*, published in 1936 under his own name. 'In the River' appeared in the *Bulletin*, 31 October 1896.

James McQueen (1934–1998) was born in Ulverstone, Tasmania. He worked in a number of jobs, from ship's cook to accountant, before becoming a full-time writer in 1977. He is the author of five novels, four children's novels and more than one hundred short stories, several of which won awards. 'Death of a Ladies' Man' was first published in *Island* in 1985. The version reproduced in this anthology is taken from his collection *Death of a Ladies' Man* (1989).

Hal Porter (1911–1984) was born in Melbourne. He lived in Hobart while working as a teacher at the Hutchins School from 1946 to 1947, and again while working at the Theatre Royal in the early 1950s. His oeuvre includes novels, poetry, drama and three volumes of autobiography, as well as short stories, with Tasmania a setting for a number of his works. He won numerous literary awards, and was made a Member of the Order of Australia for services to literature in 1982. 'Great-Aunt Fanny's Picnic' was first published in the *Bulletin*, 23 December 1961. The version reproduced in this anthology is taken from *Selected Stories* (1991).

Philomena van Rijswijk (1956–) was born in Sydney and grew up in the city's western suburbs. She moved to Tasmania in 1985 and for twenty-one years lived in the Huon Valley township of Cygnet, where her first writing studio was a blue canvas tent by the side of a creek. She is the author of two novels, and her poetry and fiction have been published in periodicals and anthologies in Australia and abroad. She now lives and writes in Hobart. 'Faith, Hope and Charity', which won a Tasmanian Writers' Centre short story award and was included in *The Best Australian Stories 2002*, was first published in *Meanjin* in 2002.

Barney Roberts (1920–2005) was born in Flowerdale, Tasmania, where, except for a brief period during World War II, he spent his whole life. He published poetry collections, short fiction and a novel, winning a New South Wales Premier's Award in 1986 for *A Kind of Cattle*, the story of his time as a prisoner of war. In 2005 he was awarded an honorary doctorate from the University of Tasmania in recognition of his contribution to literature. 'A Jar of Raspberry Jam' was first published in his collection *Where's Morning Gone?* (1987).

Margaret Scott (1934–2005) was born in Bristol, England, and migrated to Hobart in 1959. She lectured in English at the University of Tasmania from 1966 to 1989. Her literary output includes three volumes of poetry; two novels; a collection of memoir, short fiction and verse; and a non-fiction work about the response of the Tasman Peninsula community—of which she was part—to the 1996 Port Arthur massacre. She also co-edited the anthology *Effects of Light: The Poetry of Tasmania* (1985). A much-loved public figure, she made regular appearances on the ABC television shows *Good News Week* and *The Great Debate* during the 1990s. In honour of her outstanding contribution to Australian literature she was awarded the Australia Council Writers' Emeritus Award in 2005. 'Preserves' was published in the collection *Changing Countries* (2000).

Nicholas Shakespeare (1957–) was born in Worcester, England. The son of a diplomat, much of his youth was spent in the Far East and South America. His books have been translated into twenty languages and include *In Tasmania*, winner of the 2007 Tasmania Book Prize, and *Secrets of the Sea* (2007), set on Tasmania's east coast, which was longlisted for the Miles Franklin Award. A Fellow of the Royal Society of Literature, he lives in Oxford and, since 1999, has had a home in Dolphin Sands, Tasmania. 'The Castle Morton Jerry' was first published in *Island* in 2009.

H. W. Stewart (1883–?) was born in Launceston, Tasmania. His publications include *A Handbook of Launceston* (1927), as well as poetry and five short stories. 'Nectar of the Gods' was published in the *Bulletin*, 28 June 1923.

Tasma was the nom de plume of Jessie Couvreur (nee Huybers, 1848–1897). Born in London, she migrated with her parents to Hobart when she was four. She moved to Victoria with her first husband, but the marriage was not a success and she made two extended trips to Europe. In 1877 she began submitting short stories to several journals under the pseudonym Tasma. After her 1885 marriage to Auguste Couvreur, a Belgian politician, she began writing novels. 'An Old-Time Episode in Tasmania' was first published in *Coo-ee: Tales of Australian Life by Australian Ladies* (1891), edited by Mrs (Harriette Anne) Patchett Martin.

Theresa Tasmania is most likely the pen name of Lucy Anna Edgar (1838–?). Edgar was born in Hobart into a prominent Baptist family, and grew up in Victoria and Tasmania. She published *Among the Black Boys*, an account of her family's experiences in Victoria, in 1865. As Theresa Tasmania she regularly contributed short stories and poems to the *Australian Journal*, the *Tasmanian Messenger* and the *Christian Witness*. 'A "Model" Dream' was published in the *Australian Journal* in September 1869.

Rachael Treasure (1968–) was born in Hobart, and educated at Orange Agricultural College and Charles Sturt University. Before turning her hand to fiction she worked as a rural journalist, jillaroo, wool classer and sheepdog trainer. Her four novels have been published in Australia and abroad. She lives on a farm in the southern Tasmanian hamlet of Woodsdale. 'The Mysterious Handbag' first appeared in her short-fiction collection *The Girl and the Ghost-Grey Mare* (2011).

Price Warung (1855–1911) is the pseudonym of William Astley, who was born in Liverpool, England, and migrated with his family to Melbourne in 1859. Between 1875 and 1890 he worked as a journalist on regional newspapers in New South Wales, Victoria and Tasmania, before settling in Sydney. In the 1890s he was a regular contributor of stories to the *Bulletin*, and was as well known as Henry Lawson and A. B. 'Banjo' Paterson. While he published more than a hundred stories, Astley is best remembered today for his convict tales. 'How Muster-Master Stoneman Earned His Breakfast', the first of Astley's stories to appear in print, was published in the *Bulletin*, 24 May 1890. This anthology reproduces the text published in *Tales of the Convict System* (1892).

A. Werner is probably Alice Werner (1858–1935). She was born in Trieste, Italy, and as a child lived in New Zealand, Mexico, the USA and Europe, finally settling in England in 1874. Werner had a distinguished academic career, for which she was appointed Commander of the Most Excellent Order of the British Empire in 1930. 'Black Crows: An Episode of "Old Van Diemen"' was first published in *Longman's Magazine*, a British literary journal, in June 1886, and reprinted in the *Australian Journal*, September 1886, the copy text for this collection.

Rohan Wilson (1976–) was born in Launceston, Tasmania. After graduating from the University of Tasmania he spent several years teaching English in Japan, and is currently enrolled in a PhD at the University of Melbourne. His novel, *The Roving Party*, won the 2011 *Australian* / Vogel Literary Award. 'The Needle in the Shoe' is published here for the first time.

Joan Wise (1912–1985) was born in Hobart and educated at St Michael's Collegiate School. She spent her early married life on a rural property in the Derwent Valley before moving to Mt Rumney. She began publishing poetry and short fiction in the 1940s, her work appearing in the *Bulletin* and in various anthologies. In the 1970s she published two children's novels, *Trapped on Tasman* and *The Silver Fish*. 'The Conquest of Emmie' was published in the *Bulletin*, 18 January 1950.

Danielle Wood (1972–) was born and bred in Hobart. After graduating from the University of Tasmania she worked as a journalist in Tasmania and Western Australia, before completing a PhD at Edith Cowan University. Her publications include a novel, *The Alphabet of Light and Dark*, which won the 2002 *Australian* / Vogel Literary Award and the 2004 Dobbie Award for Australian women writers, and a collection of stories, *Rosie Little's Cautionary Tales for Girls*. 'None of the Above' was first published in *Island* in 2011.

Acknowledgements

We are indebted to the following: Heather Rose for the title; Toni Sherwood for locating copies of several hundred of the stories from which we made this selection; Gillian Winter for guiding Ralph Crane's early archival searches in the late 1980s, and for knowing about James Leakey and Joan Wise when we found ourselves in a cul-de-sac; Alaina Gougoulis at Text for typing stories we were unable to scan; Anica Boulanger-Mashberg for assistance with proofreading; and David Winter at Text for championing the project and for his editorial acumen. We would also like to thank the University of Tasmania for financial support.

We are grateful for permission to include the following copyright material:

Carmel Bird, 'The Woodpecker Toy Fact', from *The Woodpecker Toy Fact and Other Stories* (Fitzroy, Vic: McPhee Gribble / Penguin, 1987), reproduced by kind permission of the author;

Geoffrey Dean, 'The Meat Merchant', from *The Literary Lunch: Selected Stories* (Hobart: Roaring Forties Press, 2004), reproduced by kind permission of Caroline, Ben and Annabel Dean;

Adrienne Eberhard, 'Orange Bathers', from *Island* 85 (2001), reproduced by kind permission of the author and *Island*;

Hal Porter, 'Great-Aunt Fanny's Picnic', from *Selected Stories* (North Ryde, NSW: Collins / Angus & Robertson, 1991), reproduced by permission of Tom Thompson / ETT Imprint;

Philomena van Rijswijk, 'Faith, Hope and Charity', from *Meanjin* 61.3 (2002), reproduced by kind permission of the author;

Barney Roberts, 'A Jar of Raspberry Jam', from *Where's Morning Gone?* (Fitzroy, Vic: McPhee Gribble / Penguin, 1987), reproduced by kind permission of the Roberts family;

Margaret Scott, 'Preserves', from *Changing Countries* (Sydney: Australian Broadcasting Corporation, 2000), reproduced by kind permission of Sarah Scott, Kate North and Daniel Boddy;

Nicholas Shakespeare, 'The Castle Morton Jerry', from *Island* 117 (2009), reproduced by kind permission of the author and *Island*;

Rachael Treasure, 'The Mysterious Handbag', from *The Girl and the Ghost-Grey Mare* (Camberwell, Vic: Michael Joseph, 2011), reproduced with permission by Penguin Group (Australia);

Joan Wise, 'The Conquest of Emmie', from the *Bulletin*, 18 January 1950, reproduced by kind permission of Sue Loane;

Danielle Wood, 'None of the Above', from *Island* 124 (2011), reproduced by kind permission of the author and *Island*.

Every effort has been made to trace the copyright holders of stories included in this anthology. Where the attempt has been unsuccessful, the editors and publisher would be pleased to hear from the copyright holder concerned and to rectify any omission in future editions.

Original spelling has been retained in all stories.